Monetary Policy Implementation

Angelo Baglioni

Monetary Policy Implementation

Exploring the 'New Normal' in Central Banking

palgrave
macmillan

Angelo Baglioni
Università Cattolica del Sacro Cuore
Milano, Italy

ISBN 978-3-031-53884-1 ISBN 978-3-031-53885-8 (eBook)
https://doi.org/10.1007/978-3-031-53885-8

This Palgrave Macmillan imprint is published by the registered company Springer Nature Switzerland AG
The registered company address is: Gewerbestrasse 11, 6330 Cham, Switzerland

Paper in this product is recyclable.

Contents

List of Figures

List of Tables

CHAPTER 1

Introduction

Abstract This chapter provides the motivation and an overview of the book. During the last fifteen years, several innovations have been introduced in the art of central banking, that go under the name of "unconventional policies". They have left a durable legacy, as the tools introduced under those policies remain in the toolkit of central banks. The focus of the book is on the operational framework, showing its evolution over time. The topic is relevant for the effectiveness of monetary policy, the institutional setup of central banks, and the smooth operation of money markets and financial intermediation. The book provides a simple model of monetary policy implementation, which is used to interpret the experience of some central banks, namely: ECB, Fed, BoE, and BoJ. Finally, two very innovative topics are addressed: Central Bank Digital Currency and "greening" monetary policy.

Keywords Monetary policy · Operational framework · Interest rate steering · Quantitative easing · European central bank · Federal reserve system · Central bank digital currency

During the last fifteen years, the conduct of monetary policy has gone through several and deep changes. Starting with the great financial crisis in 2008, many central banks have introduced some innovative tools

A. Baglioni, *Monetary Policy Implementation*,
https://doi.org/10.1007/978-3-031-53885-8_1

that go under the name of "unconventional policies": large-scale asset purchases, long-term lending programs, and negative interest rates in some countries. These innovations have been introduced to address the limitations of the conventional policy coming from the zero lower bound (ZLB) for interest rates, in a macroeconomic environment featuring very low levels of inflation, frequently well below the 2% target adopted by several central banks worldwide. Given that the policy rates remained close to zero for many years, the main tool to implement monetary policy was the size of the central banks' balance sheet rather than the level of interest rates, which used to be the primary tool in the tradition of central banking. The communication policy of central banks has generally changed as well, with the adoption of the approach based on forward guidance.

The sharp (and largely unexpected) rise in inflation starting in 2021, together with the recovery from the pandemic crisis, led almost all central banks to exit their quantitative easing (QE) policies and raise the level of interest rates well above zero. The downsizing of central banks' balance sheets and the return to (nominal) positive levels of interest rates mark the "normalization" of monetary policy. The primary tool to implement monetary policy is again the level of interest rates. However, the way in which this operational target is achieved is not the old "interest rate steering" framework. It is instead a "new normal" that combines some features of the old framework with others inherited from the QE era. Indeed, the unconventional measures have left a durable legacy in the art of central banking, affecting the operational framework of monetary policy for the years to come.

This book tries to show how these innovations have changed, and possibly improved, the techniques used to implement monetary policy. The focus is on the *operational framework*, namely on the instruments used to change the stance of monetary policy, in response to the indications coming from the strategy and from the incoming information about the relevant economic variables. With a few exceptions (that will be reviewed in the next chapter) the macroeconomic literature is generally focused on the strategic issues related to monetary policy, namely its final targets and the central bank's reaction function. An example is the Taylor rule, linking the output gap and the inflation gap to the general level of interest rates. This approach leaves a basic question unanswered: how does the central bank affect the level of interest rates in the financial market? More precisely, how is the central bank able to keep the money market rate in line with its own target? This issue and others, that often remain "under the carpet" in monetary economics, will be explored in this book.

The operational framework may be perceived as a purely technical matter, which is of interest only to central bankers. I believe, instead, that it is a topic also relevant for a wider audience. Any scholar in monetary economics should be aware of the ways in which monetary policy is implemented, to be able to assess and compare the available options. Of course, central banks' operations affect the money market and thus the liquidity management of banks and other financial intermediaries: this is an issue for practitioners and for scholars in money and banking. The ongoing debate about the normalization shows that the different options on the table have several implications, in terms of effectiveness and efficiency of monetary policy implementation, and for financial stability as well. Balance sheet policies, and the exit process from them, have important consequences for the institutional setup and independence of central banks, related to the management of the huge portfolio of securities still in the hands of central banks worldwide.

Our first step will be to go through a simple theoretical model of the operational framework, highlighting the basic principles underlying the implementation of monetary policy. In this area, the institutional details play a relevant role: there is not a single way in which monetary policy is implemented worldwide. However, some common features can be identified. The model introduced in Chapter 3 is intended to be flexible enough to be applied, with some adaptations, to different geographical contexts. In particular, its application to the euro zone and the US will be shown in detail in Chapters 4 and 5, respectively, while a more synthetic exposition will be devoted to the UK and Japan in Chapter 6.

The last chapter will take up a couple of issues that are becoming more and more relevant looking ahead: the likely adoption of a *central bank digital currency* (CBDC) and the trend towards a *green* monetary policy. The first one is the response of central banks to the rapid technological innovations taking place in the payment industry, leading to the digitalization of money. The second one responds to the growing concerns about climate change and its implications for financial risks.

There are two ways to read this book. One is to follow the path suggested by the sequence of chapters, namely to go first through the theory of monetary policy implementation (after a brief review of the related literature) and then to the application of the model to the countries examined in the book, and finally to address the two most innovative issues: CBDC and green monetary policy. This way helps the reader to interpret the historical stages of monetary policy implementation in different countries and place them into a coherent theoretical framework. As an alternative, the reader can pick up one or more chapters that are of interest to her/him, without paying attention to the chapter sequence. For example, the reader interested in European matters can decide to go directly to Chapter 4: even without the theoretical back-round, he/she will be able to get a lot of (hopefully) useful information about the conduct of monetary policy in the euro area. Each chapter is written in such a way to be self-contained to a large extent.

1.1 An Overview of the Book

The next chapter will review and discuss the literature on monetary policy implementation. We will first focus on the current debate on the likely and desirable outcomes of the normalization process, and then we will go back to the older literature on the traditional interest rate steering approach. Chapter 3 will provide an analytical framework to address the implementation of monetary policy under three different approaches: (i) interest rate steering, (ii) quantitative easing, and (iii) new normal. That chapter will also address the transmission channels of monetary policy and discuss some potential side effects of the unconventional policies on financial stability.

We will start from a basic question: how does a central bank implement a monetary expansion or restriction? The typical way of doing this is by steering the level of interest rates. For this reason, the traditional operational framework is called "interest rate steering" (IRS). The central bank is able to control quite precisely the level of money market interest rates (by convention, those with a maturity up to one year). It is able to determine with even greater precision the interest rate on the shortest maturity, the overnight (O/N) maturity: this is the one at which most of the trades in the interbank market take place. The central bank is able to do so by using two levers. The first is the setting of a desired level for the O/N rate, which is the operational target of monetary policy. This level can either be communicated to the market by explicitly setting a target level for the O/N rate or it can be signaled by setting a policy interest rate (typically that applied on short-term lending operations). Such announcements define the stance of monetary policy: an increase in the target level for the O/N rate signals a monetary tightening, and a reduction signals an easing. The second lever stems from the central bank's monopoly position in the creation of base money, in particular the component consisting of banks' deposits at the central bank: bank reserves. Thanks to this position, it is able to place the supply of reserves at the level necessary for the interbank market to be in equilibrium at an interest rate level in line with its target. This monetary control mechanism is based on the relative scarcity of bank reserves, in the presence of a reserve requirement, and on the active management of the reserve supply by the central bank: frequent, even daily, interventions. In addition, this approach relies on two policy rates, that applied on bank reverses and that applied on the marginal lending facility, which provide the two boundaries (lower and upper, respectively) to the corridor of money market rates: this is why it is called "corridor system" (in addition to interest rate steering).

With the transition to *quantitative easing* (QE), the stance of monetary policy is no longer identified by the level of interest rates, but by the size of the central bank's balance sheet: this is the new operational target of monetary policy, and it is mainly affected by the asset purchase (AP) programs. A monetary expansion occurs by increasing the size of the net periodic purchases, while a monetary tightening occurs by reducing the net purchases, possibly to zero. When this happens, the central bank can still guarantee the reinvestment of the proceeds from maturing securities for a rather long period of time, in order to make the phase out of a QE program gradual and prudent. Since every purchase of securities by the central bank is matched by an issuance of base money, large-scale purchase programs end up creating a structural excess of bank reserves. The monetary control framework is thus characterized by an oversupply in the interbank market, which pushes the market rates to the lower bound of the system: this is why it is called "floor system". The floor can coincide either with the ZLB or with the interest rate applied on bank reserves (which may take even negative values, as it used to be the case for several years in the eurozone). In addition to asset purchases, the unconventional policies include the long-term lending operations (LTLOs). These differ from the traditional (short-term) lending operations for three features: (i) large scale, (ii) long maturity (up to three/four years), and (iii) some incentives for banks to lend out to firms and households the money borrowed from the central bank.

The exit process from QE policies must be gradual and predictable, in order to avoid excessive volatility in financial markets. In general, the exit strategy follows the following four steps. (1) *Tapering*: the size of net asset purchases is reduced and eventually set to zero. (2) *Roll-over*: when some securities come to maturity, the central bank buys other securities in order to keep the size of its portfolio unchanged. (3) *Interest rate tightening*: policy interest rates are increased. (4) *Quantitative tightening* (*roll-off*): the policy portfolio is progressively downsized by discontinuing the roll-over of maturing securities. The decision to exit from QE policies does not imply that a central bank comes back to the old IRS/corridor system. To the contrary, the exit process has generally opened the way to a "new normal" with the following features:

i. The level of interest rates is the primary operational target of monetary policy. The stance is signaled by setting a target level for a short-term (O/N) market rate.
ii. This target is achieved in a floor system, where the market for bank reserves features a structural excess supply: the central bank manages its securities portfolio and makes loans to the banking sector in order to keep an abundance of liquidity in the system. The relevant policy rate is the interest rate paid on bank reserves. Some empirical evidence will be provided in Chapter 3, showing that a floor system can perform better than a corridor system in keeping the market O/N rate in line with the target level set by the central bank.
iii. The new tools remain in the toolkit of central banks, which can decide to start new AP programs and rounds of LTLO whenever they decide that these can be useful to expand the stance or preserve the transmission of monetary policy. Those measures, that used to be called "unconventional", have become standard tools available to implement monetary policy in the new normal.

The next two chapters will be devoted to the experiences of the Ecb and the Fed. For each of them, we will illustrate the strategy and the evolution over time of the operational framework, going from the traditional interest rate steering approach to the unconventional measures introduced in the years of quantitative easing, and finally showing the convergence towards the new normal.

The Ecb strategy is characterized by the priority given to the price stability objective. Until 2021, it was based on an analysis named "two-pillar approach", where the two pillars were the economic analysis and the monetary analysis. From a cross-check of the information coming from these two analyses, the Ecb was able to identify the risks to price stability and to act accordingly. In July 2021, the Governing Council announced a strategy revision addressing several issues, among which the definition of price stability: since then, the 2% inflation target has become a symmetric objective, and the historical expression "below but close to 2%" has been replaced by a formulation in which the ECB commits to react to any positive and negative inflation gaps with equal aggressiveness. The 2021 strategy review included an important announcement related to the Ecb's operational framework, which marked the exit from the QE era: the primary monetary policy instrument is the set of policy rates. The Governing Council also announced that the new instruments introduced in the previous years (asset purchases and long-term lending to the banking sector) would enter its toolkit on a permanent basis. The two-pillar approach has been substituted by the "integrated analytical framework", where the assessment of the risks to price stability is based on the analysis of the real economy and the inflation outlook, and financial variables are used to assess the transmission of monetary policy and financial stability.

Since the start of the European Monetary Union (EMU) until October 2008, the Ecb followed an interest rate steering policy implemented through a corridor system. The rate applied to the main refinancing operations (MROs) was the key policy rate. The first important innovations in its operational framework were introduced by the Ecb to address the financial instability created by the 2008 crisis: the "fixed rate full allotment" mechanism to provide liquidity through the MROs, the extension of the maturity and size of the longer-term refinancing operations (LTROs), and the covered bond purchase program. The sovereign debt crisis led to the adoption of the OMT (*Outright Monetary Transactions*) program in September 2012 (anticipated by the President Draghi's famous statement "whatever it takes") with which the Ecb has de facto assumed the role of lender of last resort for the eurozone governments. At the same time, the size and maturity of the LTROs were further extended (up to three years), injecting huge amount of liquidity in the money market. The recession of 2012–2013 induced the Governing Council to decide several reductions in policy rates until the zero lower bound was reached in September 2014; actually, that barrier was broken by bringing the interest rate on the deposit facility into negative territory, starting the *Negative Interest Rate Policy*. The years between 2008 and 2014 can be seen as a long transition phase, during which the Ecb's operational framework has gradually evolved from a corridor to a floor system. The Ecb started explicitly targeting the size of its balance sheet at the beginning of 2015, when the QE policy was adopted by introducing the large-scale asset purchase program known as APP (*Asset Purchase Programme*), the main component of which was the PSPP (*Public Sector Purchase Programme*). At the same time, the *Targeted Longer-Term Refinancing Operations* (T-LTRO) have been introduced, with some technical features aimed at inducing banks to use these loans to expand the volumes of credit to the economy. After a short phase (2018–2019) in which the Ecb initiated an exit strategy from QE, asset purchases have been resumed with the *Pandemic Emergency Purchase Programme* (PEPP) introduced in 2020 to address to the pandemic crisis. The Ecb exited again QE policies in 2022 and started a normalization of its policy, by raising interest rates and reducing the size of its balance sheet. The implementation framework currently relies on excess liquidity and on the rate applied to the deposit facility as the key policy rate.

In addition to the above issues, Chapter 4 will address some specific institutional features of the EMU, which explain both the delay with which the QE policy was introduced in the euro area, compared to the US and other countries, and some limitations of government bond purchase programs. Contrary to the Fed, the Ecb does not have the option of purchasing federal debt securities. The transfer of monetary sovereignty to the Ecb was not accompanied by a similar process regarding fiscal policy. During the introduction of QE, this institutional framework created quite a few disagreements at political level and within the Ecb itself, as well as some legal disputes. In the policy debate, some concerns emerged about the monetization of public debt and the moral hazard problems it might create. After QE policies have been abandoned, there is still the problem of how to manage the large stock of government bonds held by the Eurosystem. These issues are much less controversial in the US and other countries. Finally, the Eurosystem's asset purchases have contributed to a considerable increase in the balances that each national central bank (NCB) has in the euro area interbank payment system: the "TARGET balances". This has caused a bitter controversy, as negative balances may represent a debt position accumulated by some countries against others.

Again, we note that this controversy is absent in the US, despite the fact that here too there is a central bank organized on a federal basis (Federal Reserve System) and a payment system in which the Federal Reserve Banks can accumulate bilateral debit/credit positions between each other.

The comparison between the Ecb and the Fed will be discussed in more detail in Chapter 5, devoted to the US central bank. As we shall see, the Federal Reserve System has reached a higher level of centralization than the Eurosystem: both from a governance perspective, thanks to the voting share that the Board of Governors retains within the Federal Open Market Committee (FOMC) which is the body responsible for taking monetary policy decisions, and from an operational point of view, thanks to the delegation to the New York Fed of the task of carrying out all the open market operations.

The Fed's strategy responds to the dual mandate assigned to it by the Congress: maximum employment and price stability are the two final targets, which receive equal weight in its reaction function. The 2020 revision has introduced a shift from "flexible inflation targeting" to "flexible *average* inflation targeting": this implies that, should inflation persistently fall below the 2% target, the Fed is committed to bringing it moderately above 2% for a certain period of time. In contrast, the full employment objective is now pursued asymmetrically: the Fed intends to counter only negative deviations ("shortfalls") in employment from its potential level, without reacting to any positive deviation (unless this comes together with an undesirable rise in inflation).

The US central bank introduced QE measures well before the Ecb: during the 2007/2008 financial crisis. When the Ecb introduced its QE policies in 2015, the Fed was already implementing its exit strategy. QE was implemented in the US with massive purchase programs not only of government bonds, but also of mortgage-backed securities (MBS). As a result of these programs, the size of the Fed's balance sheet increased five-fold in the period between 2007 and 2014. The injection of base money created a structural excess of bank reserves, pushing money market rates towards the lower bound and making the Fed's operational framework shift from an interest rate steering to a floor system. The US money market is segmented between two different categories of participants: banks and non-bank intermediaries. This has created a system with two floors (which generally coincide with the limits periodically set by the Fed for the federal funds target range).

The exit process from QE policies started in 2014 and took a few years to be completed. The outcome of the "normalization" of the US monetary policy is the operational framework currently used by the Fed (after a new round of normalization taking place when the exceptional measures, introduced to address the pandemic crisis, have been abandoned). Its main features are the following. (1) The monetary policy stance is signaled by communicating a target range for the federal funds rate. This operational target is achieved by setting the two "administered rates": the one on bank reserves and the one on short-term deposits (reverse repos) of non-bank intermediaries. (2) The central bank's securities portfolio is managed so as to maintain an "ample supply of reserves", such that the money market works according to a (supply driven) *two-floor system*, with no need to actively manage the base money on a daily basis. (3) Balance sheet policies remain in the Fed's toolbox. The normalization of monetary policy after a long period of QE policies, in particular the interest rate tightening, may have some destabilizing effects on the financial sector: this is what has been observed in the 2023 banking crisis in the US (that will be discussed in the last section of Chapter 5).

In addition to the US and the euro area, large-scale asset purchase programs have been introduced in past years in several countries, like: UK, Japan, Sweden, Switzerland, and Mexico. Long-term lending operations have been used in Australia, Brazil, Canada, New Zealand, the Philippines, and Korea, in addition to the countries just mentioned, to expand their balance sheets during the years of QE. In a few countries, the central bank resorted to a negative interest rate policy, namely: Japan, Sweden, Denmark, and Switzerland (in addition to the euro area). Providing a systematic exposition of the unconventional policies implemented by many central banks worldwide is not the purpose of this book. I will limit myself to extend the analysis to the Bank of England and the Bank of Japan in Chapter 6.

Starting in 2009, the BoE introduced a QE policy with large asset purchases mainly focused on government bonds (*gilts*). Since then, its operational framework is based on a structural excess of reserves: the floor system. The lower limit to money market rates is the *Bank Rate*, which is the interest rate paid on the reserves deposited by banks at the BoE. Similarly to the Ecb, the BoE has made extensive use of long-term lending operations, including incentives for banks to lend the money borrowed from the central bank to businesses and households. In 2022, the BoE started downsizing its securities portfolio within its exit strategy from

QE policies. However, the floor system has remained in place: the aggregate level of bank reserves exceeds by far the amount needed by banks to manage their day-to-day liquidity needs, keeping the money market interest rates close to the Bank Rate. This is the policy rate used by the BoE to signal the stance of its policy. In the next few years, the BoE will continue unwinding the asset purchases accumulated so far, making the supply of bank reserves decline until it will eventually approach the minimum level needed by banks. To avoid any shortage of bank reserves at that stage, the BoE has introduced a new unlimited lending facility: *Short-Term Repo* (STR). At the steady state, the stock of reserves will be determined by the demand for reserves made by the banking system: banks will be able to meet their liquidity needs through use of the STR. The outcome of this normalization process will be a "demand-driven" floor system (as opposed to the "supply-driven" floor system adopted in the US, where the stock of reserves is determined by the Fed's open market operations).

The Bank of Japan (BoJ) was the first central bank introducing a QE policy in 2001, when it started to target the size of bank reserves instead of the interest rate level, which at that time has already reached the ZLB. However, it was unable to avoid the great depression experienced by Japan in the 1990s and in the next decade: for this reason, its action has been considered late and weak by many observers. Also the reaction to the 2007/2008 financial crisis was late: only in October 2010 the *Comprehensive Monetary Easing* program was introduced, under which the BoJ purchased several categories of financial assets. However, the amounts of securities purchased were rather small and did not lead to a significant increase in the size of the BoJ's balance sheet. Kuroda's governorship marked a turning point in BoJ policy, with the introduction of the *Quantitative and Qualitative Monetary Easing* (QQE) in 2013: this program gave a remarkable acceleration to the pace of asset purchases and it led to a significant increase in the average maturity of securities under purchase. Since 2016, a negative interest rate policy has been adopted, by applying an interest rate as low as -0.1% on bank reserves. In the same year, the *QQE with yield curve control* has been introduced: the BoJ is committed to keep the yield of 10-year government bonds around zero through its (potentially unlimited) bond purchases. This approach differs from the QE programs adopted by many other central banks: instead of announcing the amount of periodical asset purchases, the BoJ announces an interest rate target and adjusts the pace of purchases accordingly; the size of the program thus becomes endogenous. Finally, the BoJ's strategy responds to its *inflation-overshooting commitment*, which envisages that the 2% inflation target should be reached on average over the business cycle. Under this regard, the BoJ has anticipated (in 2016) the *average inflation targeting* approach that would be taken by the Fed lately (in 2020).

Looking ahead, the most challenging innovation in central banking will be the introduction of a *Central Bank Digital Currency*, opening up the possibility for anyone to hold money issued by the central bank in digital format. So far, individuals can hold central bank money only in physical form, namely as banknotes and coins. The motivation behind this innovation comes from the decline in the use of cash and the proliferation of digital payment services, stablecoins, and crypto-assets, implying relevant risks for consumers. The ultimate reason to adopt a CBDC is to preserve the public nature of money, offsetting the diffusion of private e-currencies and digital means of payments. Among the available alternatives, the version of CBDC most preferred by central banks worldwide is the *digital banknote*: unremunerated, available in small amounts (i.e. with holding limits) for retail payments, and not be seen as an asset to be used for investment purposes. In addition, albeit issued by the central bank, the CBDC will be generally distributed through the banking system. These features are designed to limit the risk of disintermediating the banking sector, with potential negative implications for credit flows and financial stability. The drawback of this approach is that it will severely limit the potential of the CBDC as an additional tool for implementing monetary policy. In Chapter 7, these issues will be discussed and some national initiatives in this area will be reported, namely those taking place in China, the euro area, the UK, and the US.

Finally, we will turn to "greening monetary policy". Monetary authorities are increasingly involved in the issue of environmental sustainability, both in their capacity as prudential supervisors over the financial sector and in their responsibility to conduct monetary policy and manage their own funds. Unconventional policies, with their legacy of large amounts of financial assets in the hands of central banks, have made even more urgent the need to control their exposure to climate-related risks and to assess the impact of their investment policy on the environment. In Chapter 7, we will overview the initiatives taken by the *Network for Greening the Financial System*, a forum involving more than one hundred central banks and supervisory authorities worldwide, and we will discuss the sustainability policy of the European Central Bank. The Ecb's Action Plan has opened the way to a revision of the questionable "market neutrality" approach to investment policy, and it has introduced a roadmap leading to the inclusion of climate-related factors within the criteria used to select the securities under purchase in monetary policy operations and eligible in the collateral framework.

CHAPTER 2

The Literature on Monetary Policy Implementation

Abstract This chapter discusses the literature on monetary policy implementation. First, it focuses on the recent debate about the outcome of the ongoing normalization process, with particular attention to the euro area and the US. Despite the different views about the pros and cons of the two options on the table, either keep the floor system in place or go back to the corridor system, the first option seems to be prevailing among scholars and central bankers, for several reasons: the problems related to the unwinding of the huge excess liquidity accumulated during the years of quantitative easing policies, the difficulties in providing reliable estimates of the demand for bank reserves, and the financial stability concerns raised by a regime relying on liquidity shortage. We will then review the older literature on the traditional interest rate steering framework, which has introduced some cornerstone ideas, such as: decoupling principle, averaging provision of the reserve requirement as a stabilizing mechanism, and open mouth operations.

Keywords Normalization of monetary policy · Excess liquidity · Interest rate policy · Balance sheet policy · Minimum reserve requirement · Open mouth operations · Money market

A. Baglioni, *Monetary Policy Implementation*,
https://doi.org/10.1007/978-3-031-53885-8_2

2.1 Introduction

In monetary economics, the operational framework of monetary policy is a neglected topic. The macroeconomic literature is in general focused on the strategic issues related to monetary policy: its final targets and the central bank reaction function, linking those targets to some operational targets used by the central bank. One famous example is the Taylor rule, linking the output gap and the inflation gap to the general level of interest rates, where the latter is supposed to be under the control of the central bank: this is the framework known as "interest rate steering". More recently, when the policy rates have reached the zero lower bound (ZLB), the size of the central bank balance sheet has become an important operational target, allowing central banks to implement an expansionary stance of monetary policy: this is the "Quantitative Easing" approach (QE). Again, the attention of the macroeconomic literature has been mainly devoted to the implications of ZLB and QE for the standard macroeconomic framework and to the channels through which the asset purchase programs can affect the economy.[1]

Little attention has been paid to the understanding of the links between the tools under the direct control of central banks and their operational targets. Some contributions in this area, surveyed in this chapter, dating back to the nineties and the first decade of this century, were focused on the interest rate steering framework and were able to clarify some misconceptions prevailing in the macroeconomic tradition (the IS-LM model): first of all, the idea that the central bank needs to change the supply of (base) money to implement a change of the policy rate.[2] But even when the macroeconomic theory has evolved towards a framework where the central bank is supposed to directly set the level of interest rates (the New Keynesian aggregate supply–demand model

[1] See Joyce et al. (2012) for a survey of the literature and Mishkin (2015) for an undergraduate textbook exposition, introducing the "kinked" aggregate demand schedule. Walsh (2017) provides a more advanced treatment of the implications of the effective lower bound for the New Keynesian macro-model, including unconventional policies (forward guidance and QE). It also includes an entire chapter devoted to the operating procedures of monetary policy, but its main focus is still on the "interest rate steering – corridor system", while little space is devoted to the more recent "QE – floor system".

[2] This misconception is present in the traditional model of monetary policy implementation, which is still used even in a leading textbook like Walsh (2017) (see page 588).

with a Taylor-type reaction function) several issues remain "under the carpet". A few examples are the following. How can the central bank affect (with a high degree of precision) the level of short-term rates, where the latter is determined by the interplay between supply and demand for funds in the money market? How the so-called "non-standard" measures of monetary policy, introduced after the financial crisis of 2007/2008 and more recently as a reaction to the pandemic crisis, have changed the way in which monetary policy is implemented? Looking forward, will the management of monetary policy come back to the traditional (interest rate steering) framework or will it go towards a "new normal"?

So far, little effort has been made to place the above issues within a coherent analytical framework. This book tries to do so, by providing a simple model of the operational framework of monetary policy. Despite its simplicity, the model should be able to capture the basic principles underlying the implementation of central banking and to show the transition from the traditional approach to the more recent developments. In this area, the institutional details play a relevant role: there is not a single way in which monetary policy is implemented, and several cross-country differences emerge when looking at national experiences.[3] However, some common features can be identified, which are shared among several central banks in the world.

In the following, I am going to discuss the literature related to monetary policy implementation, trying to highlight the links between this book and the main contributions in this area. I will start by summarizing the ongoing debate about the outcome of the normalization process currently taking place, after several years of quantitative easing policies. I will then go back to the older literature mostly dealing with the traditional interest rate steering approach to monetary policy implementation. I will finally mention a number of publications released by several central banks, which have been extremely useful in writing this book.

[3] See Borio (2001): "*A hundred ways to skin a cat*".

2.2 The Debate on Normalization: Stay on the Floor or Get Up?

The exit from QE policies and the normalization of monetary policy have prompted a renewed interest for the issues related to the operational framework.

In the euro area, several contributions have addressed the basic question: what should be the outcome of the normalization process that began in 2022? Should the ECB come back to the old interest rate steering (IRS) framework with scarce bank reserves or should it continue to rely on the current floor system with excess liquidity? Some analyses have been presented at the European Parliament ahead of the Monetary Dialogue with the ECB (in September 2023).[4] With some differences, they point to the second option as more desirable or at least realistic. Let me briefly summarize them.

Whelan (2023) suggests that the ECB should continue to operate an ample reserves environment, even after substantially reducing its balance sheet in the coming years. More precisely, he suggests that the ECB should rely on a demand-driven floor system, where the abundant liquidity will be provided through the already existing refinancing operations with fixed rate full allotment. By the way, this is the operational framework adopted by the Bank of England (as we shall see in Chapter 6). The main reason behind this suggestion is that the old IRS framework relies on an accurate estimate of the daily demand for reserves, which has become even more difficult nowadays than in the past. The demand for reserves has become larger and more unpredictable, due to several years of abundant liquidity and to some regulatory innovations, first of all the Liquidity Coverage Ratio (LCR).

Blot et al. (2023) argue that the floor system has been introduced in the euro area to remedy the fragmentation of the money market during the great financial crisis (2008/2009) and the sovereign debt crisis (2011/2012). In that context, the rise of excess reserves was demand driven, especially by the banks located in the "periphery" of the euro area (notably Italy and Spain) that had lost the ability to get funding in the interbank market. The key issue is thus "whether there may still be financial stress on interbank and sovereign markets that would require the floor

[4] They are available at https://www.europarl.europa.eu/cmsdata/275048/Topic2_CompilationSept2023.pdf.

system to remain in place". As the role of interbank market in channeling liquidity among banks has sharply decreased in recent years, reverting to a corridor system would imply some risks. An additional argument in favor of the floor system is that it provides banks with a safe asset, bank reserves, that banks may want to hold (in addition to Treasury bills) for prudential and regulatory reasons. Finally, Blot et al. (2023) suggest that the ECB should rely on a demand-driven system to provide liquidity, namely through full allotment refinancing operations (as it did at the outset of the financial crisis): this would avoid the distortions on the sovereign debt markets implied by a supply-driven system relying on asset purchases.

Dabrowsky (2023) provides some arguments supporting the view that the ECB should come back to the old IRS framework with scarce reserves. However, he acknowledges that such goal, albeit desirable, is actually unfeasible, due to the sharp acceleration in quantitative tightening that would be required to implement it. He computes that at the current pace of QT (as of 2023), it would take eight years for the ECB to return to a pre-pandemic size of its balance sheet (notice that this would still imply an excess liquidity, albeit substantially reduced). Since "every monetary tightening involves a risk of financial instability", he concludes that "the ECB will not be able to return to the SRS (scarce reserves system) in the foreseeable future".

The main argument, provided by Dabrowsky (2023) in support of the old IRS framework, is related to central bank's independence. Quoting a statement from Baglioni (2023), namely "the floor system gives central banks one more degree of freedom, since the interest rate policy and the balance sheet policy become two independent instruments, that can be targeted to different objectives", he argues that a multi-task mandate of the central bank might create a conflict between some tasks (e.g. supporting growth or financial stability) and the price stability objective, thus compromising the independence of the central bank. However, this argument can be easily objected. The strategy of the ECB (as defined in its Statute) envisages the support to the general economic policies of the EU with a view to contributing to the achievement of the Union's objectives (including full employment and balanced economic growth), provided this does not conflict with price stability: thus, the mandate of the ECB is indeed multi-task, albeit with a clear hierarchy of objectives, and this is true regardless of its operational framework. Preserving the liquidity of financial institutions, acting as a lender of last resort, is also within the mandate of any central bank. Under this regard, the balance sheet policy may contribute to financial stability: asset purchases can be used to preserve the liquidity of specific market segments (e.g. asset-backed securities or sovereign bonds), leaving the macroeconomic stabilization goal (price stability and full employment) to the interest rate policy. In addition, the independence of the ECB relies on several guarantees included in its Statute, among which: the prohibition to seek or take instructions from EU institutions and national governments, the prohibition of directly financing the public sector (either by granting credit facilities to public entities or by purchasing government securities in the primary market), the long (eight years) and non-renewable term of office of the Executive Board members, and finally the economic independence relying on the ECB's own capital paid up by the national central banks. Again, these guarantees are not related to the operational framework.

Finally, Dabrowsky (2023) argues that the floor system makes the interbank market redundant, since "it is easier and less risky for commercial banks to put surplus liquidity on a central bank deposit than to lend it to other banks". This argument is in line with that made by Borio (2023), namely that the floor system with abundant liquidity has "killed" the overnight interbank market, since the central bank has taken over much of the intermediation in such market. However, this argument can be objected by considering the above-mentioned counter-argument made by Blot et al. (2023), namely that in the euro area the causality was reversed: in the context of the great financial crisis and sovereign debt crisis, "excess reserves were needed because the overnight market was already dead".

The fragmentation of the money market in the euro area, across jurisdictions and across banks, is well documented by Aberg et al. (2021). As a consequence, the aggregate demand for bank reserves increases: banks with difficult or costly access to the money market may be led to resort to central bank operations, generating a demand-driven increase in reserves; at the same time, other banks endowed with excess liquidity may prefer to store it at their central bank deposits rather than circulating it to other banks. Such fragmentation could re-emerge in the future, complicating the transition towards lower levels of reserves. Aberg et al. (2021) also argue that estimating the excess liquidity needed to operate a floor system may be difficult, due to the uncertain demand for reserves. But of course, this uncertainty makes it even more problematic to operate a corridor system, which requires a point estimation of the daily demand for reserves.

In the US, the first round of normalization took place between 2014 and 2019, when the Fed was exiting the QE policies adopted to address the great financial crisis.[5] In January 2019, the FOMC made clear that the "ample reserves regime" would be the Fed's implementation framework for the years to come.[6] This decision was based on the analysis made by the staff of the Fed. The outcome of that analysis, reported in the minutes of the FOMC meeting of 7–8 November 2018,[7] was that the corridor system worked well before the financial crisis, when reserve demand was fairly stable and largely influenced by payment needs and reserve requirements; following the crisis, there was some uncertainty whether the reserve demand would be sufficiently stable for the Fed to target the interest rate following the corridor approach. The floor system was believed to be more reliable, as in such a regime the money market rates are not sensitive to small fluctuations in the demand for and supply of reserves. FOMC participants agreed that, based on the experience of previous years, the ample reserves regime was able to provide a good control of short-term money market rates in a variety of market conditions, including those where severe liquidity strains needed to be addressed. This view has been confirmed in a speech given by the Vice President of the New York Fed (and head of the Open Market Trading Desk) Lorie Logan, stressing that the ample reserve regime is very effective at controlling short-term interest rates, and it achieves this effectiveness in a simple and efficient manner, reducing the need for active management of reserve supply, thanks to its ability to absorb shocks to the supply of or demand for reserves; in particular, it is able to accommodate the variability of the autonomous factors affecting the base money ("non-reserve liabilities" in the Fed's terminology).[8] The model presented in Chapter 3 will address in detail the reasons why the floor system is expected to be more effective in absorbing liquidity shocks and stabilize money market rates than the corridor system.

Another reason provided by the FOMC members to opt for a regime of policy implementation with abundant excess reserves is that it could enhance financial stability and reduce operational risks in the payment system. This issue has been addressed at length in a New York Fed's

[5] The second round of normalization started in late 2021, when the Fed exited the exceptionally expansive policies introduced to address the Covid-19 crisis (see Chapter 5).

[6] See Fed (2019).

[7] Available at https://www.federalreserve.gov/monetarypolicy/files/fomcminutes20181108.pdf.

[8] See Logan (2019).

Staff Report,[9] showing that the downsizing of the Fed's balance sheet up to the summer of 2019, together with some liquidity requirements inducing large US banks to maintain substantial balances at the Fed and discouraging them from incurring daylight overdrafts on their accounts at the Fed, produced significant stress in the US money market, increasing the volatility of the Treasury repo rates. This process culminated with the large and prominently reported disruption in repo markets in 16–18 September 2019, leading the Fed to revert its balance sheet normalization.[10] A number of studies (referred to in the Staff Report) show that low balances held at the Fed lead to intraday cash hoarding by banks, raising concerns over money market liquidity and potentially threatening financial stability. An ample reserve regime, to the contrary, supports financial stability because reserves have special benefits for intraday liquidity management above and beyond those of other liquid assets. As we are going to see in Chapter 5, the tension between policy normalization and financial stability has resurfaced in the spring of 2023, when a few US banks went bankrupt. To address the liquidity crisis, which from those banks threatened to spread to other US banks, the Fed has introduced a new credit line: *Bank Term Funding Program*.

In the internal debate within the FOMC over the normalization of its policy, some participants argued that the ample reserves regime has a relevant drawback, namely the large interest expenses associated with the remuneration of reserves. This might raise some difficulties related to Fed's reputation and communication. To put it with the words of Ben Bernanke: "the Fed does face an appearance problem from the fact that it is writing checks to banks".[11] In turn, the fact that banks appear to benefit at the expense of taxpayers can provide some ammunition to Congress to exert some political influence over the central bank.[12]

More generally, there are some political economy issues related to the floor system, which relies on a large central bank's balance sheet. As Plosser says, this "creates the opportunity and incentive for political actors to exploit the Fed's balance sheet to conduct off-budget fiscal policy

[9] See Copeland et al. (2021).

[10] Just to anticipate something that we are going to see in Chapter 5, the evolution of the main items of the Fed's balance sheet (bank reserves on the liability side and securities portfolio on the asset side) is shown in Figs. 5.8 and 5.9.

[11] See Bernanke and Kohn (2016).

[12] See Jordan and Luther (2022).

and credit allocation. Such actions would undermine independence and further politicize the Federal Reserve…The temptation would be to turn the Fed's balance sheet into a hedge fund, investing in projects demanded by Congress".[13] In other words, politicians may be tempted to exert pressure on the central bank and induce it to fund public bodies or private entities, thus crossing the border between monetary and fiscal policies.[14] This moral hazard argument has presumably more merit in the US than in the euro area, where the central bank enjoys very strong guarantees of independence. Even in the US this criticism, addressed to the floor system when the QE policies were in place, may become less relevant after the normalization process has been completed, since that process implies a substantial downsizing of the Fed's balance sheet. This book will not enter into these political economy issues: the floor and corridor systems will be compared on technical grounds only (in Chapter 3). However, the moral hazard argument, related to the purchases of government securities by the central bank, will be discussed in the context of the Eurosystem's institutional setup (in Chapter 4).

Despite the different views about the pros and cons of the two different approaches to monetary policy implementation, namely the corridor and floor systems, it is possible to identify a common trend in central banking. The problems related to the unwinding of the huge excess liquidity, accumulated during several rounds of QE policies, and the difficulties in providing reliable estimates of the demand for bank reserves, are leading several central banks to keep the floor system in place, albeit together with a substantial downsizing of their balance sheets. For the foreseeable future, monetary policy will rely on interest rate steering together with an abundant supply of liquidity, which promises to be more effective in controlling short-term interest rates and simpler to implement than a regime based on liquidity shortage. The latter raises also some concerns in terms of financial stability. In some countries, like the US, UK, and Canada, the outcome of the normalization process, namely a framework that relies on the floor system to steer interest rates, has been officially announced by their respective central banks.[15] In others, like the euro area and Japan, this is de facto the operational framework currently in

[13] See Plosser (2017).

[14] Selgin (2020) refers to these policies as "fiscal QE".

[15] See Fed (2022a, 2022b), Bank of England (2022), and Bank of Canada (2022).

place (as of 2023). This "new normal" in monetary policy implementation will be analyzed in Chapter 3 at a general level; that chapter will provide some arguments and some empirical evidence supporting the view that a floor system is presumably better than a corridor system, at least as far as the ability of keeping the money market rates in line with the target level is concerned. The next three chapters will address the normalization process in the euro area, the US, and UK, respectively.

2.3 The Literature on Interest Rate Steering

In the area of monetary policy implementation, the pioneering work done by Borio (1997, 2001) provided a conceptual framework to analyze the different institutional contexts at the international level. At that time, the focus was on the traditional interest rate steering approach to managing monetary policy. Even without an explicit analytical treatment, the graphical analysis by Borio made clear the distinction between two regimes: with and without a reserve requirement. Absent a reserve requirement, the demand for bank reserves (working balances) is quite inelastic to interest rates, calling for a very active management of liquidity by the central bank in order to avoid excessive fluctuations of interest rates in the money market. To the contrary, the averaging provision included in the reserve requirement provides a self-stabilizing mechanism for the overnight interbank market, calling for a less active day-to-day management of liquidity by the central bank. Borio also made clear the role of liquidity management: regulate the supply of bank reserves in order to achieve the interest rate target. Under this regard, the main task of the daily work of central banks is that of offsetting the liquidity shocks due to the autonomous factors affecting the net liquidity position of the banking system. In addition, the central bank can affect the market rates by signaling its target level for interest rates through explicit announcements. Under this approach, the target on a short-term rate is the operational objective of monetary policy, to be distinguished from the final objectives like price stability and economic growth.

Disyatat (2008) provides a discussion of monetary policy implementation, stressing that the function of open market operations is to ensure that the demand for bank reserves is satisfied. They do not play an active role in setting the interest rate level, which is set by the central bank's announcements relative to its target level for short-term interest rates. Such announcements act as a coordinating device for money market participants, and their effectiveness relies on the commitment of the central bank to implement the announced target by making open market operations, if needed: the central bank is a sort of market maker in the market for bank reserves. This signaling mechanism enables the central bank to change its target level for interest rates without making any adjustment to the quantity of base money provided through open market operations.

The last point is taken up and expanded by Borio and Disyatat (2009). They stress that distinction between "signaling" and "liquidity management operations". Under the interest rate steering approach ("interest rate policy"), the stance of monetary policy is defined in terms of a short-term rate (typically overnight) and it is signaled to the market participants by announcing the level desired by the central bank for such a rate: this announcement acts as a coordinating device for market expectations. Liquidity management operations are designed only to make such interest rate level effective: their task is to provide all the liquidity demanded by the banking system, in order to avoid large deviations of market interest rates from the predefined target level. They play a purely technical role and do not contain any information relevant for the monetary policy stance. From this approach, Borio and Disyatat derive what they call the "decoupling principle", namely: "The same amount of bank reserves can coexist with very different levels of interest rates; conversely, the same interest rate can coexist with different amounts of reserves". They also discuss the QE approach ("balance sheet policy") where the decoupling principle still holds, thanks to the ability of the central bank to sterilize the impact of its own operations (like asset purchases) on the amount of bank reserve balances by undertaking offsetting transactions.

This book (Chapter 3 in particular) builds on the contributions by Borio and Disyatat but it differs from them on several grounds. First, it provides an explicit analytical framework to analyze the implementation of monetary policy, under both the traditional interest rate steering approach and the more recent quantitative easing policies, including the negative interest rate policy. Second, such a framework is able to clarify some important qualifications to the decoupling principle. Just to anticipate what we are going to see below, under the interest rate steering approach the decoupling principle holds in one direction only. The central bank can set different levels for its target interest rate, while keeping the amount of bank reserves unchanged. To the contrary, there is only one level of reserves consistent with an announced target level of interest rate; in other words, the central bank is not free to set the supply of reserves at different levels and keep the interest rate unchanged at the same time. To the contrary, the decoupling principle works in both directions under the QE approach: the central bank can implement different levels of interest rates with the same amount of reserves as well as change the supply of reserves while keeping the target level of interest rate unchanged. This result is due to the structural excess supply in the market for bank reserves, typical of a quantitative easing policy, not to sterilization. This result in turn has a far-reaching implication. The QE policies introduce one more degree of freedom in the management of monetary policy. interest rate and quantity of base money become two independent instruments, and both can be used to define and signal the stance of monetary policy. This additional degree of freedom was not available under the traditional interest rate policy.

Guthrie and Wright (2000) (GW) made a fundamental contribution to the theory of monetary policy implementation, highlighting that a central bank can set the level of money market rates (even on maturities longer than overnight) simply by announcing a target level and threatening to implement open market operations, in case of deviations of the market rate from that target, such that the overnight rate follows the desired path: this is what they call "open mouth operations", an expression that has become standard in this literature. Provided its announcements are credible, the central bank does not need to make actual interventions to steer the short-term interest rates: the threat to do so is enough to affect the expected and actual market rate. They apply their model to the Bank of New Zealand (targeting the three-month interest rate) but their model is applicable also in many other contexts.

Building on GW, Woodford (2000) provides a clear illustration of the corridor system ("channel system" in his words) where the equilibrium in the market for bank reserves is determined by the intersection between an interest rate-elastic (downward-sloped) demand schedule and a (S-shaped) supply function. Both GW and Woodford refer to an institutional setting where there is no reserve requirement and where the central bank applies penalty rates to the two standing facilities. Banks trade in the interbank market balancing the expected cost of ending the business day either short of liquidity (being forced to apply to the lending facility) or long of liquidity (being forced to deposit some cash reserves on the deposit facility). The equilibrium market rate will be within the two boundaries set by the rates applied to the standing facilities. In particular, if the probability distribution of end-of-day balances is symmetric, the overnight rate will lie at the center of the corridor and it will be equal to the target set by the central bank. The stance of monetary policy can be changed by announcing a change of this target level, and moving the rates on the standing facilities accordingly, without altering the supply of base money.

The interest rate steering framework presented in this book (Sect. 3.2) relies on the ability of the central bank to affect the expected interest rate in the interbank market simply by announcing a target level for the overnight rate: the credibility of this announcement derives from the ability of the central bank to calibrate the supply of bank reserves to affect the market equilibrium in the desired way, in the same spirit of the GW's "open mouth operations". However, contrary to GW and Woodford, the model below will show how a corridor system can work in an institutional setting where a reserve requirement is present, as it is in many countries (like the euro area and the US until recently): in such a case, the ability of the central bank to affect the money market equilibrium relies on the features of the reserve demand schedule related to the averaging mechanism included in the reserve requirement, rather than on the penalties associated with the two standing facilities. The latter become relevant, providing a stabilization tool, only in case of extreme market conditions, either tight or soft, where some banks actually resort either to the marginal lending or to the deposit facility. In addition, we are going to see how this monetary control framework changes when a central bank adopts unconventional measures under the QE approach, leading to a floor system (Sect. 3.3). Finally, we will address the properties of the "new normal", i.e. the outcome of the normalization of monetary policy (Sect. 3.4).

Woodford (2000) also addresses the likely consequences of the progressive diffusion of digital (private) means of payment potentially able to substitute cash. His main conclusion is that such an evolution of the payment system should not alter the basic mechanism of monetary policy implementation, relying on the control of short-term interest rates.[16] Even more, the elimination of cash might make the job of central

[16] A similar conclusion is reached by Brunnermeier et al. (2019), although in their analysis that result is conditional on the assumption that the central bank money retains the role of unit of account for the economy as a whole, including the platforms where the private digital currencies can circulate.

bankers easier, by eliminating a source of volatility in the demand for base money and a source of uncertainty in the calibration of the supply of bank reserves needed to achieve a given interest rate target. This book too (Chapter 7) will explore the implications of the evolution of the payment system in a digital economy, but it will focus on the more recent and potentially revolutionary trend: the introduction of a central bank digital currency (CBDC).

The book by Bindseil (2004) provides a detailed discussion of the issues, both theoretical and institutional, related to monetary policy implementation. Building on Poole (1968), he presents a model of the corridor system, where the equilibrium interest rate in the interbank market turns out to be an average of the rates applied by the central bank to the two standing facilities, weighted by the probabilities that banks end up being either short or long of liquidity at the end of the market session, thus being forced to apply either to the lending or to the deposit facility, respectively. The central bank is supposed to implement a "neutral" management of liquidity, such that the two probabilities are perfectly balanced (each equal to ½) and the equilibrium market rate is exactly in the middle of the corridor. The central bank is able to change the stance of monetary policy by changing the rates on the standing facilities, without altering the liquidity provided through its open market operations.[17] Despite some similarities with the corridor model of GW and Woodford, Bindseil's model differs from their approach, and from my own, as it does not assign any role to the ability of the central bank to affect market expectations by announcing its target rate.[18]

Bindseil's model incorporates the reserve requirement, but with one important difference from my own. It relies on the "martingale property" for the interbank interest rate: the expected day-to-day change is zero. Such property, in turn, relies on the assumption that banks engage in inter-temporal arbitrage operations without limits, so that the daily

[17] The same model is used in the book by Bindseil and Fotia (2021), which provides an extensive survey of monetary policy implementation techniques, including those used in unconventional policies.

[18] Bindseil himself acknowledges this point when stating that his symmetric corridor approach "has nothing to do with the idea of open mouth operations made popular by GW" (page 89).

demand for bank reserves is perfectly elastic. As we shall see, this assumption is unrealistic: inter-temporal arbitrage trades are limited and the elasticity of the demand schedule is finite.

In their chapter in the *Handbook of Monetary Economics*, Friedman and Kuttner (2010) (F-K) observe that the standard macroeconomic "new Keynesian" model, by "taking the interest rate as a primitive" or "adding to the model a Taylor-type interest rate rule", does not give "any clue to how the central bank actually goes about setting its chosen policy interest rate". Even when trying to address this issue, "the traditional account of how this process works involves the central bank's varying the supply of bank reserves" in order to achieve a change of the level of interest rates (pp. 1–2). F-K provide an extensive discussion and empirical evidence showing that this is not the case: the central bank is able to move the market interest rate by announcing its target level and making the demand (not the supply) for bank reserves to shift, much like in Fig. 3.7. The central bank is able to do so by affecting expectations, provided its announcement is credible, and it does not need to change the amount of supplied reserves: this is the decoupling principle, although F-K do not use this term. In the F-K approach, like in my own, this implementation mechanism relies on the averaging facility included in the reserve requirement, making the demand for reserves depend on the difference between the current and the expected overnight interest rates (within the same maintenance period). However, they do not explicitly model the microeconomic optimization problem leading to such a demand schedule; a simple way of addressing this issue will be introduced in Sect. 3.2.

F-K also discuss the policy response to the 2007–2009 financial crisis, leading to a large expansion of central banks' balance sheets and to an implementation framework where the interest rate in the interbank market is driven from the center of the "corridor" down to the rate paid on bank reserves. They stress that this evolution enables the policymaker to have two independent instruments: the targeted interest rate level and the quantity of bank reserves supplied (the decoupling principle again). Building on the experience accumulated since the financial crisis, I will be able to introduce an explicit distinction between the "corridor" and the "floor" systems and to show the crucial differences between them. I will also address the implementation of a negative interest rate policy (NIRP).

The opportunities implied by a floor system were actually anticipated by the article of Goodfriend (2002), where he proposed to introduce the remuneration of the reserve balances deposited by banks at the central bank: a policy that the Fed has introduced six years later (in October 2008). He clearly stated that this innovation would enable the central bank to have two independent instruments to implement its policy: interest rate and quantity of reserves (provided the amount of reserves is large enough to satiate the market for bank reserves, so that the market rate sticks to the rate paid by the central bank on reserves, which becomes the policy rate). In his approach, the central bank can target the two instruments to different goals: the interest rate policy can be finalized to macroeconomic stability, and the bank reserves policy can address financial stability or the funding of the public sector. This approach has potential far-reaching implications and it will be discussed in Chapter 3. In a related paper, Goodfriend (2000) analyzes how the two instruments, NIRP and reserves policy, can be used, by exploiting different transmission channels, to overcome the limitation set by the ZLB to monetary policy. In order to implement the NIRP, he proposes to introduce a carry tax on bank reserves and cash. The modern version of this proposal might be the introduction of a CBDC with a negative remuneration. The implications of a remunerated (or unremunerated) CBDC will be discussed in Chapter 7.

2.4 Central Banks' Publications

In addition to the literature reviewed above, this book builds on the publications released by several central banks with the purpose of illustrating their own operational frameworks. A remarkable example is given by the papers written by the staff of the Fed's Board of Governors, which provide a lot of information about the implementation of monetary policy in the US; in particular, they highlight the transition from the old regime of active reserve management to the ample reserve regime that characterizes the Fed's new normal: see Ihrig et al. (2015a, 2015b, 2017, 2020a, 2020b). Rostagno et al. (2019) and Hartmann–Smetz (2018) provide a detailed account of twenty years of monetary policy management in the euro area; Altavilla et al. (2021) focus on the non-standard measures adopted by the Ecb since 2014; Alvarez et al. (2017) provide many technical details and data on the policy instruments used by the Ecb. Bank of England (2011, 2014, 2023a, 2023b) provides a description of the implementation framework adopted by the BoE and of its evolution in recent times. Gravelle et al. (2023) compare the corridor and floor systems in the context of the Canadian process to exit QE policies, finding that the latter is preferable under several dimensions: that paper has provided the basis for the decision taken by the Bank of Canada to keep the floor system in place even after the quantitative tightening process has been completed. BIS (2019) provides a cross-country analysis of the unconventional tools introduced by several central banks in recent years. Bech and Malkhozov (2016) survey the implementation of NIRP in Europe.[19]

References

Aberg, P., Corsi, M., Grossmann-Wirth, V., Hudepohl, T., Mudde, Y., Rosolin, T., & Schobert, F. (2021). *Demand for central bank reserves and monetary policy implementation frameworks: The case of the Eurosystem* (ECB Occasional Paper no. 282).

Altavilla, C., Lemke, W., Linzert, T., Tapking, J., & von Landesberger, J. (2021). *Assessing the efficacy, efficiency, and potential side effects of the ECB's monetary policy instruments since 2014* (ECB Occasional Paper No. 278).

Alvarez, I., Casavecchia, F., De Luca, M., Duering, A., Eser, F., Helmus, C., Hemous, C., Herrala, N., Jakovicka, J., Lo Russo, M., Pasqualone, F., Rubens, M., Soares, R., & Zennaro, F. (2017). *The use of the Eurosystem's monetary policy instruments and operational framework since 2012* (ECB Occasional Paper No. 188).

Baglioni, A. (2023). Monetary policy implementation: Which "new normal"?. *Journal of International Money and Finance*, available on-line: https://www.sciencedirect.com/science/article/pii/S0261560623001997

Bank of Canada. (2022, April). *Bank of Canada provides operational details for quantitative tightening and announces that it will continue to implement monetary policy using a floor system*. Market notice.

Bank of England. (2011). *The UK quantitative easing policy: Design, operation and impact* (Quarterly Bulletin 2011/Q3).

Bank of England. (2014). *The Bank of England's Sterling monetary framework*. London.

Bank of England. (2022). *Explanatory Note: Managing the operational implications of APF unwind for asset sales, control of short-term market interest rates and the Bank of England's balance sheet*. London.

Bank of England. (2023a). *Bank of England market operations guide: Our objectives*. London.

Bank of England. (2023b). *Bank of England market operations guide: Our tools*. London.

[19] These are just a few examples. Many other references to publications and public statements released by central banks will be given throughout this book.

Bech, M., & Malkhozov, A. (2016, March). How have central banks implemented negative policy rates. *BIS Quarterly Review*.

Bernanke, B., & Kohn, D. (2016, February 16). *The Fed's interest payments to banks*. Brookings commentary.

Bindseil, U. (2004). *Monetary policy implementation*. Oxford University Press.

Bindseil, U., & Fotia, A. (2021). *Introduction to central banking*. Springer.

BIS. (2019). *Unconventional monetary policy tools: A cross-country analysis*. Paper no.63 of the Committee on the Global Financial System, Bank for International Settlements, Basel.

Blot, C., Creel, J., & Geerolf, F. (2023, September). *Excess liquidity in the euro area? Assessment and possible ways forward* (Monetary Dialogue Paper requested by the ECON Committee of the European Parliament).

Borio, C. (1997). *The implementation of monetary policy in industrial countries: A survey* (BIS Economic Paper no. 47).

Borio, C. (2001). *A hundred ways to skin a cat: comparing monetary policy operating procedures in the United States, Japan and the euro area* (BIS Working Paper no. 9).

Borio, C. (2023). *Getting up from the floor* (BIS Working Paper no. 1100).

Borio, C., & Disyatat, P. (2009). *Unconventional monetary policies: An appraisal* (BIS Working Paper no. 292).

Brunnermeier, M., James, H., & Landau, J.-P. (2019). *The digitalization of money* (NBER Working Paper n. 26300).

Copeland, A., Duffie, D., & Yang, Y. (2021). *Reserves were not so ample after all* (Federal Reserve Bank of New York Staff Report No. 974).

Dabrowsky, M. (2023, September). *Excess liquidity in the euro area: Sources and remedies* (Monetary Dialogue Paper requested by the ECON Committee of the European Parliament).

Disyatat, P. (2008). *Monetary policy implementation: Misconceptions and their consequences* (BIS Working Paper no.269).

Fed. (2019, January). *Statement regarding monetary policy implementation and balance sheet normalization*, Federal Open Market Committee.

Fed. (2022a, January). *Principles for reducing the size of the Federal Reserves' balance sheet*, Federal Open Market Committee.

Fed. (2022b, May). *Plans for reducing the size of the Federal Reserves' balance sheet*, Federal Open Market Committee.

Friedman, B. M., & Kuttner, K. N. (2010), Implementation of monetary policy: How do central banks set interest rates? *Handbook of Monetary Economics, 3*, 1345–1438.

Goodfriend, M. (2000). Overcoming the zero bound on interest rate policy. *Journal of Money, Credit, and Banking, 32*(4), 1007–1035.

Goodfriend, M. (2002). Interest on reserves and monetary policy. *FRBNY Economic Policy Review, 8*(1), 77–84.

Gravelle, et al. (2023). *Reviewing Canada's monetary policy implementation system: Does the evolving environment support maintaining a floor system?* (Staff Discussion Paper 2023–10). Bank of Canada.

Guthrie, G., & Wright, J. (2000). Open mouth operations. *Journal of Monetary Economics, 46*, 489–516.

Hartmann, P., & Smets, F. (2018). *The first twenty years of the ECB: Monetary policy* (ECB Working Paper no. 2219).

Ihrig, J., Meade, E., & Weinbach, G. (2015a). Rewriting monetary policy 101: What's the Fed's preferred post-crisis approach to raising interest rates? *Journal of Economic Perspectives, 29*(4), 177–198.

Ihrig, J., Meade, E., & Weinbach, G. (2015b). *Monetary policy 101: A primer on the Fed's changing approach to policy implementation* (Finance and Economics Discussion Series 2015-047). Board of Governors of the Federal Reserve System, Washington, DC.

Ihrig, J., Mize, L., & Weinbach, G. (2017). *How does the Fed adjust its securities holdings and who is affected?* (Finance and Economics Discussion Series 2017-099). *Board of Governors of the Federal Reserve System*, Washington, DC.

Ihrig, J., Senyuz, Z., & Weinbach, G. (2020a). *The Fed's ample-reserves approach to implementing monetary policy* (Finance and Economics Discussion Series 2020-022). Board of Governors of the Federal Reserve System, Washington, DC.

Ihrigh, J., Senyuz, Z., & Weinbach, G. (2020b). *Implementing monetary policy in an "ample-reserves" regime: When in crisis (Note 3 of 3).* FEDS Notes. Board of Governors of the Federal Reserve System, Washington, DC.

Joyce, M., Miles, D., Scott, A., & Vayanos, D. (2012). Quantitative easing and unconventional monetary policy—An introduction. *Economic Journal, 122*, F271–288.

Jordan, J., & Luther, W. (2022). Central bank independence and the Federal Reserve's new operating regime. *Quarterly Review of Economics and Finance, 84*, 510–515.

Logan, L. (2019, April 17). *Observations on implementing monetary policy in an ample-reserves regime*. Federal Reserve Bank of New York.

Mishkin, F. (2015). *Macroeconomics: Policy and practice*. Pearson Education.

Poole, W. (1968). Commercial bank reserve management in a stochastic model: Implications for monetary policy. *Journal of Finance, 23*, 769–791.

Plosser, C. (2017). *The risks of a Fed balance sheet unconstrained by monetary policy* (Economics Working Paper 17102). Hoover Institution—Stanford University.

Rostagno, M., Altavilla, C., Carboni, G., Lemke, W., Motto, R., Saint Guilhem, A., & Yiangou, J. (2019). *A tale of two decades: The ECB's monetary policy at 20* (ECB Working Paper no. 2346).

Selgin, G. (2020). *The menace of fiscal QE*, CATO Institute, Washington, DC.

Walsh, C. (2017). *Monetary theory and policy* (4th ed.). MIT Press.
Whelan, K. (2023, September). *The future of ECB liquidity policy* (Monetary Dialogue Paper requested by the ECON Committee of the European Parliament).
Woodford, M. (2000). *Monetary policy in a world without money* (NBER Working Paper no. 7853).

CHAPTER 3

The Operational Framework of Monetary Policy: A Simple Model

Abstract This chapter provides a model of monetary policy implementation under three operational frameworks. The first one is the traditional interest rate steering—corridor system, based on the active management of a scarce supply of bank reserves. The second is the floor system, relying on an ample supply of reserves: this is the approach introduced with quantitative easing policies targeting the size of central bank's balance sheet. The third one is the new normal, where the operational target is the interest rate and this is pursued under a floor system: after exiting QE policies, central banks maintain an excess liquidity in the market, albeit lower than before. The decoupling principle implies that, in a floor system, interest rate and balance sheet policies become two independent instruments. Some empirical evidence shows that the floor system is more effective than the corridor system in keeping money market interest rates in line with the announced target level. The chapter also addresses the transmission channels of monetary policy and the potential tensions between financial stability and monetary policy.

Keywords Corridor system · Floor system · New normal · Interbank market · Decoupling principle · Negative interest rate policy · Transmission channels · Financial stability

A. Baglioni, *Monetary Policy Implementation*,
https://doi.org/10.1007/978-3-031-53885-8_3

3.1 Introduction

How does the central bank control the level of interest rates in the financial market? Once the interest rate has reached the zero lower bound (ZLB), as it did for several years in the past, what are the tools available to the central bank to implement its policy? How can monetary policy affect the economic variables on which its ultimate objectives are defined, such as the inflation rate and the level of economic activity? This chapter will try to answer these questions by introducing a simple model of the operational framework and by discussing the transmission channels of monetary policy.

The analysis of the operational framework focuses on the technical ways in which the central bank can change the stance of monetary policy, by making either an expansionary or a restrictive intervention, in response to the indications coming from its strategy and to the information about the relevant economic variables. We will distinguish between three operational frameworks. The first is the more traditional one, which was in place for many years until the great financial crisis of 2007/2008. It relies on the control of interest rates: this is why it is labeled "interest rate steering" (IRS). For the reasons that will be explained below, this monetary control framework goes also under the name of "corridor system".

The second one relies on a wide range of innovative instruments, which collectively go under the name of "unconventional monetary policy". They include large-scale purchases of securities and long-term lending to banks: these policies, referred to as Quantitative Easing (QE), target the size of the central bank balance sheet. But they also include the possibility of bringing interest rates into negative territory, albeit within certain limits, following the Negative Interest Rate Policy (NIRP). The huge amounts of liquidity, injected into the financial system through the unconventional policies, have implied the introduction of a new implementation framework: the "floor system". In the toolbox of innovative monetary policies, communication has also become part of the mix. It is not that it was absent in the traditional scheme, but it has assumed an increasingly important role in recent years: central banks rely on forward guidance to guide market participants' expectations.

The unconventional policies have been introduced to overcome the limitations of the traditional IRS framework in a world of low inflation and interest rates close to the ZLB. Starting in 2022, most central banks ended their QE programs and started a "normalization" of their policies, also as a reaction to the ongoing inflation. During this process, they have raised the level of interest rates well above the ZLB and they have started reducing the size of their securities portfolio and of their balance sheet, introducing the so-called "Quantitative Tightening" (QT). This process did not lead central banks to resume the old IRS approach to monetary policy implementation. Its outcome has been instead a "new normal" that combines some features of the old framework with some important innovations introduced in the years of the unconventional policies, which left a durable legacy. In the new normal, the level of interest rates is again the operational target of monetary policy. However, this is achieved within a floor system with an ample supply of bank reserves, which has substituted the old active management of a scarce supply of reserves. This chapter will provide some empirical evidence supporting the view that the floor system is superior to the corridor system as a way to control the level of money market interest rates. This is the reason, albeit not the only one, why central banks may want to continue relying on the floor system even when they have abandoned QE policies.

A section of this chapter will be devoted to the transmission channels of monetary policy. In this respect, too, things have changed over time. Conventional monetary policy mostly relied on the "interest rate channel", exploiting the central bank's ability to affect the whole yield curve while acting directly only on short-term rates. In contrast, the unconventional monetary policies rely more on other channels. Long-term lending operations to banks, by their very nature, exploit the "bank lending channel". Securities purchases influence, directly or indirectly, the market price of financial and real assets, working through the "asset price channel". Finally, monetary policy can influence, albeit in different ways depending on the operational scheme adopted, the exchange rate, thus acting through the "foreign channel".

Finally, we will address the potential tensions between monetary policy and financial stability. Unconventional policies, in particular, have been criticized for creating an incentive to undertake risky investments in search for yield: the "risk-taking channel". The policy normalization, relying on a substantial increase in interest rates after a long period of near-zero rates, can also have negative effects on some financial intermediaries. Under this regard, the attribution of tasks across the different policymakers (central bank, regulatory and supervisory authorities) is crucial. These issues will be discussed in the final section of this chapter.

Let me conclude this introduction with a caveat. The technical ways in which monetary policy is implemented differ from country to country.[1] Therefore, it is not possible to have a single model describing in detail every local institutional design. It is possible, however, to have an analytical model able to show how the implementation of monetary policy is carried out in general, taking advantage of the fact that there are some common principles and tools, albeit with some minor cross-country differences. The theoretical framework, introduced in this chapter, will be applied to analyze the implementation of monetary policy in the euro area and in the US, in the next two chapters respectively. Some hints on the implementation of monetary policy in the UK and Japan will be given in Chapter 6.

3.2 Interest Rate Steering and Corridor System

3.2.1 The Market for Bank Reserves

The traditional approach to monetary policy implementation, prevailing in most countries until the 2007/2008 financial crisis, relies on the ability of the central bank to control the short end of the yield curve of interest rates, by exploiting an announcement effect and by managing the supply of bank reserves: these are the balances held by banks on their current accounts with the central bank. On the one side, reserves are a perfectly liquid asset for banks, which can be used for settling payments in real time. On the other side, they are a liability of the central bank, which retains a monopoly position as an issuer of base money.

Under the interest rate steering framework, the operational target of monetary policy is the level of interest rates in the interbank market, where banks can trade their reserves with each other. Most of the trades in this market are made on the overnight (O/N) maturity, and central banks typically target the O/N rate.[2] However, the expectations theory

[1] The title of an interesting study devoted to this topic some years ago contained the suggestive words "A hundred ways to skin a cat": see Borio (2001), which analyzed the traditional interest rate steering framework from a comparative perspective. For an international comparison of unconventional monetary policies, see BIS (2019).

[2] O/N is the shortest maturity in financial markets with explicit trades. An intraday (hourly) interest rate can be implicitly defined by the intraday pattern of the O/N rate: see the evidence provided by Furfine (2001) for the US and by Baglioni and Monticini (2008) for the euro area.

of interest rates implies that the rates on longer maturities are affected by the expectations of market participants about the future path of monetary policy: thus, central banks are able to affect medium- to long-term interest rates through their communication policy.

Let us denote by i the interbank O/N interest rate, and by i^* the target set by the central bank. The latter can implement its target in two complementary ways. First, through communication: the stance of monetary policy is signaled to market participants by announcing the target level (i^*) for the market rate. Such announcement can be either explicit (e.g. the Federal Funds target in the US) or implicit. In the latter case, the target is signaled by setting the level of a *policy rate*: the interest rate applied to some operations made by the central bank (e.g. the rate on the main refinancing operations of the Ecb). Second, by managing the supply of bank reserves in such a way that the money (O/N) market clears at an equilibrium interest rate equal to i^*. In doing so, the central bank exploits its monopoly position as supplier of the aggregate amount of bank reserves. This monopoly power is what makes the central bank announcements credible. The fine tuning of the supply of bank reserves, through frequent interventions in the money market, is called "active management", which is a typical feature of this operational framework. As we shall see, the ability to control the supply of bank reserves is not perfect, due to the presence of a stochastic component in the so-called "autonomous factors" affecting the stock of base money. However, we can safely assume that on average the central bank is able to reach its target, and market participants are aware of this, so the expected value of the market O/N rate is equal to that target:

$$E(i) = i^*. \tag{3.1}$$

In the following, we are going to address in turn: (i) the demand for bank reserves, (ii) the supply of bank reserves, (iii) the equilibrium in this market, and (iv) the implementation of monetary policy.

3.2.2 *Demand for Bank Reserves*

The interest rate in the interbank market (i) is the opportunity cost of holding reserves with the central bank. The management of reserves by banks balances two objectives: (i) minimize this opportunity cost and (ii) minimize the deviations of their balance on current accounts from some target level. The latter is determined by the technical features of the payment system and by the regulation. Historically, the shift from end-of-day net settlement systems to real-time gross settlement (RTGS) systems has determined a significant increase in the amount of liquidity needed to settle payments.[3] More recently, regulatory liquidity requirements have contributed to further increase banks' holdings of liquid assets, including reserves with the central bank.[4]

Let us define the daily demand for bank reserves as the (end-of-day)[5] desired balance on banks' current accounts with the central bank. The representative bank will have a demand for reserves, denoted by R^D, which is determined by the minimization of the following loss function:

$$\min_{R^D} L = \frac{1}{2}\left(R^D - \overline{R}\right)^2 + \alpha R^D \bullet i \tag{3.2}$$

where $\overline{R}$ is the target level of reserves, needed for settlement and regulatory purposes. The behavioral parameter α captures the weight that bank managers assign to the objective of minimizing the opportunity cost of reserves by engaging in trades in the money market.

The First Order Condition (FOC) of the above problem defines the demand for bank reserves as:

$$R^D = \overline{R} - \alpha \bullet i \tag{3.3}$$

Not surprisingly, the demand for bank reserves is a negative function of the market interest rate, which is the opportunity cost of holding reserves with the central bank. The target set on bank reserves ($\overline{R}$) is presumably rather rigid, due to technical and regulatory reasons. Therefore, the interest rate elasticity of the demand schedule is quite low.

Many central banks pay an interest on reserves. Let us label this rate of interest by i_R, which in general can take either positive or zero or even negative values. This is the reservation rate for interbank market

[3] See Baglioni (2006).

[4] Central bank reserves are included in the range of assets of extremely high liquidity and credit quality (Level 1 assets) that can be used to comply with the Liquidity Coverage Ratio (LCR). Indeed, a large share of Level 1 assets is made up of bank reserves with the central bank: see EBA (2020) for evidence in Europe.

[5] Intraday balances do not generally matter, neither for regulatory purposes nor for internal banks' targets.

participants: no bank will ever lend money in the market at a rate lower than i_R, since it can always deposit money overnight at the central bank at such a rate. Should the market rate hit this lower bound, the demand for reserves would become perfectly elastic: banks would be willing to hold any amount of money at the central bank, since the *net* opportunity cost of holding reserves $(i - i_R)$ would be zero. Therefore, the demand for reserves can be written as follows:

$$R^D = \overline{R} - \alpha \cdot i \quad if \quad i > i_R,$$
$$R^D \to \infty \quad if \quad i = i_R.$$

The above simple formulation relies on the implicit assumption that there is no reserve requirement. Now, we can include it into our framework by assuming that banks are required to hold an amount of reserves at least equal to some threshold level as a ratio to deposits taken. If we denote by k the reserve coefficient, the reserve requirement $(\widehat{R})$ in some period may be written as:

$$\widehat{R} = kD_{-1} \tag{3.4}$$

where D_{-1} is the level of bank deposits at the end of the previous period. The requirement may include an "averaging rule". In such a case, a bank is not obliged to hold a balance at least equal to $\widehat{R}$ in each business day on its current account with the central bank. To the contrary, the *average* of the end-of-day balances over some specified period (called "maintenance period") has to be at least equal to $\widehat{R}$. This implies that a bank is allowed to end some business days with a balance lower than $\widehat{R}$, provided such reserve deficits are compensated by a reserve surplus in some other days within the maintenance period. Let us denote days by $t = 1,...,T$, where T is the length of the maintenance period. A bank has to meet the following constraint:

$$\frac{1}{T}\sum_{t=1}^{T} R_t \geq \widehat{R} \tag{3.5}$$

where R_t is the end-of-day balance on its current account.[6] If this constraint is not met, a bank incurs in a penalty: the central bank applies

[6] Notice that what matters for the reserve requirement is the end-of-day balance on banks' current accounts. The intraday balance can take values below $\widehat{R}$ (even negative)

a penalizing (above market level) interest rate to the shortfall. A current account balance exceeding the requirement is also penalizing: while the required balance ($\widehat{R}$) is supposed to be remunerated at market rates, the interest paid on excess reserves (if any) is generally lower than that. The risk of incurring in one of these costs can be significant, due to the randomness of the payment flows and to liquidity shocks possibly hitting some banks.

The averaging rule allows banks to engage in the so-called "inter-temporal arbitrage", in order to minimize the opportunity cost of holding reserves with the central bank, namely the O/N interbank interest rate (i). As we noted above, the interbank market is the market where banks can lend their reserves to each other. Now, suppose that in day t a bank manager expects a decline of the interbank rate in the following day: $i_t > E_t(i_{t+1})$, where $E_t(\cdot)$ is the expectation operator with the information available at time t. He can earn an expected profit by lending money in the interbank market today and borrowing tomorrow; the today reserve deficit on the settlement account ($R_t < CR$) will be compensated by the planned tomorrow reserve surplus ($R_{t+1} > CR$). This deal makes the demand for reserves (R_t^D) of such bank to go down in the current day. Of course, the opposite expectation ($i_t < E_t(i_{t+1})$) will lead to an arbitrage deal opposite to the previous one, thus making the current demand for reserves go up. This reasoning shows that there is an inverse relationship between the demand for bank reserves and the current level of the interbank interest rate, for a given level of the expected O/N rate.

As I will show below, the averaging rule plays an important stabilizing role in the money market, since the inter-temporal arbitrage operations increase the elasticity of the demand for bank reserves. As a consequence, the impact of liquidity shocks on market rates is limited, reducing the need for the central bank to make frequent open market operations.

To derive the daily demand for bank reserves, let us momentarily consider for simplicity a two-day maintenance period: $T = 2$.[7] Under this assumption, constraint (5) boils down to $\frac{1}{2}(R_1 + R_2) \geq \widehat{R}$. The

without any consequence. We are implicitely assuming that $\widehat{R} > \overline{R}$: the amount of reserves held to meet the requirement is large enough to manage payments. This implies that the marginal demand for reserves is determined by the requirement.

[7] This way of simplifying the problem was first suggested by Campbell (1987). In this two-day example, I am assuming that $i > i_R$ (where i_R is the interest on excess reserves) to focus on the case where the net opportunity cost of holding reserves is strictly positive.

demand for reserves in the first day (R_1^D) is determined by two conflicting objectives: set the end-of-day balance on the current account as close as possible to $\widehat{R}$, in order to avoid the risk of incurring in the above-mentioned penalties; (ii) minimize the opportunity cost of the reserve requirement, by exploiting inter-temporal arbitrage opportunities, if any. Therefore, the problem faced by a representative bank can be written as the minimization of the following loss function:

$$\min_{R_1^D} L = \frac{1}{2}\left(R_1^D - \widehat{R}\right)^2 + \beta\left[R_1^D i_1 + R_2 E_1(i_2)\right] \tag{3.6}$$

where β is the weight attached to the second target: the higher the value of this behavioral parameter, the higher the willingness of a bank to engage in inter-temporal arbitrage deals. After substituting the constraint ($R_2 = 2\widehat{R} - R_1^D$) into the objective function, from the FOC we obtain:

$$R_1^D = \widehat{R} + \beta[E_1(i_2) - i_1] \tag{3.7}$$

This reserve demand schedule, represented in Fig. 3.1, goes through the point with coordinates ($\widehat{R}$,$E_1(i_2)$): when the current level of the interbank interest rate equals the expected rate, there is no room for inter-temporal arbitrage, so $R_1^D = \widehat{R}$. If, to the contrary, the current rate is higher (lower) than the expected rate, inter-temporal arbitrage opportunities will induce banks to decrease (increase) their demand for reserves: so for any given level of the expected rate, the demand for reserves is an inverse function of the current overnight interest rate. The higher is the banks' willingness to engage in inter-temporal arbitrage, the larger is the elasticity of the reserve demand schedule (its slope is$-1/\beta$). In the limit case where$\beta \to \infty$, the demand schedule is perfectly elastic, and the O/N rate satisfies the "martingale property": $i_t = E_t(i_{t+1})$, so the expected change of the O/N rate is zero. At the opposite extreme, if $\beta = 0$ the demand is rigid and equal to the amount due to meet the reserve requirement. The empirical evidence suggests that β generally takes a positive and finite value. The evidence also shows that β is decreasing throughout the maintenance period, and the reason behind this result is quite intuitive. In the first days of the period, banks have a large room for compensating any reserve deficit/surplus in later days within the same period. This room gets smaller as long as the end of the period approaches. In the last day of the period, any deficit/surplus would force a bank either to borrow or to deposit money overnight at the central bank at penalizing rates:i_{ML},i_R respectively (see below).[8]

The demand schedule (Eq. 3.7) can be easily extended to the more general case where $T > 2$. Suppose to be in any day $t > 1$ of the maintenance period. First of all, we have to compute the average balance required over the time span going from day t to day T, that we denote as$\widehat{R}_t$.[9] To this aim, we can rewrite the constraint (Eq. 3.5) as $\sum_{t=1}^{T} R_t = T \bullet \widehat{R}$, or equivalently as:

$$\sum_{j=1}^{t-1} R_j + \sum_{j=t}^{T} R_j = T \bullet \widehat{R} \tag{3.8}$$

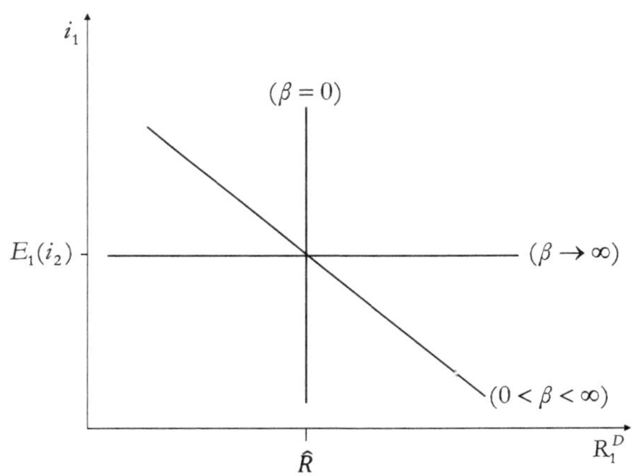

Fig. 3.1 Demand for bank reserves: an example with two-day maintenance period

[8] See Bartolini et al. (2002a) for a formal treatment of this point. For empirical evidence on the interest rate elasticity of the daily demand for bank reserves, see: Hamilton (1996), Bartolini et al. (2002b), and Angelini (2008), and other studies referred to in Friedman and Kuttner (2010). Hamilton (1996) also provides a model, based on the frictions in the interbank market, able to explain why the martingale property does not hold in practice.

[9] Of course, in the first day it is: $\widehat{R}_1 = \widehat{R}$.

from which

$$\frac{1}{T-(t-1)}\sum_{j=t}^{T} R_j = \frac{1}{T-(t-1)}\left[T \bullet \widehat{R} - \sum_{j=1}^{t-1} R_j\right] \tag{3.9}$$

which defines $\widehat{R}_t$ as:

$$\widehat{R}_t \equiv \frac{1}{(T-t+1)}\left[T \bullet \widehat{R} - \sum_{j=1}^{t-1} R_j\right] \tag{3.10}$$

In the last day of the maintenance period ($t = T$) the above expression boils down to:

$$\widehat{R}_T = T \bullet \widehat{R} - \sum_{j=1}^{T-1} R_j \tag{3.11}$$

We can now reformulate problem (Eq. 3.6) as:

$$\min_{R_t^D} L = \frac{1}{2}\left(R_t^D - \widehat{R}_t\right)^2 + \beta\left[R_t^D i_t + \sum_{j=t+1}^{T} R_j \bullet E_t(i_j)\right] \tag{3.12}$$

s.to: $R_t^D + \sum_{j=t+1}^{T} R_j = T \bullet \widehat{R} - \sum_{j=1}^{t-1} R_j$.

By exploiting assumption (Eq. 3.1), we can substitute i^* for $E_t(i_j)$ in the above problem.[10] After substituting the constraint into the objective function, the problem can be written as:

$$\min_{R_t^D} L = \frac{1}{2}\left(R_t^D - \widehat{R}_t\right)^2 + \beta\left[R_t^D i_t + i^* \bullet (T \bullet \widehat{R} - \sum_{j=1}^{t-1} R_j - R_t^D)\right] \tag{3.13}$$

Finally, from the FOC we can derive the following daily demand for bank reserves:

$$R_t^D = \widehat{R}_t + \beta\left[i^* - i_t\right] \tag{3.14}$$

[10] I am implicitly assuming that i^* is constant within the maintenance period. This is a quite realistic assumption. In the euro area (as we shall see in the next chapter) the maintenance period is defined in a way able to avoid that, once a maintenance period has started, a decision by the Governing Council, changing the policy rate, may be taken within the same period. In the US, before the suppression of the reserve requirement, the length of the maintenance period was quite short: two weeks, implying a low probability that a policy decision, changing the Federal Funds target, could be taken within an ongoing period.

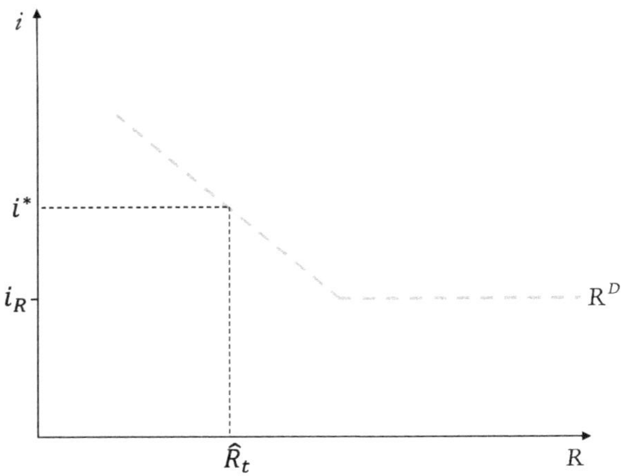

Fig. 3.2 Demand for bank reserves

This formulation holds for $1 \leq t < T$. In the last day of the maintenance period, by definition no inter-temporal arbitrage operation can be done. Then, the demand for reserves is perfectly rigid and it equals the amount due to satisfy the reserve requirement: $R_T^D = \widehat{R}_T$, where the latter is given by equation (Eq. 3.11).

Equation (3.14) has been derived under the implicit assumption that $i > i_R$, where i_R is the interest rate paid on excess reserves, i.e. the current account balances exceeding the reserve requirement. This is quite realistic in the corridor system, where the interest paid on excess reserves (if any) is generally below market rates, which in turn are close to the center of the corridor. For completeness, we have to consider also the case where $i = i_R$: in such a case, the net opportunity cost of holding reserves vanishes and the demand for reserves becomes perfectly elastic. Summing up, the daily demand for bank reserves is given by Eq. (3.14) as long as $i > i_R$, and $R^D \to \infty$ if $i = i_R$: see Fig. 3.2.

3.2.3 *Supply of Bank Reserves*

So far, we have examined the demand for bank reserves, which is given by the balances targeted by banks on their current accounts. Now we come to the supply of reserves, i.e. the existing aggregate amount of reserves, which is under the control of the central bank.

As it is well known, the "base money" (BM) is defined as the sum of the sight liabilities of the central bank. Base money can be held by financial intermediaries and the general public in two ways: bank reserves (R) and cash (C):

$$BM = R + C \tag{3.15}$$

The central bank issues base money through its open market operations. OMOs can be carried out either through repurchase agreements (repos) or through outright transactions. Repos enable the central bank to implement a temporary creation of base money, by buying today some securities from banks (paying by crediting the relative amount on their current accounts) and selling them back at a future date (debiting their accounts). They are secured loans: the central bank receives some securities as collateral for the money lent to banks. Normally repos are rolled over at maturity, so the central bank can manage the stock of base money by making a new deal for an amount either larger than the old one (positive net issue of base money) or smaller (negative net issue). Outright purchases/sales of securities imply a definitive creation/destruction of base money.

In addition to OMOs, central banks generally rely on a Marginal Lending (ML) facility: they stand ready to lend (overnight) any amount requested by some banks at a penalty interest rate (i_{ML}), higher than the "normal" level of the market O/N rate.[11] Since no bank will be willing to borrow in the market at an interest rate above i_{ML}, this rate sets a ceiling on the money market rates. On the other side, as we noted above, the interest paid on reserves (i_R) sets a floor to the money market rates, since it is the reservation rate for market participants. Taken together, the two rates (i_R, i_{ML}) define the so-called "corridor" for the money market rates: the O/N rate volatility is curbed within these two boundaries. Moreover, the ML facility has an impact on the stock of base money: when some

[11] Several central banks ask banks to deposit a collateral to obtain marginal lending. In such a case, there is actually a limit to the amount that a bank can borrow, which is given by the amount of available eligible securities. In general, banks hold a large amount of securities, in order to avoid that the collateral constraint becomes binding. Therefore, this constraint is not formally introduced into our framework.

banks apply to it, their current accounts are credited, so some base money is temporarily (overnight) issued.

In addition to the above-mentioned operations, there are other factors that can affect the stock of bank reserves. Since they do not depend on monetary policy, they are called "autonomous factors". The first one is the Public Sector (PS). In many countries, the public sector holds an account with the central bank, which acts as the settlement agent for the payments of the public administration. When the public sector receives some payments, say some tax revenues, these are credited in its own account. At the same time, some banks' accounts are debited, since taxes are normally paid through the banking system: so some base money is withdrawn from the system. The opposite happens when the public sector makes some payments.

The second autonomous factor is the foreign channel, which is strictly related to the balance of payments and to the interventions of the central bank in the foreign exchange market, which in turn will depend on the exchange rate policy, if any. Suppose, for example, that the central bank buys foreign currency and sells the domestic currency to avoid an appreciation of the latter: the official reserves in foreign currency of the country will increase, and the stock of base money, issued by the central bank, will increase accordingly. An intervention aiming to avoid a depreciation of the domestic currency will have the opposite impact.

Summing up, the stock of base money is determined as follows:

$$BM = OMO + ML - PS + FC, \tag{3.16}$$

where the sign of each item derives from the above discussion.

Equations (3.15) and (3.16) together imply that the supply of bank reserves is:

$$R^S = OMO + ML - PS + FC - C. \tag{3.17}$$

Cash in circulation must be subtracted from available reserves, since banks have to convert part of their current account balances into cash, depending on the needs of their customers. Therefore, cash can be considered as an autonomous factor affecting the stock of bank reserves. By denoting the autonomous factors as

$$AU = FC - PS - C, \tag{3.18}$$

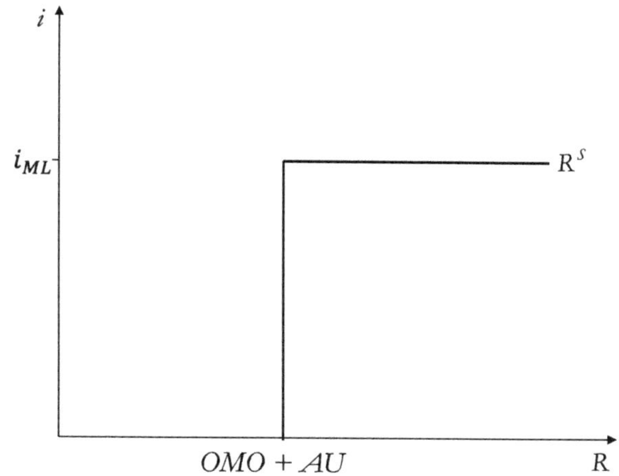

Fig. 3.3 Supply of bank reserves

the supply of reserves can be written as:

$$R^S = OMO + ML + AU, \tag{3.19}$$

which is represented in Fig. 3.3. The vertical segment shows the stock of base money issued through OMOs and by the autonomous factors up to some date. The horizontal line shows the potentially unlimited increase in base money triggered by the activation of the ML facility: this happens when the market O/N rate shows a tendency to go above the upper bound i_{ML}. More formally:

$$R^S = OMO + AU \quad \text{if} \, i < i_{ML}$$
$$R^S \rightarrow \infty \quad \text{if} \, i = i_{ML}$$

3.2.4 Money Market Equilibrium

In order to implement the announced target for the O/N interest rate level (i^*), the central bank should set the supply of bank reserves at such a level to match the aggregate level of demand at rate i^*. This is a complex task for the central bank's operative desk, due to the volatility of the autonomous factors, mainly related to the daily flows of payments of the public sector: tax revenues, interest and principal payments on public debt, public employees' wages, etc. The central bank makes a daily forecast of the amount of base money created/absorbed by the autonomous factors. Such a forecasting activity, which is at the core of the active management of reserves made by the central bank, is necessarily affected by some errors. To account for this problem in our model, let us introduce a random component into the autonomous factors by writing them as follows:

$$AU_t = \overline{AU}_t + \widetilde{\varepsilon}_t \tag{3.20}$$

where the daily size of the autonomous factors (AU_t) is made up of two components: $\overline{AU}_t$ is the predictable component and $\widetilde{\varepsilon}_t$ is a forecast error with zero mean. The daily supply of reserves becomes:

$$R_t^S = OMO_t + ML_t + \overline{AU}_t + \widetilde{\varepsilon}_t \tag{3.21}$$

Now, let us focus on a "normal" day, where there is no particular tension in the market, so $i < i_{ML}$ and the ML facility is not activated.[12] Then, the expected value of the supply of reserves is:

$$E(R_t^S) = OMO_t + \overline{AU}_t \tag{3.22}$$

In the interbank market, individual banks trade their reserves with each other. However, for the money market equilibrium, what matters is the aggregate demand for reserves. The central bank manages the supply of reserves to match the aggregate level of demand at rate i^*. Formally:

$$E(R_t^S) = R^D(i^*) \tag{3.23}$$

The guarantee of making open market operations, if needed, to make the O/N interbank market clear at the level i^* of interest rate is crucial to affect the expectations of market participants. They know that if a significant amount of trades at a rate $i > i^*$ take place, the central bank will inject base money into the system in order to make the market rate to converge to i^*. Of course, the opposite will happen starting with $i < i^*$.

[12] Some individual banks might apply for the ML facility, but the aggregate recourse to it is assumed to be negligible as long as the market O/N rate does not show a tendency to go above its upper bound i_{ML}.

Therefore, market participants anticipate that the only equilibrium level of the O/N interest rate is i^*. Temporary deviations are possible, due to the volatility of the autonomous factors. But on average the interbank O/N rate will be equal to i^*. This justifies the initial assumption, made in Eq. (3.1), about the expected level of the interbank market rate.

Figure 3.4 provides a picture of the equilibrium in the daily market for bank reserves. At the equilibrium point, the current market rate (i_t) equals the expected rate (i^*), so banks do not engage in any inter-temporal arbitrage trade and the demand for reserves is given by the requirement: $R_t^D = \widehat{R}_t$ in Eq. (3.14). This, together with Eq. (3.22), implies that the equilibrium condition (3.23) can be written as follows:

$$OMO_t = \widehat{R}_t - \overline{AU}_t \tag{3.24}$$

The right-hand side of Eq. (3.24) is called "net liquidity position" of the banking system. Central banks make open market operations to match the amount of reserves needed by the banking system to satisfy the reserve requirement (due on average from day t until the end of the maintenance period) net of the base money created/subtracted from the system by the autonomous factors.

This framework relies on a relative scarcity of bank reserves and on the active management of the stock of base money by the central bank,

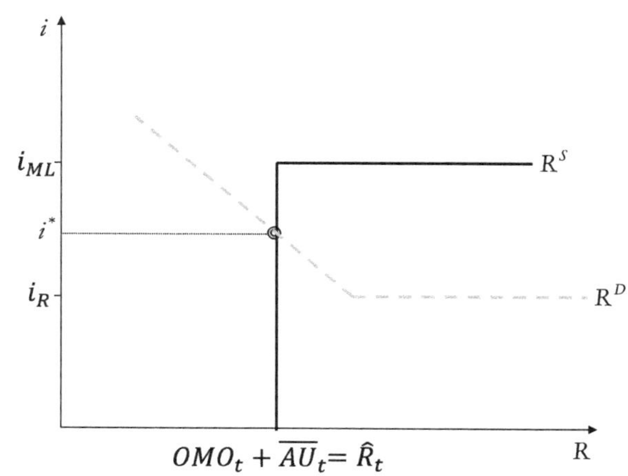

Fig. 3.4 Corridor system: the money market equilibrium

making frequent interventions in the money market, even on a daily basis. The target set by the central bank for the O/N interest rate (i^*) provides an anchor to the interbank market. This mechanism is generally able to keep the market rate in line with the target level with a good degree of precision, albeit not perfectly. The two rates (i_R, i_{ML}) provide the lower and upper bounds to the corridor of interest rates: they play an active role only in rather exceptional circumstances, when there is either an aggregate excess or lack of liquidity.

An important implication of this operational framework is that, since the central bank targets the interest rate level, the supply of bank reserves becomes endogenous. Bank reserves are a liability of the central bank, which can decide the amounts to be issued. However, the central bank commits to supply all the quantity of reserves needed to make sure that the money market clears at i^*. As a consequence, the money supply, which is linked to the base money through the money multiplier, is endogenous as well. In other words, *monetary policy cannot have two independent targets: interest rate level and quantity of money*. This principle will no longer apply under the quantitative easing framework, as we shall see in the next section.

We can now understand why the reserve requirement, in particular the averaging rule, used to be a useful tool for central banks under the traditional interest rate steering approach. The reason is that the averaging facility introduces a self-stabilizing property into the monetary control framework. To see this point, remember that the stock of bank reserves is affected by the volatility of the autonomous factors, which are not under the direct control of the central bank. The latter makes a forecast of such factors in order to offset them in its day-to-day liquidity management, but it can make mistakes. The unpredictable component of the autonomous factors is captured by $\tilde{\varepsilon}_t$: the forecast error introduced above. This is equal to zero on average, but it can sometimes take sizable positive or negative values. We call these deviations from zero "liquidity shocks". Let a negative liquidity shock ($\varepsilon_t < 0$) take place: for example, an amount of tax payments larger than expected. Starting from the initial equilibrium point, where the supply of bank reserves matches the reserve requirement ($OMO_t + \overline{AU}_t = \widehat{R}_t$), this shock makes the stock of reserves to shift to the left, going down to $R_t' = OMO_t + \overline{AU}_t + \varepsilon_t < \widehat{R}_t$: Fig. 3.5 shows in bold

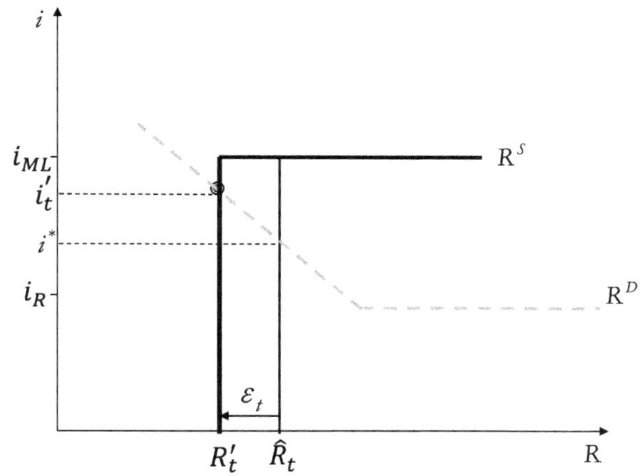

Fig. 3.5 Liquidity shock

the new supply schedule.[13] This creates an excess demand at the initial interest rate i^*. This tension in the money market will make the interest rate increase up to i'_t. This increase is smaller, the larger the elasticity of the demand for reserves, which in turn is related to the willingness of some banks to exploit inter-temporal arbitrage opportunities[14]: they can lend money today in the interbank market, thus reducing their demand for reserves, expecting to borrow at a lower rate in the next days of the maintenance period. This behavior reduces the excess demand for reserves and consequently the impact of the liquidity shock on the O/N market rate. This self-stabilization property enables the central bank to intervene in the money market less frequently than it should do in the absence of the averaging facility.

The corridor system relies on two additional stabilizing tools: the ML facility and the interest paid on reserves. They play an active role when the level of interest rates in the money market tends to go outside the boundaries of the corridor: i_R, i_{ML}. This can happen, in particular, when the end of the maintenance period approaches: in those days, for the

[13] We are implicitly assuming that the liquidity shock is temporary, as it is generally the case, so it affects the money market only in day t.

[14] The higher is the value of the parameter β, the flatter is the demand schedule R_t^D.

reasons explained above, the demand for bank reserves becomes more rigid and the self-stabilizing mechanism provided by the averaging facility is less effective (it is not available at all in the last day of the period). To show the point, let us take up again the example of a negative liquidity shock: see Fig. 3.6. Absent the ML facility, such shock would produce an increase in the market O/N rate up to i_t'. This will not happen since banks can borrow money from the central bank at rate i_{ML}. The activation of the ML facility implies an endogenous injection of reserves into the system (from R_t' toR_t'') able to reduce the gap between the reserve requirement and the supply of reserves: from $\widehat{R}_t - R_t'$ to $\widehat{R}_t - R_t''$ (where $R_t'' = OMO_t + ML_t + \overline{AU}_t + \varepsilon_t$). As an outcome, i_{ML} will be the clearing rate for the O/N interbank market. The alternative case of a positive liquidity shock (e.g. an interest/principal payment on Government debt) can be easily seen by using Fig. 3.4 again. Imagine to shift the vertical line rightward up to a point where it intersects the horizontal segment of the reserve demand schedule. The abundance of liquidity will exert a downward pressure on the O/N interbank rate, but this will not go below i_R, since the latter is the reservation rate for market participants.

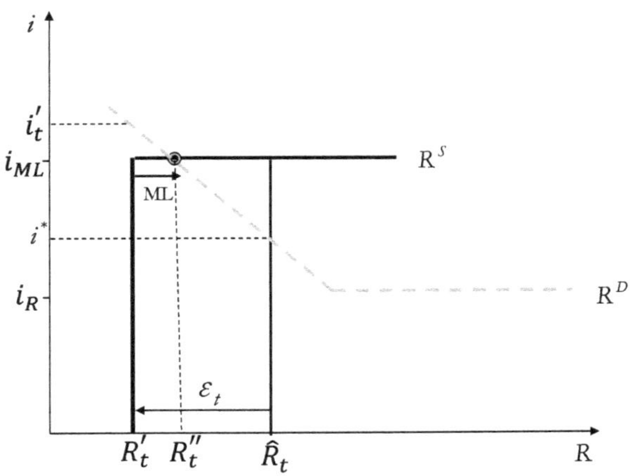

Fig. 3.6 Activation of the marginal lending facility

3.2.5 Monetary Policy Implementation

Under the interest rate steering framework, the stance of monetary policy is signaled to market participants by announcing the target level (i^*) for the market (O/N) interest rate. This announcement affects the demand for bank reserves and it is able to move the market rate in the desired way, ***without the need to change the supply of base money***: what matters is the impact of the announcement on expectations, namely on the expected O/N rate (see Eq. 3.1). Figure 3.7 can help understand this point. Let us start from an equilibrium point A, where the target and market interest rates are at level i_0^*. Now, let the central bank announce a reduction of its target to i_1^*. This makes the demand schedule for reserves (Eq. 3.14) to shift downwards from R_0^D to R_1^D. The equilibrium in the interbank market (Eq. 3.23) is reached for a lower level of the market interest rate (from $i = i_0^*$ to $i = i_1^*$) and for the same level of bank reserves: $\widehat{R}_t$. The amount of base money that the central bank should supply through its open market operations remains the same (see Eq. 3.24). In the figure, this process is shown by a change of the equilibrium from point A to point B, which lie on the same vertical line corresponding to the existing stock of bank reserves. This argument shows that the central bank is able to change the equilibrium level of interest rates in the money market while keeping the supply of bank reserves unchanged: this "***decoupling principle***" is an important feature of the operational framework.

It is worth stressing that, under the interest rate steering framework, the decoupling principle works in one direction only: ***the central bank can implement different levels of interest rate with the same level of bank reserves, but not*** vice versa. On the one hand, the central bank can set different levels for its interest rate target (i^*) while keeping the supply of bank reserves constant. On the other hand, there is only one amount of reserves able to match the quantity demanded at a level of interest rate equal to the announced target: $\widehat{R}_t$. The size of open market operations should always meet the net liquidity position of the banking system: if they fail to do so, the market rate would differ from the target rate. This conclusion is consistent with the above observation that monetary policy cannot have two independent tools: interest rate and supply of money. Once the target on the interest rate has been set, the amount of base money must be set accordingly. If, to the contrary, the central bank wanted to set a target on the quantity of money, it should give up the target on interest rates.

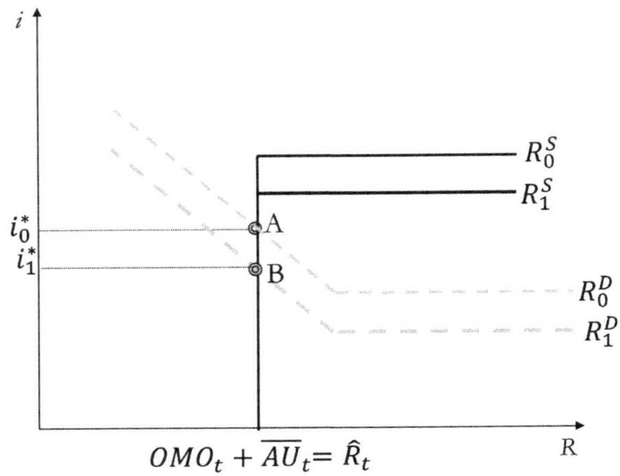

Fig. 3.7 Monetary policy implementation: expanding the stance

The above feature implies that the management of liquidity does not have any signaling role under the interest rate steering approach. The monetary policy stance is signaled by setting the target level for the O/N interest rate. To the contrary, the purpose of liquidity management is to make sure that such a target is achieved, and that the volatility of autonomous factors or sudden changes of the demand for reserves do not make the effective interest rate diverge significantly from its target level. To make an example, this issue became quite relevant at the outset of the financial crisis, since August 2007, and even more one year later following the Lehman Brothers crash. In such circumstances, several central banks reacted by injecting huge amounts of liquidity into the money market, in order to offset the liquidity hoarding behavior of financial institutions, leading to a demand for reserves well beyond the reserve requirement.[15] Such kind of behavior can be introduced into our simple model by considering a rightward shift of the reserve demand schedule,[16] which must be accommodated through open market operations (from OMO_t to OMO'_t) in order to keep the equilibrium interest rate unchanged: Fig. 3.8 shows

[15] Ashcraft et al. (2011) document the huge increase in the demand for reserves in the US interbank market during the financial crisis, due to precautionary reasons.

[16] In Eq. (3.14) a constant term should be added to $\widehat{R}_t$.

the point. This injection of reserves does not per se mean a change of the monetary policy stance; it is rather a way to preserve the correct transmission of monetary policy to the short end of the yield curve. Of course, such an intervention has also a financial stability rationale, namely to avoid a liquidity crisis of the banking system. The central bank acts as the lender of last resort for banks, in addition to managing the monetary policy.

In the next section, we are going to see that the decoupling principle works in both directions with the QE policy: under this approach, interest rates and supply of base money become two independent tools to implement the desired stance of monetary policy. As a consequence, the central bank can signal a change in the stance either by announcing a change of the target level for interest rates or by altering the supply of liquidity injected into the system through asset purchases and/or lending operations. Therefore, the management of liquidity will assume a signaling role.

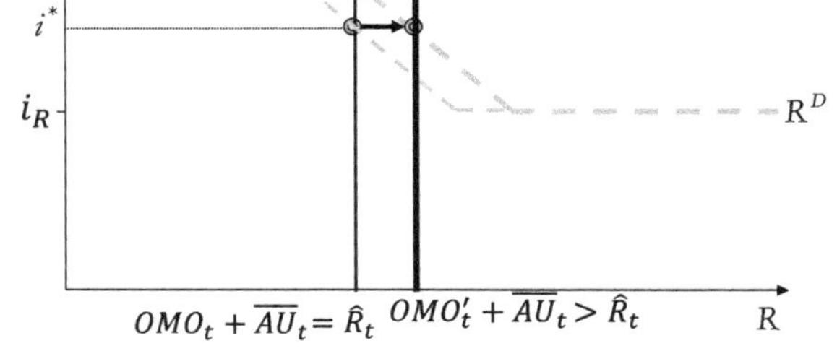

Fig. 3.8 Liquidity management

3.3 Quantitative Easing and Floor System

3.3.1 The New Tools of Monetary Policy

The so-called "unconventional monetary policy" relies on four innovative tools:

1. Large-scale asset purchases (AP).
2. Long-term lending operations to the banking system (LTLO).
3. Forward guidance (FG).
4. Negative interest rate policy (NIRP).

The first two instruments identify the operational framework known as Quantitative Easing (QE).[17] Under this framework, the operational target of monetary policy is the size of the central bank balance sheet: in particular, the size of the AP and LTLO operations plays a crucial role in identifying and signaling the stance of monetary policy. This does not imply that the level of interest rates becomes irrelevant: however, when the level of the policy rate remains close to the ZLB for long periods, it plays a minor role. Differently from traditional OMOs, including both repos and outright purchases, APs are outright transactions. They are unusual also for their size, and they cover a wide range of securities eligible for purchase: government bonds, corporate bonds, covered bonds, and Asset Backed Securities (ABS). LTLOs differ from traditional lending operations for three features: (i) large scale, (ii) long maturities (up to four years in the euro area), and (iii) some technical features creating an incentive for banks to lend out to firms and households the money received from the central bank.

There is a crucial difference between LTLOs and APs. While the latter enable the central bank to take full control of the size of its own balance sheet, the former do not. In an AP program, it is the central bank who decides the amount of securities under purchase: the contribution of the program to the increase in the central bank balance sheet is exogenous and it is in the hands of the central bank itself. To the contrary, the central bank can only decide the potential size of an LTLO program. The effective size depends on the ratio between the amount of loans actually taken by banks and the borrowing allowance made available by the central bank:

[17] Sometimes the LTLOs are labelled as "credit easing" policy.

the so-called "take-up ratio", which in turn depends on banks' behavior. In addition, LTLO programs often include a prepayment option, allowing banks to pay back loans before maturity. Therefore, the actual size of LTLOs is endogenous, up to some limits set by the central bank.

QE policies have been introduced with two main purposes: (i) preserve the correct transmission of monetary policy and (ii) support aggregate demand by expanding the stance of monetary policy. The first rationale for unconventional measures emerged under the pressure of the great financial crisis of 2007/2008 and later during the sovereign debt crisis in Europe: in such circumstances, the provision of liquidity to financial intermediaries turned out to be crucial to avoid disruptions in the flow of credit to the economy. The second motivation comes from the ZLB: when interest rates approach this level, the central bank cannot rely only on interest rates to implement a further expansion of its monetary policy stance. Recently, a new wave of QE measures has been taken to limit the disruptive impact of the pandemic crisis on the business cycle.

Together with QE measures, FG has become an essential element of modern monetary policy. In the past, many central bankers made use of what the Fed Chairman Alan Greenspan called "constructive ambiguity": the underlying idea was that the central bank should retain an informational advantage over market participants about its own future moves. Today, to the contrary, central banks try to make their future actions as predictable as possible through their communication policy, in order to anchor expectations. When the interest rate level reached the ZLB, a way to expand further the stance of monetary policy was to convince market participants that such a level would be maintained for a long time, at least until a satisfactory economic recovery would be observed. Since QE measures have been introduced, the communication policy has become essential to provide information about their features, like: the size of periodical net asset purchases, the range and maturity of assets under purchase, and the policy related to the reinvestment of the proceeds from maturing securities (the latter is quite relevant as part of the exit strategy from QE). Also the features of the LTLO operations, like the interest rate applied and the conditions determining the size of the borrowing allowance, have become quite relevant in the communication policy of some central banks. All this information contributes to signal the stance of monetary policy. We can distinguish between a "calendar-based" and an "outcome-based" FG. The former, for example, provides an explicit date when a program is expected to be terminated. The latter makes the adoption or the end of a policy measure contingent on the attainment of some macroeconomic targets, such as the convergence of inflation and/or employment towards some specific levels.

3.3.2 The Floor System

QE policies have produced a remarkable change of the operational framework. As we have seen above, the interest rate steering approach relies on the scarcity of bank reserves together with an active management of the supply of reserves. The reserve requirement can play a crucial role, together with the technical features of the payment system, in shaping the demand for reserves. To the contrary, the QE approach relies on a large excess supply of reserves, which becomes a structural feature of the monetary control framework. Under this approach, a reserve requirement becomes redundant: as we shall see, in a "floor system" the demand for reserves is perfectly elastic in the relevant range, since the net opportunity cost of holding reserves with the central bank drops to zero. Therefore, there is no point in creating an artificial demand for reserves by imposing a regulatory requirement. Indeed, in some countries like the US and UK the reserve requirement has been abolished altogether. It is still present in the euro area, but it does not play anymore a relevant role in the determination of the money market equilibrium. The following model of the operational framework under QE can include both cases: where the reserve requirement is present or not. To this aim, it relies on a flexible formulation of the daily demand for bank reserves: the demand is given by either Eq. (3.3) or (3.14) as long as $i > i_R$, and $R^D \to \infty$ if $i = i_R$.

On the supply side, the traditional OMOs, namely the frequent interventions in the money market, do not play a relevant role anymore in the provision of base money. The great part of the liquidity created by the central bank comes into the system through AP and LTLO programs. Therefore, we modify Eq. (3.19) above as follows:

$$R^S = AP + LTLO + ML + AU \tag{3.25}$$

which is represented in Fig. 3.9, where the vertical segment shows the stock of base money issued through APs and LTLOs, as well as by the autonomous factors, up to some date. The figure is drawn under the

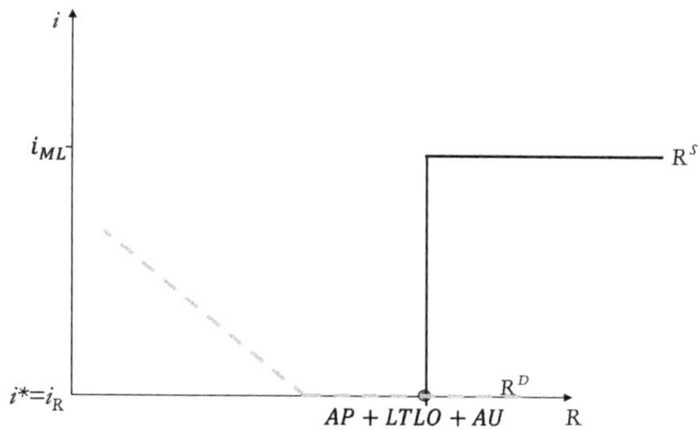

Fig. 3.9 Floor system: the money market equilibrium under QE

assumption that $i_R = 0$, since QE policies have generally been implemented when the policy rates have reached the ZLB. Of course, the model holds also for positive levels of the interest paid on bank reserves.

The equilibrium in the money market, shown in Fig. 3.9, features a structural excess supply of bank reserves, labeled "excess liquidity". The amount of reserves accumulated through time, injected into the system through AP and LTLO programs, exceeds by far the needs of the banking system to settle payments and to meet regulatory reserve (if any) and liquidity requirements. This excess supply in the market for bank reserves exerts a downward pressure on their price, pushing it to the lower bound provided by the interest rate on reserves (i_R), which is the reservation rate for interbank deals. For this reason, this operational framework is called "floor system".

In a floor system, the money market equilibrium differs considerably from that of a corridor system. Instead of being stabilized at the center of the interest rate corridor, the market rate sticks to the bottom level, which coincides with the rate paid on bank reserves. The latter becomes the crucial policy rate, sending to market participants the signal about the target level for the O/N rate: $i^* = i_R$. Market participants are aware that the equilibrium in the interbank market features an excess supply, with the O/N interest rate sticking to $i^* = i_R$. Therefore, the central bank is able to affect market expectations: Eq. (3.1) still holds. However, the rationale behind that assumption differs now from Sect. 3.2: in the traditional framework it was the central bank's guarantee of making an active management of reserves in order to implement its target i^*; in the new framework it is the "satiation" of the market for bank reserves, of which market participants are aware.

Another important difference between the two operational frameworks has to do with the *decoupling principle*. This works in one direction only under the interest rate steering framework. The central bank can set different interest rate levels for the same stock of base money, but not vice versa: once a target has been set for the interest rate level, the supply of reserves has to be managed accordingly. Under QE, instead, this principle works in *both directions*, enabling the central bank to have an additional degree of freedom in managing monetary policy. It can set different interest rate levels for the same amount of liquidity created through its own operations. But it can also change the size of such operations, affecting the stock of base money, without altering the target for interest rates. Therefore, the central bank has two independent instruments to implement and signal the stance of its policy: interest rate and quantity of money. By looking at Fig. 3.9 again, it is easy to see that the central bank can change the target level for interest rates (i^*) by changing the policy rate i_R, thus moving up or down the equilibrium point (marked by the circle), without changing the amount of liquidity created through AP and LTLO operations. It can also alter the size of AP and LTLO programs while keeping the interest rate target unchanged: the vertical bar in R^S can be moved to the right or to the left without altering the equilibrium level of interest rate. This property derives from the existence of a large excess of bank reserves, acting as a buffer in the money market. The decoupling principle plays a crucial role when a central wants to exit a QE policy (as we shall see in Sect. 3.4).

The existence of a large excess of reserves has another relevant implication. The volatility of the autonomous factors, affecting the stock of base money, does not have any significant impact on the money market equilibrium, thanks to the buffer provided by the excess reserves.[18] Therefore, there is no need to introduce a stabilizing tool, such as the reserve requirement together with the averaging facility, which instead used to play a relevant role under the traditional interest rate steering framework. For the same reason, the central bank does not need to implement an

[18] This is the reason why the volatility of the autonomous factors has not been explicitly considered in this section, contrary to what has been done in the previous section.

active management of bank reserves by making frequent operations in the money market.

3.3.3 *Negative Interest Rate Policy*

The NIRP was adopted in recent years by the central banks of several countries: Japan, Sweden, Denmark, Switzerland, and in the euro area. Those central banks have resorted to this policy, generally as a complement to QE measures, in order to expand further the stance of their policy, after lowering the level of interest rates down to zero. We can introduce the NIRP into our QE framework by assuming that the interest rate applied to bank reserves becomes negative: $i_R < 0$ (see Fig. 3.10). The aim of this measure is to drive the interest rates in the money market into a negative territory, by exploiting the property of a floor system, where the equilibrium O/N rate is equal to the lower bound: i_R.

There are two channels through which the NIRP can contribute to expand the stance of monetary policy. The first one is the interest rate channel: by driving down, even below zero, the level of interest rates in the money market, the central bank tries to affect the whole yield curve. To this aim, the forward guidance can play an important role, by convincing financial market participants that the policy rates will remain at very low (even negative) levels for a long time. The second channel is the bank lending channel: since holding money "idle" on their accounts with central bank is costly, the NIRP should introduce an incentive for

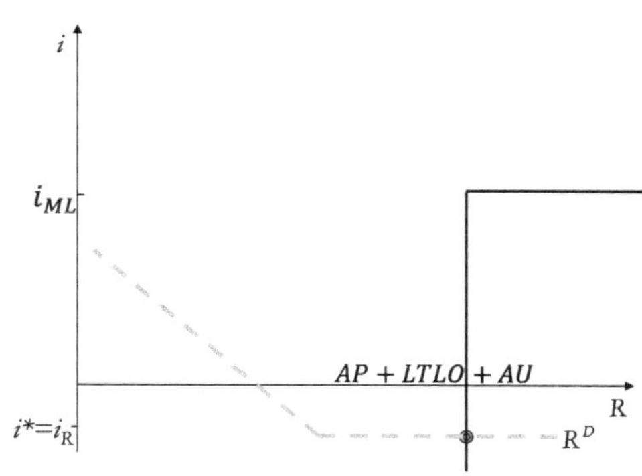

Fig. 3.10 Negative interest rate policy

banks to lend out to firms and households the abundant liquidity received through AP and LTLO operations.

A negative side effect of the NIRP is that it hurts the profitability of the banking sector. Under this regard, it must be stressed that, even if banks circulate the money received from the central bank by making loans to the non-financial sector of the economy, at the end of the day the liquidity must be deposited with the central bank. An example may be useful to clarify this point. Imagine that bank A lends some money to a firm, which in turn uses that money to make a payment to a supplier holding an account at bank B. The settlement of the payment through the banking system implies a transfer of reserves from bank A to bank B, but the aggregate amount of reserves is unaffected. In accounting terms, the sum of all the items recorded on the asset side of the central bank balance sheet, due to AP and LTLO operations, must be balanced on the liability side by an equal amount of bank reserves. This implies that the negative interest rate applied to such reserves is a sort of tax levied by the central bank on the banking sector. It is quite difficult for banks to translate such a tax on their depositors by paying them a negative rate of interest. To limit the impact of this tax on the banking sector, some central banks (e.g. the Ecb) have introduced a two-tier remuneration scheme for bank reserves: these are applied a zero rate of return up to some threshold level, beyond which they are applied a negative rate. More generally, by keeping the level of interest rates in the economy very low, the NIRP contributes to the compression of the interest rate margin, thus making a negative contribution to the profitability of the banking sector. A lower level of profitability, in turn, can have a negative impact on the accumulation of regulatory capital, thus reducing the ability of the banking sector to provide loans to the economy. For that reason, it is possible to identify a "reversal interest rate level". Pushing the policy rate below that level can be counter-productive: instead of expanding the stance of monetary policy, the opposite effect would be obtained.[19]

[19] The idea of a "reversal interest rate" has been introduced by Brunnermeier and Koby (2018). An estimate for the euro area, around −1%, has been provided by Pariès et al. (2020).

3.4 The New Normal

3.4.1 Exit Strategy and Normalization

The unconventional policies, addressed in the previous section, have been implemented by several central banks to overcome the limitations of the traditional IRS framework in a world of low inflation and interest rates close to the ZLB. The strong inflationary pressures, arising between 2021 and 2022, have dramatically changed this picture and induced almost all central banks to end their QE programs and to start a "normalization" of their policy. During this process, they have raised the level of their policy rates, driving the general level of (nominal) interest rates well above the ZLB.

The historical experience shows that the exit from QE policies must be carefully designed and communicated to avoid a destabilizing impact on financial markets. The episode known as "Taper Tantrum" shows this point pretty well. In May 2013, the Fed's Chairman Ben Bernanke announced that the Fed was planning to reduce, starting in July of the same year, the size of the monthly purchases of securities under the QE3 program (started in 2012). The announcement came as a surprise and triggered a sharp increase of volatility in financial markets: the rate of return on 10-year government bonds raised by 100 basis points in less than one month. This market reaction induced the Fed to delay the exit from QE until 2014.

Through time, central banks have learnt to implement the exit process from QE in a gradual and predictable way, in order to avoid excessive volatility in financial markets. Typically, the exit strategy follows four steps. (1) *Tapering*: the size of periodic net purchases of securities is gradually reduced and finally set to zero. (2) *Roll-over*: when some securities in its policy portfolio come to maturity, the central bank buys other securities (generally of the same kind) in order to keep the size of the policy portfolio unchanged. (3) *Interest rate tightening*: policy interest rates are increased. (4) *Quantitative tightening* (*roll-off*): the size of the policy portfolio decreases as long as the central bank reduces and finally stops the roll-over of maturing securities. Those steps can be taken at different times, enabling the central bank to implement a gradual exit strategy: in particular, the interest rate tightening can be started after the tapering phase, and the start of the quantitative tightening (QT) can be delayed even further. This is made possible by the decoupling principle (that we have seen in the previous section). Both the Ecb and the Fed have taken this opportunity when implementing and communicating their exit strategies from QE (as we are going to see in the next chapters).

The decision to exit from QE policies does not imply that a central bank comes back to the old operational framework: interest rate steering and corridor system. To the contrary, QE policies have left a durable legacy, opening the way to a "new normal" in monetary policy implementation, with the following features:

i. The level of interest rates is the primary operational target of monetary policy. The stance is identified and signaled by setting (either explicitly or implicitly) a target level for a short-term market rate, typically the O/N rate. However, the way in which this target is achieved is not the old interest rate steering with an active management of (scarce) reserves: the corridor system of Sect. 3.2. The new normal relies instead on the floor system. Therefore, the crucial policy rate is the interest rate paid on bank reserves (i_R): by setting this rate, the central bank is able to affect the market rate.
ii. The market for bank reserves features a structural excess supply. The central bank manages its portfolio of securities and/or makes loans to the banking sector in order to keep an abundance of liquidity in the system. The equilibrium of the interbank market in the new normal can be represented as shown in Fig. 3.11, which differs from QE (Fig. 3.9) for three reasons. First, the policy rate (i_R) is generally at some positive level, following the interest rate tightening typically implemented during the exit process from QE policies. Second, OMOs replace APs and LTLOs: when AP and LTLO programs have been abandoned, the way to adjust the size of the central bank's balance sheet is by using the standard OMOs, including repos and outright trades in the securities market as well as short-term (collateralized) loans to banking institutions.[20] Third, the structural excess liquidity is typically lower in the new normal than under the QE policy. The reason is that the purpose of central bank's operations is to keep the amount of liquidity at a level sufficient to maintain the market for reserves "satiated", accounting for

[20] In the transition from the QE to the new normal framework, the pace of the "roll-off" (i.e. the share of securities holdings that are not reinvested at maturity) can play an important role in determining the size (and composition) of the central bank's securities portfolio and of its balance sheet.

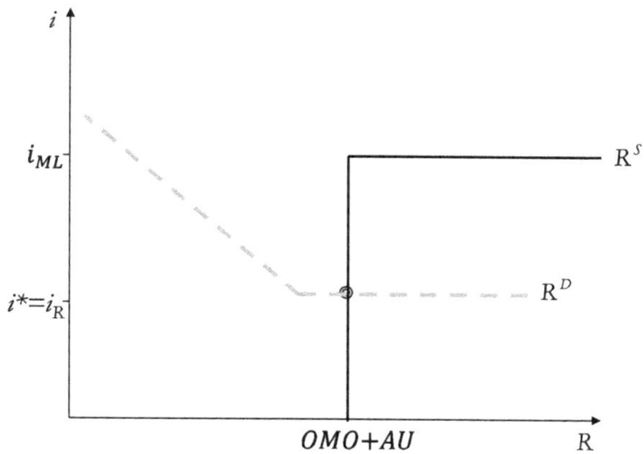

Fig. 3.11 Floor system: the money market equilibrium in the *new normal*

the dynamics of the autonomous factors; they are not targeted at expanding the size of the central bank's balance sheet, as it used to be under QE.

iii. The new tools remain in the toolkit of central banks, which can decide to start new AP programs and rounds of LTLO whenever they decide that these can be useful to expand the stance of their policy. Balance sheet policies, able to alter the size and composition of central bank's assets, can be seen as a complement to the interest rate management. The forward guidance can still be used to signal the future path of monetary policy, although some central banks have adopted a "meeting-by-meeting" approach: they prefer to take decisions based on incoming data, without making pre-commitments on the future level of policy rates. Therefore, those measures, that used to be called "unconventional", have become standard tools that can be used to manage monetary policy in the new normal.

At this point, it may be useful to provide a schematic representation of monetary policy implementation under the three operational frameworks considered in this chapter: see Table 3.1. Under both IRS and new normal, the central bank signals the stance of its policy by steering the level of short-term interest rates. However, they differ in the way this

Table 3.1 Operational frameworks

	IRS	*QE*	*New normal*
Operational target	Short-term interest rate	Size of central bank balance sheet	Short-term interest rate (balance sheet policies still available)
Monetary control framework	Corridor system	Floor system	Floor system

operational target is achieved: corridor system and floor system, respectively. The balance sheet policies, inherited from the QE experience, remain available in the new normal.

The balance sheet policies can be used for different purposes (as we are going to see in the next chapters): Fig. 3.12 provides a schematic view. They can play a purely technical role, namely that of providing enough liquidity to keep the market for bank reserves "satiated" at the steady state, i.e. when the excess supply of reserves has been driven down to the minimum level needed in a floor system. But they can also be used to signal the stance of monetary policy: in such a case, the size of the central bank's balance sheet is used as an instrument to complement the interest rate policy. This role has become evident in the transition phase, when central banks have implemented their exit strategy from QE: the quantitative tightening has been added to the interest rate tightening during the normalization process. The composition of the balance sheet can be used to preserve the correct transmission of monetary policy: in the euro area, the *Transmission Protection Instrument*[21] and the deviations from the "capital keys principle" in managing the Eurosystem's securities portfolio respond to this need. Open market operations can be used to preserve the liquidity of specific market segments (e.g. ABS). Finally, the composition of the (corporate) securities portfolio held by a central bank can be managed to pursue sustainability goals: this goes under the name of "greening monetary policy".

[21] Asset purchases under TPI should only temporarily affect the size of the Eurosystem balance sheet, leaving the monetary policy stance unaffected. See the Ecb press release of 21 July 2022.

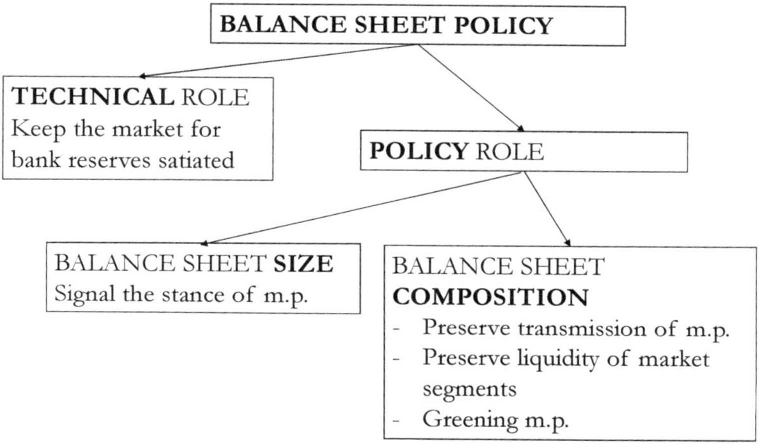

Fig. 3.12 Balance sheet policies in the new normal

3.4.2 *Floor Versus Corridor Systems: A Comparison*[22]

Why central banks have generally decided, in normalizing their policies, to rely on the floor system to target the level of interest rates, instead of resuming the old IRS/corridor system approach? There can be different answers to this question. One reason is related to the difficulty of downsizing the huge portfolio of securities, most of which government bonds, accumulated through the asset purchase programs of the previous years: a complete sell-off of those securities (either by selling them or by not rolling-over maturing securities) might have destabilizing effects on some segments of financial markets. But there can be other reasons why a floor system is preferable to a corridor system.

First, the floor system gives central banks one more degree of freedom in managing their policy. The analysis of the previous sections has shown that in the corridor system the decoupling principle works one way only: in particular, there is only one amount of reserves able to meet the

[22] There is an ongoing debate over the most desirable outcome of the normalization process: this literature has been reviewed and discussed in Chapter 2. This sub-section (and the next one) is intended to provide some further elements hopefully useful to assess the merits of the floor system over the corridor system (and to assess supply-driven versus demand-driven floor systems).

liquidity demanded by the banking system at a level of interest rate equal to the target set by the central bank As a consequence, monetary policy cannot have two independent operational targets: interest rate level and quantity of (base) money. To the contrary, in the floor system the decoupling principle works both ways, implying that the central bank is endowed with two independent tools: interest rate policy and balance sheet policy.

In principle, these two instruments can be targeted to different objectives. The level of the policy rate can be used to signal the stance of monetary policy, targeting some macroeconomic variables (price stability and full employment), letting the balance sheet policy to pursue other goals. As an alternative, both instruments, interest rate and balance sheet policies, can be used for the same target, e.g. price stability. Of course, this additional degree of freedom opens the way to a new issue: how to coordinate those tools? For example, which is the most appropriate mix between interest rate tightening and quantitative tightening during a process leading to a more restrictive stance of monetary policy? This issue is rather new and it deserves more analysis and experience in monetary policy making.

The second reason why the floor system is superior to the corridor system is that in the former the ability of the central bank to keep the money market rates in line with the announced target level is higher than in the latter. As we have seen in this chapter, the corridor system relies on the ability of the central bank to forecast the daily liquidity conditions of the banking system, and such forecasts are necessarily subject to some errors, due to the volatility of the autonomous factors affecting the stock of available bank reserves. In turn, these liquidity shocks introduce an undesired volatility of money market rates.[23] In the floor system, to the

[23] ECB (2002) provides an estimate of the forecast errors made by the Ecb itself: they account for about 30% of the volatility of the autonomous factors, which is a remarkable size. As expected, the government's deposits with the Eurosystem are the main source of liquidity shocks and of forecast errors. Bindseil et al. (2006) stress that forecasting excess reserves is a significant challenge for the implementation of monetary policy and that even small forecast errors can have a significant impact on the level and volatility of short-term interest rates; they support this view with a model of bank reserve management and with data for the euro area. Schnabel (2023) argues that, after several years of large excess reserves, largely determined by central bank's asset purchases rather than banks' liquidity choices, the ability to provide an accurate estimate of the demand for bank reserves is presumably lower than in the past, making even more difficult to steer interest rates in a corridor system.

contrary, the liquidity shocks do not have any significant impact on the money market rates, since they are absorbed by the buffer provided by the excess supply of reserves. Therefore, in the corridor system the volatility of the O/N market rate, around the target level set by the central bank, is expected to be larger than in the floor system.

This prediction can be tested for the euro area, by analyzing the volatility of the market rate Eonia (Euro Overnight Index Average) around the target level signaled by the Ecb to market participants by announcing its policy rates. As a preliminary analysis, we can look at the data reported in the following figures. Figure 3.13 provides a picture of the corridor of interest rates for the period 2003/6/6–2005/12/5: the Eonia rate shows a remarkable volatility around the policy rate (the MRO rate was the relevant policy rate at that time, when the Ecb implemented its policy following the traditional IRS approach). Figure 3.14 provides an analogous picture for the period 2016/3/16–2019/9/17: except for a couple of spikes, the volatility of the Eonia rate seems to be much lower than in the previous period. Notice also that the relevant policy rate in the more recent period is the rate applied to the Deposit Facility: this is consistent with an operational framework relying on excess liquidity (floor system).[24]

To check that the impression provided by the above pictures is correct, I will present some statistical analysis. In doing so, I will compare two periods: 2004/1/26–2008/10/7 and 2015/1/28–2022/10/19. The first period provides a sample for the corridor system. It begins with the date when the reform of the maintenance period of the minimum reserve requirement has been introduced in the euro area (as we are going to see in the next chapter): since then, the maintenance period goes from the settlement day of the MRO, following a meeting of the Governing Council devoted to monetary policy decisions, to the day before the settlement day of the MRO, following the next meeting of the Governing Council devoted to monetary policy decisions. This way of defining the maintenance periods rules out the possibility that, once a period has begun, a change of the policy rates might take place within the same period. As a consequence, expectations of changes of the policy rates within the period, leading to an undesired volatility of money market

[24] Both periods have been selected in such a way that the policy rate is constant in each of them, to facilitate the visualization of the volatility of the market rate around the policy rate.

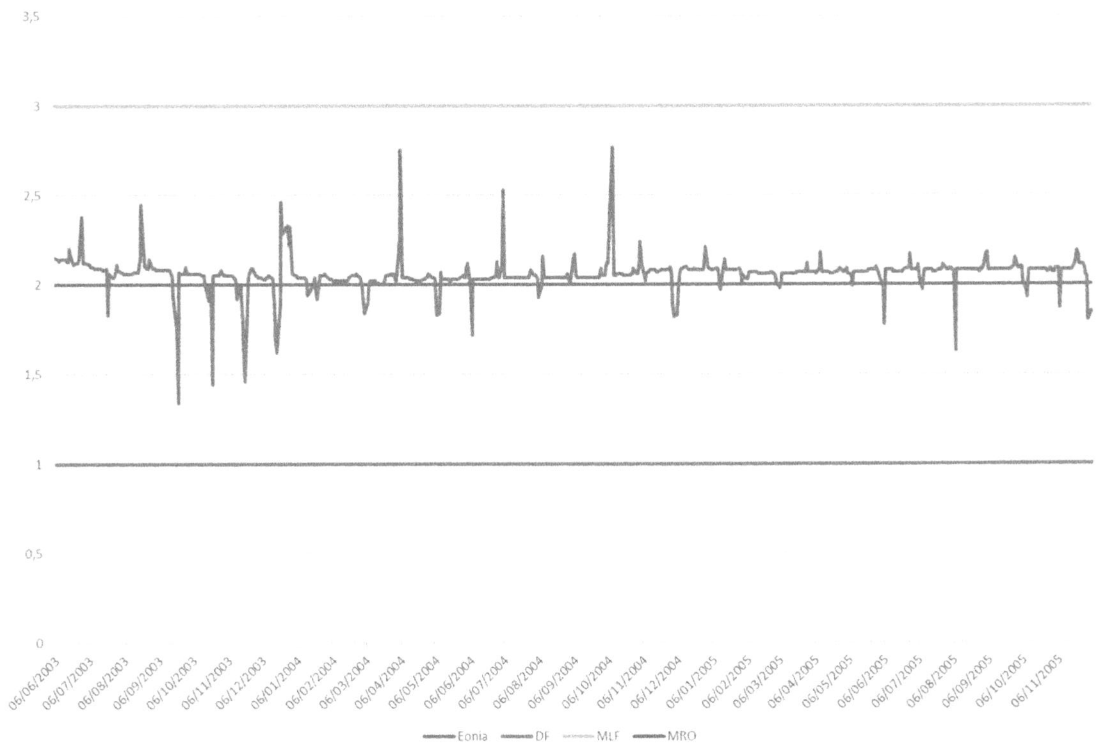

Fig. 3.13 Euro area: volatility of market rate in the *corridor* system (percentage points, daily data 2003/6/6–2005/12/5) (*EONIA* [Euro OverNight Index Average]: interest rate in the interbank O/N market. *MRO*: interest rate applied to the Main Refinancing Operations [minimum bid rate]. *DF*: interest rate applied to the deposit facility. *MLF*: interest rate applied to the marginal lending facility. *Source of data:* Ecb, Statistical Data Warehouse)

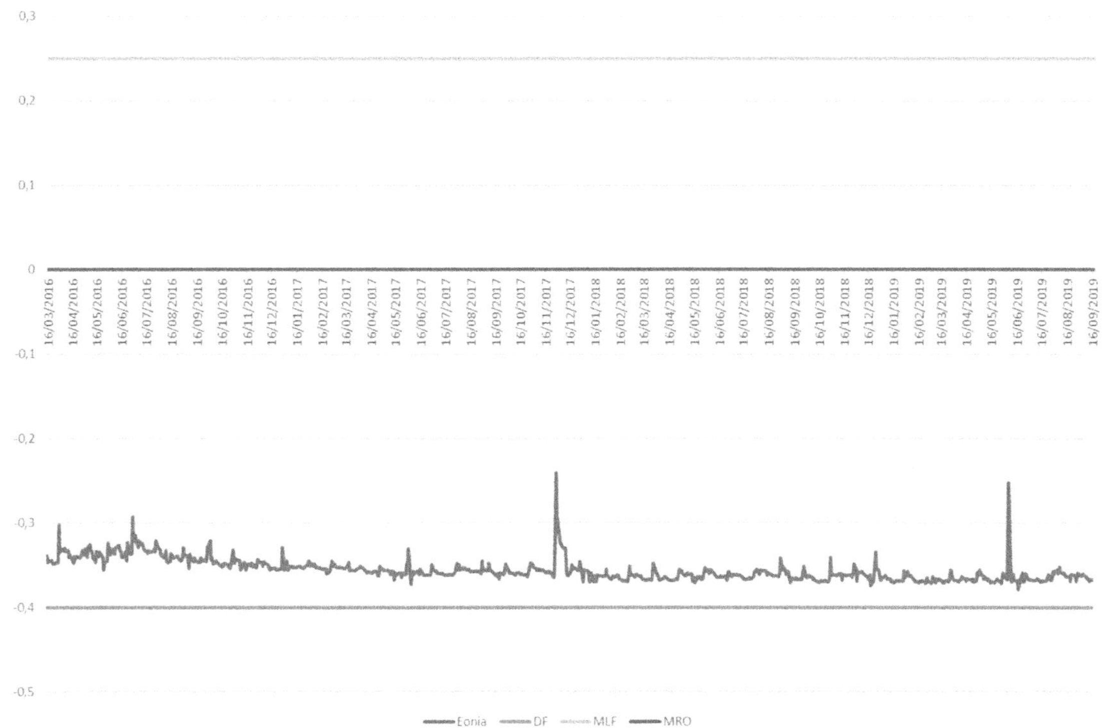

Fig. 3.14 Euro area: volatility of market rate in the *floor* system (percentage points, daily data 2016/3/16–2019/9/17) (*EONIA* [Euro OverNight Index Average]: interest rate in the interbank O/N market. *MRO:* interest rate applied to the Main Refinancing Operations [fixed rate]. *DF:* interest rate applied to the deposit facility. *MLF:* interest rate applied to the marginal lending facility. *Source of data:* Ecb, Statistical Data Warehouse)

rates, are avoided by definition. For our purposes, this enables us to focus on the volatility of the O/N rate due to technical factors only, ruling out any volatility due an expected change of the stance of monetary policy. The first period ends with the introduction, in October 2008, of the fixed rate full allotment mechanism for MRO operations: this date marks the end of the corridor system relying on the shortage of liquidity, and it marks the beginning of a long transition period towards the floor system relying on excess liquidity. The second period provides a sample for the floor system: it begins with the adoption of the Asset Purchase Program (APP), marking the introduction of QE policies in the euro area. During 2022 the net asset purchases (made under both the APP and the pandemic program PEPP) have been discontinued, but the money market has continued to exhibit the excess liquidity typical of the floor system, thanks to the complete roll-over of the Ecb's securities portfolio.[25]

For each period, the daily spread between the market O/N rate[26] and the relevant policy rate[27] has been computed. Table 3.2 shows some statistics for the spread in the two periods. In the first period, the spread was 8 basis points on average, and it was half than that in the second period (see column A).[28] The difference in mean between the two sample periods shows a high statistical significance (based on the *t*-test). The standard deviation of the spread, computed over the whole sample periods, shows a sharp decline in the second period (column C). The difference in volatility between the two sample periods shows a high statistical significance (based on the *F*-test). The decline in volatility turns out to be even more remarkable as an outcome of the following, more accurate, analysis: the standard deviation of the daily spread has been computed within each maintenance period of the minimum reserve requirement. Column D reports the average of such standard deviations for each of the two sample periods, showing a huge decline in the second one. This evidence supports the prediction that the ability of the central

[25] All these developments will be explored in the next chapter.

[26] The market O/N rate in the euro area is the Eonia rate until 1 October 2019, and the Ester rate (plus 8.5 basis points to make the two series consistent) afterwards.

[27] In the first period, the relevant policy rate is the minimum bid rate on the MROs; in the second period, it is the rate applied to the Deposit Facility.

[28] Of course, the mean has been computed on the absolute value of the daily spread, to avoid compensations between negative and positive values.

bank to keep the money market rates in line with the announced target level is higher in the floor system than in the corridor system.

A possible objection to the above analysis is that the volatility of the O/N market rate is heavily concentrated in the last days of the maintenance period, when the demand for bank reserves becomes more rigid since banks' treasury departments are more pressed by the need to meet the reserve requirement. This volatility is quite evident in Fig. 3.13, where periodic ample swings can be observed. Actually, the elasticity of the reserve demand schedule is decreasing throughout the maintenance period, for the reasons that we have seen in Sect. 3.2.2. To control for this issue, the above analysis has been replicated by dropping the observations in the last three days of each maintenance period throughout both the sample periods. The results are shown in Table 3.3. The volatility of the spread between the market rate and the policy rate shows a remarkable reduction in the 2004–2008 interval when the last three days of each maintenance period are excluded from the analysis. Nevertheless, the difference in mean and volatility between the two sample periods remains large and highly significant, confirming the previous results. Notice also that dropping the last three days of the maintenance period does not have any impact on the mean and standard deviation of the spread in the

Table 3.2 Statistics of daily market-policy rate spread

	(A) ***Mean***	*(B)* ***Median***	*(C)* ***Stand. Dev*** *(over whole sample periods)*	*(D)* ***Stand. Dev*** *(within maintenance periods)*
2004–2008 (n. obs.: 1207)	0,08 (95% conf.int.: 0,07–0,08)	0,07	0,09	0,07
2015–2022 (n. obs.: 1981)	0,04 (95% conf.int.: 0,04–0,05)	0,04	0,05	0,01
t-test (with different variances) H_0: difference in mean = 0 *P*-value = 0				
F-test H_0: difference in variance = 0 *P*-value = 0				

Table 3.3 Dropping the last three days of the maintenance period

	(A) **Mean**	(B) **Median**	(C) **Stand. Dev** *(over whole sample periods)*	(D) **Stand. Dev** *(within maintenance periods)*
2004–2008 (n. obs.: 1018)	0,07 (95% conf.int.: 0,07–0,08)	0,07	0,07	0,04
2015–2022 (n. obs.: 1791)	0,04 (95% conf.int.: 0,04–0,05)	0,04	0,05	0,01
t-test (with different variances) H_0: difference in mean = 0 *P*-value = 0 *F-test* H_0: difference in variance = 0 *P*-value = 0				

2015–2022 interval. The reason is that the above-mentioned pattern of the elasticity of the demand for bank reserves used to be quite relevant in the corridor system, but it is not anymore so in the floor system, where the demand for reserves is perfectly elastic in the relevant range of values, i.e. around the money market equilibrium (see Fig. 3.9).

3.4.3 Supply-Driven Versus Demand-Driven Floor Systems

So far, we have identified a floor system as an operational framework where the market for bank reserves is "satiated": the supply of reserves exceeds the level needed by the banking system for settlement and regulatory purposes. The latter may be due to a reserve requirement, if any, and to the liquidity requirements (namely the Liquidity Coverage Ratio). The excess reserves make the equilibrium interest rate in the interbank market to stay close to the floor of the system, provided by the interest paid by the central bank on bank reserves: this is the shadow price of lending in the interbank market (see Fig. 3.11). A further distinction can be made between "supply-driven" and "demand-driven" floor systems. This has become quite relevant in the normalization process taking place after the QE era: some central banks (like the Fed) have opted for a supply-driven system, and others (like the Bank of England) for a demand-driven system.

In a supply-driven system, the central bank manages its portfolio of securities in such a way to keep an abundance of liquidity in the money market. Remember that any purchase/sale of securities by the central bank has an impact on the base money. By trading in the market,[29] the central bank can keep the stock of reserves at a level exceeding the needs of the banking system. Since such trading activity is completely in the hands of the central bank, the stock of reserves is driven by the decisions of the monetary authority related to the management of its own securities portfolio. This is the reason why it is labeled "supply driven".

In a demand-driven system, the central bank makes (secured short-term) loans to the banking system, with two features. First, the amount of liquidity available through these lending operations is potentially unlimited (the only limit may come from the amount of available collateral, but this is not binding in general): this is needed to make the market rate to stick to the floor of the system. Second, the interest rate charged on central bank loans is the same as that applied for remunerating bank reserves deposited at the central bank: this is needed to make the loan facility appealing for banks. In an equilibrium where the market rate sticks to the floor, namely the interest on reserves, no bank would be willing to borrow from the central bank at a higher rate, unless it was forced to do so, for example because of limited access to the money market. This system relies on the willingness of banks to tap the loans made available by the central bank, borrowing all the amount needed (for operational and regulatory reasons) and possibly even more for precautionary reasons: since the estimate of the level of needed reserves is prone to errors, banks may want to build up a buffer of excess liquidity, given that the borrowing rate is not penalizing. In any case, the aggregate stock of bank reserves is determined by the demand of central bank loans by the banking system: this is why it labeled "demand-driven".

The supply-driven system has a clear advantage over the demand-driven system. In the former, the supply of base money is exogenous, since it

[29] During the normalization process, such trades can include the partial reinvestment of the proceeds from maturing securities (partial "roll-over").

is set by the central bank. In the latter, to the contrary, it is endogenous, since it depends on the behavior of banks.[30] Actually, some banks might fear to incur in a "stigma effect" by applying for loans at the central bank. Some banks might "free-ride" on other banks, economizing in their borrowing from the central bank and relying on the market in case of an unexpected liquidity shock. This kind of behaviors might create situations where the aggregate stock of reserves is scarce, leading banks to bid in the money market at rates higher than the floor rate: in such case, the ability of the monetary authority to steer the market interest rate at the desired level would be impaired.

Another difference between the two systems is the following. In the supply-driven system, the central bank has to manage its own portfolio of securities in order to keep an excess supply of reserves, accounting for the dynamics of the autonomous factors: under this regard, the balance sheet policy has a purely technical role. In the demand-driven system, the task of keeping the stock of reserves at an adequate level is assigned to another instrument: the (short-term) lending operations This solution leaves the central bank free to adjust the size of its securities portfolio as needed for policy purposes: the balance sheet policy can be used—together with the interest rate policy—to define the monetary policy stance. This property of the demand-driven system can be appreciated in the exit phase from the expansionary policies of the QE era: such system allows the central bank to reduce the size of its securities portfolio to the extent needed to signal a more restrictive stance and address inflationary pressures. This might not be feasible in the supply-driven system, once the size of the securities portfolio has been driven down to the minimum level needed to maintain the money market "satiated".

Finally, the demand-driven system may be preferable in those countries where the interbank market suffers some fragmentations and the distribution of liquidity is not even across the banking sector. In such a case, central bank loans can meet the liquidity needs of those banks located in areas where reserves are relatively scarce. This property can be appreciated in the euro area, where excess reserves are not evenly distributed

[30] Remember that a similar argument has been made when comparing APs and LTLOs in Sect. 3.3.1.

across banks and are largely concentrated in two countries: Germany and France.[31]

3.5 The Transmission Channels of Monetary Policy

Monetary policy pursues some final targets, such as price stability and support to the economic activity. In defining its strategy, the central bank must assign relative weights to those objectives and must decide how to calibrate the stance of monetary policy. In this chapter, we have examined the tools available to the central bank to implement its strategy: the operational framework identifies what levers the central bank can move to increase the degree of monetary tightening or easing. In this respect, the shift from the traditional interest rate steering approach to the unconventional policies and eventually to the new normal has represented a historic turning point in the conduct of monetary policy.

There is a considerable "distance" between the instruments directly used by the central bank, in the operational management of monetary policy, and its ultimate objectives: there is generally no direct link between those variables. For example: how does the level of the overnight interest rate affect price stability? What is the ability of a government bond purchase program to provide support to the real economy? To answer these questions, it is necessary to analyze the relationships between the instruments and the ultimate objectives: these links go under the name of "transmission channels" of monetary policy. They often involve other intermediate variables, such as long-term interest rates and the amount of bank credit available to the economy: variables over which the central bank exerts some influence, albeit less direct than over its own instruments, and which in turn have a sufficiently stable relationship with the final objectives.

This section is devoted to a quick illustration of the transmission channels of monetary policy. The purpose is not to provide an in-depth and exhaustive treatment, but rather to focus on those aspects that have gained importance since the adoption of unconventional policies. We can classify the transmission channels as follows:

[31] See Schnabel (2023).

1. Interest rate channel.
2. Bank lending channel.
3. Asset prices channel.
4. Foreign (exchange rate) channel.

It should be pointed out immediately that the channels just listed are not alternative to each other. They are instead complementary to each other: several transmission channels can operate at the same time, enhancing the effectiveness of monetary policy.

3.5.1 Interest Rate Channel

In the AD-AS (aggregate demand–aggregate supply) model of the economy generally presented in macroeconomics textbooks,[32] the nexus between monetary policy and the real economy is through the general level of interest rates: this nexus identifies the "interest rate channel" in the transmission of monetary policy. The central bank reacts to any deviations of some macroeconomic variables, namely inflation rate and output level, from their respective target values by acting on the interest rate: an increase (decrease) of its level represents a restriction (loosening) of the monetary policy stance. This impulse is transmitted to the economy thanks to the fact that a key component of aggregate demand, investment activity, depends on the cost of financing.

The macroeconomic models are often simplified on the financial side and do not distinguish between different interest rates: by maturity, by issuer, and by financial instrument. To understand the transmission channels of monetary policy, some distinctions need to be introduced. Let us start with that between short-term rates and long-term rates. Monetary policy acts on short-term rates. The operational target is the overnight interest rate, to which the money market rates (those with maturities up to one year) are closely linked. In contrast, investment activity is affected by the cost of long-term financing, with maturities in the range of several years. For this reason, the central bank aims to condition the entire term structure of interest rates: this is done by acting on the expectations of financial market participants, which in turn affect the yield curve of interest rates. According to the expectations theory of the term structure

[32] See, for example, Mishkin (2015).

of interest rates, the financial market equilibrium requires that long-term rates be equal to the average of short-term rates currently observed and expected for future periods. Through its communication policy, which signals the future path of monetary policy, the central bank contributes to the formation of expectations regarding the future levels of short-term interest rates, and in this way it is able to affect the current level of long-term rates.

3.5.2 *Bank Lending Channel*

Another distinction is that between different debt instruments. A company can finance itself by borrowing from a bank or by issuing bonds in the market. These two funding sources are not perfect substitutes: the relationship built over time between the firm and the bank allows the latter to acquire some information that cannot be easily transferred to the market. This is especially true for small/medium-sized firms, which are therefore highly dependent on bank financing. This distinction allows us to identify a specific channel of monetary policy transmission: the bank lending channel. This assigns a special role to the banking system in transmitting a monetary policy impulse to the real economy: in particular, an expansionary intervention is transmitted through an increase in the supply of bank loans to firms. This can occur for two reasons: (1) because banks have more liquidity available, and (2) because the opportunity cost of lending, represented by financial market interest rates, is reduced. The first issue can be captured by extending the traditional Keynesian macroeconomic model to account for the banking sector, particularly for the expansion of deposits and lending resulting from an expansionary monetary policy intervention.[33] The second one can be analyzed using a microeconomic approach, in which a bank must choose whether to lend to firms or invest in the bond market. The choice is made by comparing the marginal revenue on loans with the prevailing interest rate in the

[33] See Bernanke and Blinder (1988), who extend the IS-LM model to include the responsiveness of investment to the interest rate on bank loans, in addition to that of the bond market. The model thus reformulated is called CC-LM, where the Commodities and Credit relationship takes the place of the traditional IS (Investment and Saving).

financial market: the latter represents the opportunity cost of lending to firms, and monetary policy acts on this cost.[34]

The banking channel has become more relevant with the inclusion of the long-term lending operations (LTLOs) in the toolbox of central banks, for several reasons: their unusual size and maturity, and some technical features of these operations. With these loans, the central bank has become a stable source of funding for the banking system, in addition to depositors and financial markets, with the aim of inducing banks to expand the volume of their loans. This goal has also been pursued by including precise incentives to use central bank funding to support the level of bank loans: we will see in the next chapter that these incentives have been part of some programs (Targeted—LTLOs) implemented by the Ecb; similar programs have been adopted by other central banks, such as the Bank of England.

The effectiveness of the bank lending channel encounters a limitation in the prudential regulation of the banking system, which imposes a minimum ratio of capital to (risk-weighted) assets, by virtue of the international Basel Agreements transposed into the legislation of many countries (in Europe through EU Directives). The ability to offer loans depends not only on the availability of funding sources (deposits and bank bonds) but also on the size of banks' own capital: when this is relatively low and many banks are constrained by regulatory solvency ratios, an expansionary monetary policy may have little effect through the banking channel. Thus, a delicate problem of coordination between prudential regulation and monetary policy arises.[35]

3.5.3 Asset Price Channel

Monetary policy has an impact not only on interest rates, but also on financial and real asset prices. The market price of a bond is (in equilibrium) equal to its present value, which in turn is given by the sum of the coupon and principal payments that the holder will receive, discounted by the market interest rate. If the level of the market rate declines

[34] For a microeconomic analysis of the bank lending channel, based on the "Klein - Monti" model of the banking firm, see Baglioni (2007).

[35] On the regulation and supervision of bank solvency, see the Basel Committee website: www.bis.org/. For an analysis of how regulatory capital constraints can interfere with the transmission of monetary policy, see Baglioni (2007).

(increases), the present value of a bond goes up (down). Lower interest rates encourage the financing of leveraged positions in the stock market, thus supporting the prices of stocks traded in that market. It also makes real estate mortgages less expensive, thereby encouraging the purchase of real estate properties by businesses and households and helping to drive up real estate prices: both industrial and residential ones. Thus, an additional transmission channel of monetary policy emerges through asset prices: the "asset price channel".

A rise in asset prices has two implications. The first one mainly concerns businesses. These often borrow money by pledging collateral assets, such as securities and real estate properties. The provision of collateral may be required by the creditor, typically a bank, to protect itself against credit risk: should the borrower be unable to meet its own obligations, the bank can seize the assets received as collateral. It can be shown that collateral can also help reduce the problems arising from informational asymmetries between borrowers and lenders. It introduces a potential cost to the borrower, which materializes in the event of default. He thus has an incentive to limit the level of risk with which he employs the borrowed funds: collateral thus limits the borrower's moral hazard, originating from the fact that his management choices are not perfectly observable by the lender. It can also help solve adverse selection problems in the screening of borrowing firms. By helping to keep moral hazard and adverse selection problems under control, the provision of collateral makes it possible to limit credit rationing: this is a serious market failure, which occurs when banks do not extend credit to many applicants, regardless of the interest rate they are willing to pay.[36]

The value of available assets that can be pledged as collateral thus conditions a firm's ability to obtain credit: its "debt capacity". This is where monetary policy comes in. If a reduction in interest rates supports asset prices, then it helps increase the market value of the securities and real estate properties that can be pledged as collateral, thus increasing the debt capacity of firms. The expansionary effect of monetary policy comes through an increased ability of firms to finance their business and especially their investment, supporting aggregate demand and the business cycle.

[36] On the theory of credit rationing and the role of collateral, see Freixas and Rochet (2008).

The second implication of a change in asset prices has to do with households. These hold bonds and stocks directly or indirectly through asset management products, such as mutual funds. They are also often homeowners. The value of their wealth, both financial and real, contributes (together with income) to determine the level of consumption. If the market value of financial and real assets rises, following a reduction in interest rates, households' wealth will increase, possibly inducing them to consume more. Monetary policy thus acts through a wealth effect, supporting aggregate demand for consumption goods. Household consumption may also be supported by their increased debt capacity in the presence of rising house prices: this is a relevant phenomenon in some countries (other than continental Europe), notably the US.

The asset price channel, similarly to the bank lending channel, has become even more relevant with the shift from the traditional interest rate steering policy to the unconventional monetary policy, particularly with the adoption of asset purchase (AP) operations. By purchasing large quantities of securities in the market, the central bank directly supports their price. Not only that, but it also supports the price of a wide range of assets, both financial and real, that are not under purchase. In fact, the liquidity injected through AP operations is used by the entities that receive it, mainly banks and other financial intermediaries, to purchase assets in the market, rebalancing the composition of their portfolios towards less liquid assets than money: that is why we speak in this case of a "portfolio rebalancing" effect. As a result, the price of corporate bonds increases: companies can thus finance themselves in the bond market by paying lower yields to their lenders. It also becomes cheaper to issue new shares, thanks to rising stock prices. The market value of the assets that firms can pledge as collateral increases as well: as we have seen, this increases their ability to finance investment (debt capacity). Finally, households feel wealthier and are willing to consume more (wealth effect).

3.5.4 Foreign Channel

Finally, an additional channel of monetary policy transmission is the foreign channel, which works through the exchange rate between the domestic and foreign currencies.[37] Suppose that the central bank wants to expand the stance of its policy by reducing the level of interest rates: more precisely, its policy rates, which in turn affect the general level of interest rates on domestic financial assets. These assets will then become less attractive compared to foreign assets, and investors will be induced to alter the composition of their portfolios by including a larger share of foreign assets. This process will produce a devaluation of the domestic currency, which will be sold by investors to buy foreign currency. The devaluation will make the domestic goods more competitive (cheaper) compared to those produced abroad. As a consequence, our exports will increase and our imports will decrease: the trade balance (a component of the aggregate demand) will improve. The bottom line is that the devaluation introduces an additional channel through which lower interest rates can exert an expansionary impulse on the domestic income.

In AP operations, the central bank buys securities in the domestic financial market and injects liquidity into the financial system. This money will be used (in part) by the financial intermediaries to purchase foreign assets. The reallocation of portfolios will generate a capital outflow that will lead to a depreciation of the domestic currency, providing support for our net exports. When the QE policy was introduced in the euro zone, the first transmission channel to operate was the foreign one: the external value of the euro began to decline even before the Ecb started its asset purchase operations (in early 2015), as a result of the announcements that preceded the actual adoption of QE.

3.6 Monetary Policy and Financial Stability

3.6.1 The Risk-Taking Channel

The unconventional policies adopted by several central banks, starting from the great financial crisis of 2007/2008, have been often criticized for their potential side impact on financial stability.[38] The argument goes as follows. When interest rates are kept close to zero for many years,

[37] I am implicitly assuming flexible exchange rates: this is generally the case in Western countries.

[38] See the extremely interesting discussion of this matter by Ben Bernanke (2022, chapter 14), and the references therein.

people are induced to take more risk in order to gain a positive and significant expected return on their investments. This holds for households and financial intermediaries as well. Savers may be induced to undertake more risk than they are used to, for example by buying more shares or other risky securities, sometimes under the pressure of their financial advisors. Some financial institutions may be forced to shift their portfolios to a riskier mix of securities to get a positive return on their assets, since they have to repay a fixed return on their liabilities: think, for example, of a pension fund which has promised a predefined stream of payments to retired people. This *risk-taking channel* introduces a tension between price stability, which is the primary objective of monetary policy, and financial stability.

The risk-taking channel does not work only through the above-mentioned *search-for-yield* effect, which is related to the permanence of interest rates to a very low level for a long time. The other source of instability is the abundance of liquidity injected into the financial system through large-scale asset purchases and long-term loans to the banking sector. These large amounts of liquidity can be used by banks to expand their supply of loans to "marginal" borrowers with a low credit quality, thus increasing the average riskiness of their loan portfolios. When investors use this large supply of funds to buy financial assets, they can fuel a "stock-market bubble", where securities prices increase more than is justified by fundamental factors. These events often come together with a "real estate bubble", where the prices of real estate properties increase well above their historical average: this kind of bubble can be fueled both by the abundance of funds and by the low level of the interest rates applied to mortgage loans. Both credit booms and bubbles (in the stock market and in the real estate sector) may suddenly be stopped by some adverse event. For example, a remarkable increase in bad loans (as a ratio to total loans) may induce banks to adopt stricter lending criteria, leading to a credit crunch. A negative shock to the economy, e.g. an increase in energy prices, may lead to a massive sell-off in the stock exchange, making a stock-market bubble revert into a market bust.

Credit booms and crunches, as well as bubbles and busts in the stock exchange and in the real estate sector, are a relevant source of financial instability. Financial intermediaries can suffer heavy losses on bad loans or on their securities when these have to be quickly liquidated at a discount (*fire-sale*). Some financial institutions might go bankrupt under the pressure of creditors withdrawing their funds (*bank run*), with a potential contagion effect on other intermediaries. Households may be hit by a reduction of their wealth, due to a decrease in the market value of their financial assets or of their house. All these events can amplify the fluctuations of the business cycle, introducing an undesired pro-cyclical component into the QE policies. During a boom, when asset prices increase, firms benefit from a higher debt capacity and invest more; households feel wealthier and consume more (remember what we said about the asset price channel in the previous section). During a bust, the opposite happens. This is the reason why financial instability is a relevant problem not only for the financial sector, but even more broadly for the whole economy.

3.6.2 *Exit from QE Policies and Side Effects on Banks*

In past years, the above arguments have been made to highlight the potential negative side effects of unconventional monetary policies when they were in place. Recently, more attention has been given to the negative consequences of those policies when they have been abandoned: the exit process from QE policies is a delicate matter and it can create severe stress to the stability of the financial sector. The banking crisis that occurred in the US between March and May 2023 (see Chapter 5 for details) highlighted the potential tension between monetary policy and financial stability. Many commentators attributed the difficulties of several US banks to the Fed's aggressive increase in interest rates since March 2022, after a long period of near-zero rates. This criticism was focused on the abrupt reversal of monetary policy, with negative repercussions on the financial system.

This view seems somewhat simplistic. In general, rising interest rates can have two effects on banks, one positive and one negative. On the one hand, the rise in rates on floating-rate assets and newly acquired fixed rate assets leads to an increase in revenues. It is true that funding costs also increase, but generally more slowly than lending rates, thanks to the market power enjoyed by financial institutions. Consequently, the interest margin increases in a rising rate environment. On the other hand, rising interest rates negatively affect the market value of fixed rate assets held by banks, such as medium- to long-term securities. Which effect prevails? It depends on banks' business model and their ability to manage risks (interest rate, market, and liquidity risks) as well as on the efficacy of supervisors in signaling critical situations and imposing corrections accordingly.

The business model of the three US banks (Silicon Valley Bank, Signature Bank of New York, and First Republic Bank) that went bankrupt in the first half of 2023 was very particular. They had experienced considerable growth in size within a few years, funded mainly by collecting uninsured deposits from a few, often interconnected, entities. This made the funding of these banks particularly fragile, exposing them to rapid and massive bank runs. Their business was highly concentrated on a few sectors: high-tech companies, crypto-asset intermediaries, and real estate lending. This exposed the banks to some shocks that hit those sectors in particular. The management of those banks underestimated the liquidity and interest rate risks they were exposed to. When market interest rates rose, the banks suffered large losses in the value of the securities in their portfolios. Under the pressure of money withdrawals by some large depositors, they were forced to liquidate part of the securities portfolio at a loss, inducing other depositors to withdraw their deposits and thus starting a downward spiral. The supervisory authorities were late in pointing out the critical issues to banks' managers and in taking action to induce them to adopt the necessary corrective measures. In this respect, a crucial role was played by the deregulation that took place in 2018, which raised the asset size threshold, above which banks are applied the *Enhanced Prudential Standards* (EPS), from USD 50 billion to USD 250 billion.

The 2023 US banking crisis took place in an environment of rising interest rates, which created severe difficulties to some intermediaries. However, the main cause of the crisis has to be found in the deficiencies of the management of those banks that went into trouble and in the lack of adequate supervisory actions. For many other financial institutions, in the US and in other countries, the increase in interest rates has been beneficial: they have enjoyed larger interest margins, thus increasing their profitability and their soundness accordingly. The potential losses, due to the decline of market value of their securities holdings, did not become effective losses to a large extent: this has been made possible by an appropriate liquidity management, preventing those banks from being forced to liquidate their securities holdings before maturity.

Financial stability is a task that must be pursued by prudential policies: both regulation and supervision. Despite its increasing complexity, financial regulation is not always effective[39] and supervisory actions are not always timely and adequate. Banking crises show that prompt corrective actions at the micro-level are needed to prevent that some critical situations, originated by the mismanagement of single financial institutions, lead to their collapse. A crucial role is also played by the lender of last resort function of the central bank: by providing liquidity to troubled banks, the central bank can avoid them to liquidate some illiquid assets at a loss, thus preventing a liquidity crisis from degenerating into an insolvency. Under this regard, it must be noted that the *Bank Term Funding Program* has been introduced by the Fed too late to prevent the situation of Silicon Valley Bank and Signature Bank from precipitating (we will come back on this in Chapter 5). Macro-prudential policy should contribute to stabilize the financial system by taking a counter-cyclical stance: increasing bank capital requirements in good times and decreasing them during a downturn of the business cycle. To the contrary, counter-cyclical capital buffers have not been actively used by the macro-prudential authorities so far, at least in Europe. The bottom line is that, in order to enhance financial stability, some improvements are still needed in the area of prudential regulation and supervision, despite all the positive developments that have taken place in recent years. Within a framework where each task is assigned to a specific policy, financial stability should be a matter of regulatory and supervisory policy, while monetary policy should focus on its ultimate goals, namely price stability and macroeconomic stabilization.

References

Angelini, P. (2008). Liquidity and announcement effects in the euro area. *Giornale degli Economisti, 67*(1), 1–20.

Ashcraft, A., Mc Andrews, J., & Skeie, D. (2011). Precautionary reserves and the interbank market. *Journal of Money, Credit and Banking, 43*(7), 311–348.

Baglioni, A. (2006). The organization of interbank settlement systems: Current trends and implications for central banking. In S. Schmitz and G. Wood (Eds.), *Institutional change in the payments system and implications for monetary policy*. Routledge.

[39] For a discussion of banking regulation in the European context, see Baglioni (2016).

Baglioni, A. (2007). Monetary policy transmission under different banking structures: The role of capital and heterogeneity. *International Review of Economics and Finance, 16*, 78–100.

Baglioni, A. (2016). *The European Banking Union. A critical assessment*. Palgrave Macmillan.

Baglioni, A., & Monticini, A. (2008). The intraday price of money: Evidence from the E-MID interbank market. *Journal of Money, Credit and Banking, 40*(7), 1533–1540.

Bartolini, L., Bertola, G., & Prati, A. (2002a). Day-to-day monetary policy and the volatility of the Federal Funds interest rate. *Journal of Money, Credit and Banking, 34*(1), 137–159.

Bartolini, L., Bertola, G., & Prati, A. (2002b). *The overnight interbank market: Evidence from the G7 and the euro zone* (CEPR Discussion Paper n. 3090).

Bernanke, B. (2022). *21st century monetary policy*. Norton.

Bernanke, B., & Blinder, A. (1988). Credit, money and aggregate demand. *American Economic Review, 78*(2), 435–439.

Bindseil, U., Camba-Mendez, G., Hirsch, A., & Weller, B. (2006). Excess reserves and the implementation of monetary policy of the ECB. *Journal of Policy Modeling, 28*, 491–510.

BIS. (2019). *Unconventional monetary policy tools: A cross-country analysis*. Paper no. 63 of the Committee on the Global Financial System, Bank for International Settlements.

Borio, C. (2001). *A hundred ways to skin a cat: Comparing monetary policy operating procedures in the United States, Japan and the euro area* (BIS Paper no. 9).

Brunnermeier, M., & Koby, Y. (2018). *The reversal interest rate* (NBER Working Paper n. 25406). Cambridge, MA.

Campbell, J. (1987). Money announcements, the demand for bank reserves, and the behavior of the Federal Funds rate within the statement week. *Journal of Money, Credit and Banking, 19*(1), 56–67.

EBA. (2020, December). *EBA Report on liquidity measures under Article 509(1) of the CRR*, European Banking Authority.

ECB. (2002, May). *The liquidity management of the ECB* European Central Bank Monthly Bulletin.

Freixas, X., & Rochet, J.-C. (2008). *Microeconomics of banking*. MIT Press.

Friedman, B. M., & Kuttner, K. N. (2010). Implementation of monetary policy: How do central banks set interest rates? *Handbook of Monetary Economics, 3*, 1345–1438.

Furfine, C. (2001). Banks as monitors of other banks: Evidence from the overnight Federal funds market. *Journal of Business, 74*, 33–57.

Hamilton, J. D. (1996). The daily market for federal funds. *Journal of Political Economy, 104*(1), 26–56.

Mishkin, F. (2015). *Macroeconomics: Policy and practice*. Pearson Education.
Pariès, M., Kok, C., & Rottner, M. (2020). *Reversal interest rate and macroprudential policy* (ECB Working Paper n. 2487).
Schnabel, I. (2023, 27 March). *Back to normal? Balance sheet size and interest rate control*, speech at Columbia University, New York.

CHAPTER 4

The European Central Bank: Twenty-five Years of Single Monetary Policy in the Euro Area

Abstract The analytical framework introduced in Chapter 3 is applied here to the implementation of monetary policy in the euro area. The traditional ECB's operational framework was the interest rate steering—corridor system. Starting with the financial crisis of 2007/2008, the ECB has introduced a first set of "unconventional measures": the years between 2008 and 2014 can be seen as a transition phase, during which the ECB's implementation framework has evolved from a corridor to a floor system (albeit unofficially). With the adoption of APP and T-LTROs in 2015, the ECB started to explicitly target the size of its balance sheet. In the euro area, QE policies have been complemented by the negative interest rate policy. New QE measures have been adopted in 2020–2021 as a reaction to the pandemic crisis. In 2022, the ECB exited QE policies and started a normalization process. Despite a downsizing of its balance sheet, the ECB currently maintains an excess liquidity; the deposit facility rate is the key policy rate. Those different stages are discussed in this chapter and some descriptive evidence is provided. I will also address the strategy of the ECB and some issues related to the specific institutional framework of the euro area.

Keywords ECB's strategy · Longer-Term Refinancing Operations · Outright Monetary Transactions · Asset Purchase Program · Pandemic Emergency Purchase Program · Transmission Protection Instrument · TARGET balances

A. Baglioni, *Monetary Policy Implementation*,
https://doi.org/10.1007/978-3-031-53885-8_4

4.1 Introduction

The analytical framework introduced in the previous chapter can be applied to the implementation of monetary policy by the European Central Bank (Ecb) since January 1st 1999: the first twenty-five years of single monetary policy in the euro area. Since the start of the European Monetary Union (EMU) until October 2008, the Ecb followed an interest rate steering policy implemented through a corridor system. The rate applied to the main refinancing operations (MROs) was the key policy rate, signaling the stance of monetary policy.

The financial crisis of 2007/2008, culminated with the Lehman Brothers' crash in September 2008, has induced the Ecb to introduce some relevant innovations into its operational framework, among which: the "fixed rate full allotment" mechanism to provide liquidity through the MROs, the extension of the maturity and size of the longer-term refinancing operations (LTROs), and the covered bond purchase program. This first set of "unconventional measures" has been followed by some other important innovations, that have been introduced as a reaction to the sovereign debt crisis taking place in 2010–2012, among which: the Outright Monetary Transactions (OMT) program and the further extension (up to three years) of the LTROs' maturity. The years between 2008 and 2014 can be seen as a long transition phase, during which the Ecb's operational framework has gradually evolved from a corridor to a floor system.

With the adoption of QE policies (asset purchase programs and targeted long-term lending operations) in 2015, the Ecb started to target the size of its balance sheet and the floor system has definitely become the implementation framework. In the euro area, QE policies have been complemented by the negative interest rate policy. After a short exit phase from QE (2018–2019), new QE measures have been adopted in 2020–2021 as a reaction to the pandemic crisis.

The Ecb exited QE policies in 2022 and started a normalization of its policy including, in addition to an interest rate tightening, a downsizing of its balance sheet and of the level of excess liquidity. The Ecb currently implements its policy in an ample reserves regime, where the money market rates are in line with the deposit facility rate: this has become the relevant policy rate signaling the stance of monetary policy.

In this chapter, I will discuss those different stages of monetary policy implementation in the euro area and provide some descriptive evidence.[1] Before doing so, I will address the strategy of the Ecb, which has remained rather stable over time: so far, only two revisions have been made (in 2003 and 2021). The final section will address some issues related to the specific institutional framework of the euro area.

4.2 The Strategy of the Ecb

4.2.1 The Primary Objective: Price Stability

The ECB's monetary policy strategy is centered on the final target assigned to it by the Treaty on the Functioning of the EU (Art. 127): price stability. This is the overriding objective of monetary policy in the euro area. It is not the only one, as the Treaty itself assigns the ECB the task of supporting the general economic policies in the Union with a view to contributing to the achievement of the Union's objectives, which also include full employment and balanced economic growth,[2] albeit under one precise condition: without prejudice to the objective of price stability. The Treaty thus defines a clear hierarchy of objectives: first comes price stability; then comes the task of contributing to sustainable growth and full employment, provided this does not conflict with price stability.

What exactly is meant by "price stability"? The Treaty establishes a general principle, which then needs to be given a quantitative content in order to have a transparent strategy that can guide the expectations of economic agents. The ECB itself took up this task in 1998, even before it was fully operational, establishing that price stability is to be understood as "year-on-year growth in the Harmonised Index of Consumer Prices (HICP) for the euro area of less than 2 percent". A few years later, in 2003, the Governing Council of the ECB felt the need to further specify this definition, stating that its objective is to keep the inflation rate "below, but close to, 2% over the medium term". This clarification contains two important elements, which are worth exploring further: an

[1] For a detailed description of the first two decades of the Ecb's experience, see Rostagno et al. (2019). For an assessment of the efficacy of the "non-standard" measures adopted by the Ecb since 2014, see Altavilla et al. (2021) and Neri and Siviero (2018).

[2] Within the objectives of the Union set out in Article 3 of the Treaty on the European Union.

inflation target that is not generically below 2%, but close to that point value; and a medium-term time horizon.

To understand the first element, one must first recall the context in which the Maastricht Treaty, the one that gave birth to the European Monetary Union, was signed in 1992. At that time, the policy debate was strongly influenced by the experience of the 1970s and 1980s, which were characterized by high and variable inflation. In Italy, for example, the inflation rate in that period was often well above 10%, with peaks around 20%. Similar situations occurred in several other European countries. This explains why the Treaty gave the ECB such a strict mandate, giving price stability priority over other possible monetary policy objectives: high and variable inflation has significant economic and social costs. However, deflation also carries high costs. This is why, when clarifying its strategy in 2003, the ECB set an inflation target close to 2%[3]: a positive inflation target, coordinating the expectations of economic agents on this level, helps to avert a deflationary spiral.

The fact remains that a target, thus defined, contains a potential asymmetry. Since it is not defined precisely, but rather as a range of possible values limited at the top by a ceiling (2%), it suggests that the ECB wants to react more aggressively to upward deviations of observed inflation from 2%, rather than to downward deviations. Such a target indicates a more aggressive strategy towards a positive inflation gap than a negative inflation gap. On closer inspection, it is even difficult to quantify exactly a negative inflation gap, since inflation rates below (albeit close to) 2% are deemed tolerable, according to this strategy. Conversely, an inflation rate above 2% certainly identifies a positive inflation gap, such that the central bank would have to implement a more restrictive stance of monetary policy. Over the years, especially in the face of the deflation risks experienced in some euro area countries over the past decade, this asymmetry has become a critical element of the ECB's strategy: this was one of the factors that led the ECB to revise its strategy in 2021 (see below).

The second aspect, which helps to define the ultimate goal of price stability, is the medium-term horizon. This means that the ECB is not committed to keeping the inflation rate close to 2% every month. This is because the inflation rate can be influenced by sudden and temporary

[3] According to some statements of the ECB top management at the time, the term "close to 2%" can be translated into a range between 1.7% and 1.9% (see Rostagno et al., 2019).

factors, against which it is neither possible nor advisable to react. It is not possible because monetary policy is transmitted to the real economy with long delays: it cannot be expected to have immediate effects that counteract an unexpected shock. It is not advisable because if the central bank wanted to completely—and immediately—neutralize the impact of an inflationary shock, this behavior would probably have strong repercussions on the real economy, in the presence of a trade-off between inflation gap and output gap: it is better to maintain a certain degree of flexibility. Therefore, the pursuit of the price stability objective should be measured over a medium-term horizon, which can be roughly identified as a period between one and two years (this is by nature an arbitrary indication).

The fact that the ECB's overriding objective is price stability, defined as a consumer inflation rate close to 2%, does not mean that its strategy qualifies as "inflation targeting". Pure inflation targeting involves a rather rigid reaction function, whereby the central bank responds mechanically to any deviation of inflation from its target level: the inflation gap. If there is an inflation forecast above the target, for example, it has to raise the policy interest rate. This scheme gives the central bank a single target and leaves it very little room for maneuver. There is also a "flexible inflation targeting", described by the Taylor rule, which assigns the central bank the task of balancing two objectives: price stability and real economic activity. According to this rule, the central bank reacts to the values assumed by the inflation gap and the output gap. Although it comes closest to the ECB's approach, even the Taylor rule does not seem adequate to describe its strategy. With respect to these reaction functions, the ECB approach is characterized by two features. First, the hierarchy of objectives: in the euro area, price stability is by statute the primary objective of monetary policy; support for real economic activity and employment is a target as well, provided it does not conflict with price stability. Second, the ECB retains a margin of discretion in deciding whether to change the stance of its policy, based on a comprehensive analysis of the economic system, which includes a broad spectrum of variables and information. In this framework, developments in monetary and credit aggregates play a relevant role in assessing risks to price stability: this is a distinctive aspect of the ECB's strategy.

4.2.2 *The "Two-Pillar" Approach*

Until recently (July 2021), in making its decisions the Governing Council of the ECB used to rely on an analysis that goes by the name of the "two-pillar approach". The two pillars are: (1) economic analysis, (2) monetary analysis. From a cross-check of the information coming from these two analyses, the ECB was able to identify the risks to price stability and to act accordingly.

Economic analysis considers a wide range of indicators. There are many factors influencing price dynamics: it depends on the interaction between supply and demand for goods, services and production factors throughout the economic system. In addition to information on price and cost developments, trends in the real economy, as measured by changes in GDP and industrial production, are monitored: a weakening of the business cycle, for example, signals a downward risk to the inflation outlook. Since it is important to have a forward-looking view, valuable information can come from sample surveys, which attempt to measure producers' and consumers' expectations. Financial variables, such as the yield curve, can also provide information on market expectations, in particular on expected inflation. On the cost side, prevailing labor market conditions can give useful indications on wage developments. Energy and commodity prices are followed very closely, as they are very volatile: shocks often come from these markets that can significantly alter production costs. Finally, international developments are relevant: for example, a slowdown in a geographical area, which is an important outlet market for goods produced in the euro area, represents a downside risk for the domestic economy. Exchange rate developments are also important. A reduction in the external value of the euro, for example, constitutes an inflationary shock: it makes imported goods (including raw materials, oil and intermediate goods produced abroad) more expensive and it increases the competitiveness of goods produced in the euro area, thereby supporting aggregate demand. Processing all this information allows the ECB staff to formulate its macroeconomic forecasts, which include: GDP and its components (consumption, investment, trade balance), employment, price and cost dynamics, and the public sector balance sheet.

Monetary analysis is a complement to economic analysis: it can provide useful indications from a long-term perspective, given that the link between money and prices is very delayed. Actually, monetary analysis has two components: monetary analysis (strictly speaking) and credit analysis. The first refers to the definition of money adopted by the ECB (in line with the international standard): see Table 4.1. It is a "concentric circles" definition: the more liquid component (including only cash and overnight deposits) is M1, while the broadest aggregate (also including less liquid financial assets such as money market fund shares and repos) is M3, which in fact includes all bank liabilities with a maturity of up to two years; M2 is an intermediate aggregate. Given that the individual components of money have a high degree of substitutability, one normally looks at the broader aggregate (M3) whose dynamics are not affected by any shifts in the public's portfolios from one liquid financial instrument to another. However, the analysis of the individual components of M3 and the narrower aggregate (M1) can also give useful indications. The important thing is to understand why money shows a specific pattern, distinguishing between the different reasons for holding money. For example, an abnormal increase in M3 could be due to a speculative motivation, i.e. a greater preference for liquidity in the face of higher volatility in the yields of other financial assets (equities and bonds): in this case, high money holdings are not motivated by transactions (purchases of goods and services) and therefore do not contain an inflationary potential.

Credit analysis considers the development of bank credit to businesses and households. In continental Europe, the banking sector is still the main source of funding for the real sector of the economy and therefore an important channel for the transmission of monetary policy. Financing conditions (quantity, interest rates, and collateral) can be a constraint on investment decisions and economic activity. Therefore, the ECB monitors the dynamics of bank lending, but not only. Observing the volumes

Table 4.1 Euro area: definition of money

	M1	*M2*	*M3*
Currency in circulation	×	×	×
Overnight deposits	×	×	×
Deposits with an agreed maturity of up to 2 years		×	×
Deposits redeemable at notice of up to 3 months		×	×
Repos			×
Money market fund shares			×
Debt securities with a maturity of up to 2 years			×

traded in the credit market does not provide sufficient information, as they depend on the interaction between credit supply and demand: a reduction in credit volumes could be the result of weak demand from businesses and not necessarily reflect a credit crunch by banks. For this reason, the Eurosystem conducts a quarterly sample survey (the Bank Lending Survey) which relies on questionnaires sent to banks to identify current and expected conditions in the credit market. This survey is able to show, for example, whether (on average) banks intend to tighten their criteria for granting credit: stricter selection of borrowers, demand for more collateral, application of higher interest rates.

The information coming from the monetary analysis can be combined ("cross-checked") with that coming from the economic analysis to outline the macroeconomic scenario within which the ECB Governing Council takes its decisions. This complex analysis helps to understand whether, given the forecasts made, the risks to the inflation and economic outlooks are either on the downside or on the upside (or balanced). Based on these elements, the Council decides whether it is necessary to increase or reduce (or leave unchanged) the degree of monetary accommodation, activating the instruments at its disposal.

The ECB strategy, briefly described here, has remained essentially unchanged for more than twenty years. From the introduction of the single currency (1999) to 2020, the only revision of the strategy took place in 2003, including two innovations. The first was a more precise quantitative definition of price stability, which we have already discussed. The second was the decision to abandon the reference value (4.5% year on year) for money growth (M3). Until then, this threshold was considered a useful indicator (albeit not a target): money growth above the threshold was interpreted as a signal of upside risk to the inflation outlook, to be assessed together with the other evidence coming from the economic and monetary analyses. Over time, it was realized that, given the considerable volatility of money patterns in several periods, the indication of a precise threshold value could be misleading (especially if it was mistakenly understood as an intermediate target for monetary policy). It was therefore decided to no longer refer to a precise value in monetary analysis and in the central bank's communication policy.[4]

[4] For a detailed account of the strategy review that took place in 2003 and of the internal ECB debate that accompanied it, see Rostagno et al. (2019).

4.2.3 The 2021 Strategy Review

In January 2020, the ECB started a second revision of its strategy, which was concluded in July 2021 (see ECB 2021a, 2021b). The most significant change concerns the definition of price stability: the 2% inflation target has become a *symmetric* objective, to be pursued over the medium term; positive and negative deviations from this target are considered equally undesirable. The historical expression "below but close to 2%" has been replaced by a formulation in which the ECB commits to react to any positive and negative inflation gaps with equal aggressiveness. In addition, when the economy is very close to the zero lower bound for interest rates, the ECB leaves open the possibility that the current inflation rate may be moderately above 2% for a certain period of time: this is intended to anchor inflation expectations at the 2% target and to prevent inflation expectations from falling below the target. The ECB thus intends to have an inflation buffer as a safety margin against the risk of deflation. This formulation of the price stability target responds to the need of correcting the above-mentioned asymmetry in the definition formulated in 2003. The strategy revision has been elaborated in a period (up to mid-2021) when the inflation rate was still below the 2% target and the interest rates were close to the ZLB: hence the need to avoid that negative deviations from the inflation target would become entrenched. After a short time, the sudden increase of the price dynamics made the opposite problem arise: namely that of avoiding inflationary expectations well above target become entrenched.

The 2021 strategy review included an important announcement related to the ECB's operational framework: the primary monetary policy instrument is the set of policy rates. This announcement marked the exit from the QE era, where the operational target of monetary policy was the size of the central bank's balance sheet. The Governing Council also announced that, alongside policy interest rates, the new instruments introduced in the previous years—purchases of financial assets, long-term lending to the banking system and forward guidance—would enter its toolkit on a permanent basis. Actually, the exit from the unconventional measures and the rise of the policy rates (taking place in 2022–2023) went together with the transition from the forward guidance to the "meeting-by-meeting" approach to decision-making and communication:

the Governing Council retains the freedom to react to incoming information at every meeting, taking "data-dependent" decisions; no (or very little) anticipation about future decisions is released.

The "two-pillar" approach has been modified as well. The cross-checking between the information coming from the economic and from the monetary analyses to assess the risks to price stability has been discontinued. The assessment of the risks for economic growth and price stability is instead based on the analysis devoted to the real economy and to the inflation outlook. The analysis of financial and monetary conditions provides information useful to assess the transmission of monetary policy through the credit channel and to detect any vulnerability that might threaten financial stability: the latter is seen as a precondition for price stability. The reasons why monetary aggregates play less of a role in the new framework have to be found in the instability of the link between money and prices, making money growth a less reliable indicator of possible inflation risks than it used to be in the past. Hence, "since the 2021 strategy review, the Governing Council has based its policy decisions on an integrated assessment of all relevant factors. While this assessment is still built on an economic analysis on the one hand and a monetary and financial analysis on the other, it recognizes that a distinct monetary pillar is no longer essential for successfully conducting monetary policy".[5] The transition from the old two-pillar approach to the new "integrated analytical framework" is reflected in the way in which the analysis, underlying the ECB's decisions, is communicated in the *Monetary policy statement* released right after the meetings of the Governing Council.

Looking ahead, house prices should become part of the inflation measurement process, complementing the consumer price index already in use. The revision of the strategy also touched upon the environmental sustainability, addressing the issues labelled "greening monetary policy" (which will be discussed in Chapter 7). From now on, the ECB will make periodic strategy reviews.

[5] See Schnabel (2023), who discusses the reasons why the link between money growth and inflation has become unstable in recent years.

4.3 The Traditional Operational Framework: Interest Rate Steering

The traditional interest rate steering approach, followed by the Ecb until 2008, relied on the corridor system that we have introduced in Chapter 3. Monetary policy was implemented by using the following tools: open market operations (OMOs), standing facilities, and reserve requirement.

Within OMOs, the main role was played by the weekly Main Refinancing Operations (MROs): repos made every week with a maturity of one week. Liquidity was allotted through a tender procedure: an auction with a minimum bid rate.[6] This was the policy rate, through which the Ecb was able to signal the desired stance of its policy. Although the Ecb did not have an official interest rate target, the minimum bid rate on the MROs was perceived by financial market participants as the Ecb's target for the O/N interbank rate (i^* in the notation of the model introduced in Chapter 3) which was its operational target. These operations were the main source of liquidity creation: see Fig. 4.1. Another relevant source of liquidity was provided by the Longer-Term Refinancing Operations (LTROs) with a maturity of three months: these were a stable source of funding for the banking system but they did not convey any signal related to the monetary policy stance. Finally, fine-tuning operations provide a flexible tool to inject and absorb liquidity in exceptional circumstances.

The OMOs are complemented by the two standing facilities: Marginal Lending Facility (MLF) and Deposit Facility (DF), enabling banks either to borrow money (by pledging collateral) or deposit money at the central bank on the overnight maturity. The DF is available until half an hour past the closing time of the interbank payment system (TARGET2).[7] Banks can switch their balances from their current accounts to the DF at the end of the business day and have the liquidity available again on their current accounts at the start of business on the next day. Therefore, although current account balances are not remunerated, the interest paid on the DF is de facto a remuneration of the excess reserves, i.e. the reserve balances exceeding the reserve requirement: this is labeled i_R in the model presented in the previous chapter.

[6] Actually, the tender procedure has been introduced in July 2000. Before then, liquidity was allotted at a fixed rate through the MROs.

[7] In the last day of the reserve maintenance period, the DF is available until one hour past the closing time of TARGET2.

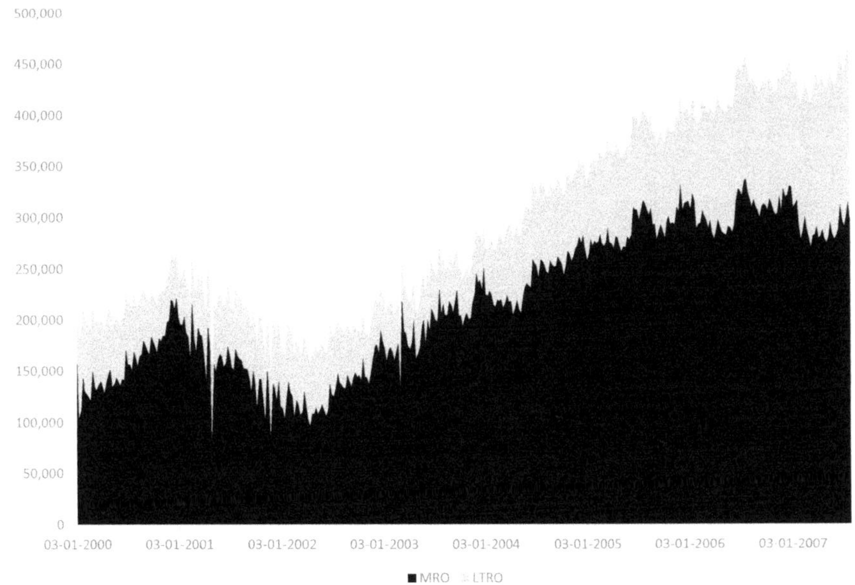

Fig. 4.1 Euro area: sources of liquidity in "normal times" (stocks in euro millions, weekly data 2000/1/3–2007/7/31) (*MRO* base money injected through Main Refinancing Operations; *LTRO* base money injected through Longer-Term Refinancing Operations. *Source of data* Ecb, Statistical Data Warehouse)

The minimum reserve requirement plays an important role in this operational framework: as we have seen in the previous chapter, the averaging facility makes the daily demand for bank reserves depend on the difference between the expected and current levels of the O/N interest rate: see Eq. (3.14). This interest rate elasticity provides a stabilizing mechanism, enabling the central bank to intervene less frequently in the money market than it should do otherwise. This explains why the MROs of the Ecb have a weekly frequency, while other central banks have to make daily operations (even more than one in the same business day). In the euro area, the reserve requirement is applied to all bank liabilities with a maturity up to two years. The reserve coefficient used to be 2% until 2011, when it was lowered to 1%. The requirement has to be met on average over a maintenance period. Each period begins on the settlement day of the first MRO following a Governing Council meeting (dedicated to monetary policy decisions)[8] and it ends just before the MRO, following the next GC meeting, will be settled. This way of defining the maintenance period (introduced in 2004) rules out the possibility that, once a period has begun, a monetary policy decision might be taken within the same period. This feature avoids the instability due to possible rumors about imminent policy decisions, making the expected policy rate change and the position of the demand for reserves shift accordingly.[9] Actually, this kind of instability was observed before 2004, when the maintenance period used to be defined on a calendar basis (from the 24th of a month to the 23rd of next month). Until recently, minimum reserve balances were remunerated at the same interest rate paid on the MROs.[10] Shortfalls are applied a penalty rate.

Figure 4.2 provides a picture of the corridor of interest rates in the money market in "normal times", before the financial crisis of 2007/2008. The market O/N rate (Eonia) is generally very close to the target

[8] The Ecb Governing Council meets about every six weeks to take monetary policy decisions. Additional meetings are held to take decisions other than those related to monetary policy.

[9] Remember that the position of the reserves demand schedule depends on the expected interest rate within the same maintenance period, since this is the time horizon for any inter-temporal arbitrage trade (see Sect. 3.2).

[10] The interest rate paid on minimum reserves has been lowered to the DF rate in October 2022 and to zero with the Governing Council decision taken in July 2023 (effective as of September 2023).

level signaled by the Ecb: the rate applied to the MROs. The volatility that can be observed is generally limited to the last day(s) of the maintenance period of the reserve requirement. As we have discussed in Sect. 3.2, in those days the demand for bank reserves becomes more rigid than in other days, so any liquidity shock can have quite a substantial impact on market rates. In any case, the rates applied to the two standing facilities provide an upper and a lower bound to market rates. This framework has been effective in stabilizing the money market rates around the target set by the Ecb: the market condition normally observed is consistent with the theoretical equilibrium identified by the model presented in Sect. 3.2 and visualized in Fig. 3.4.

In the interest rate steering framework, the stance of monetary policy is identified and signaled by the interest rate target. To the contrary, the management of liquidity has only a technical role: that of offsetting the volatility of the autonomous liquidity factors and any significant shift of the demand for reserves schedule, as we have discussed in Sect. 3.2.5. In the tradition of the Ecb, this approach goes under the name of "separation principle", and it has been stressed even at the outset of the financial crisis, when the Ecb introduced the first set of "unconventional measures" aimed at preserving the liquidity of the financial system.[11]

4.4 The International Financial Crisis and the Enhanced Credit Support Measures

The first set of innovations, labeled "Enhanced Credit Support Measures", has been introduced by the Ecb in the most acute phase of the 2007/2008 financial crisis, with the aim of preserving the stability of the financial system. Their specific purpose was to avoid that a liquidity crisis might impair the transmission of monetary policy through the banking system, given the central role of banks in providing credit to the economy of the euro area. They include the following five measures.

[11] In the press conference, following the Governing Council meeting of 6 September 2007, President Trichet said: "let us not confuse the appropriate functioning of the money market and the monetary policy stance".

Fig. 4.2 Euro area: interest rate corridor in "normal times" (percentage points, daily data 2000/1/3–2007/7/31) (*EONIA* [Euro OverNight Index Average]: interest rate in the interbank O/N market; *MRO* interest rate applied to the Main Refinancing Operations [fixed rate until 2000/6/27, minimum bid rate afterwards]; *DF* interest rate applied to the deposit facility; *MLF* interest rate applied to the marginal lending facility. *Source of data* Ecb, Statistical Data Warehouse)

a. MROs with a "fixed rate full allotment". Since October 2008, the liquidity provided to the banking system through the MROs (and through the LTROs as well since March 2009) is allocated at a fixed rate and without any limitation: banks can borrow any amount they need from the central bank (provided they have enough collateral). This procedure, replacing the tender procedure, has been introduced as a provisional measure, but it is still in place. With the full allotment procedure, the creation of base money through monetary policy operations has become officially endogenous: it is completely determined by the demand for liquidity of the banking system. Actually, the supply of base money was de facto endogenous even before then: the Ecb retained the power to set the supply of reserves, but this was to be set as a function of the interest rate target (see the discussion in Sect. 3.2.4). With the adoption of the full allotment procedure this endogeneity has become explicit.
b. Extension of the maturity of the LTROs. Between 2008 and 2009, the maturity of the LTROs has been increased from 3 to 12 months. The size of these operations has been increased as well, and they have gradually become much more relevant than the weekly MROs as a source of liquidity (see Fig. 4.3). By increasing the average maturity of monetary policy operations, the central bank has become a stable source of funding for the banking system of the euro area.
c. Collateral framework. The range of assets eligible as collateral in monetary policy operations has been widened, in order to facilitate the access to central bank funding by all banks.
d. Covered bond purchase program (CBPP). This was the first asset purchase program adopted by the Ecb (in 2009), with the aim of providing liquidity to the market for covered bonds, that was hit by a "dry up" during the financial crisis.
e. Currency swaps. To be able to provide liquidity in US dollars to banks located in the euro area, the Ecb agreed on currency swaps with the Fed in 2007 and 2008. Similar agreements have been signed with other central banks in the following years.[12]

Through the above measures, the Ecb was able to accommodate the huge increase of the demand for reserves by the banking system: the

[12] More details on currency swaps will be given in the next chapter.

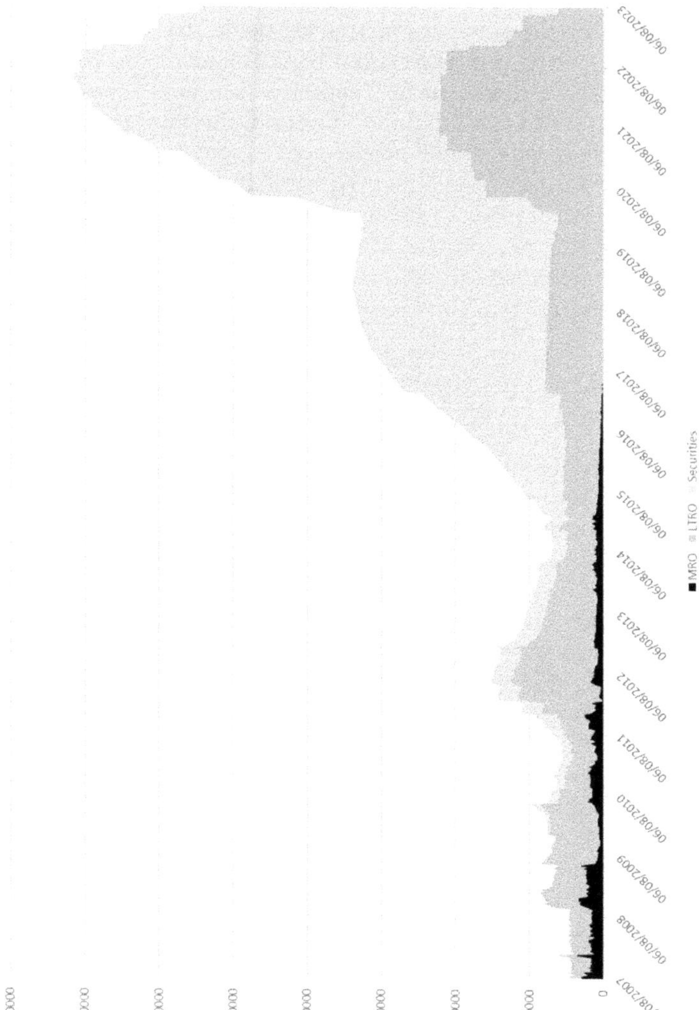

Fig. 4.3 Liquidity creation through unconventional monetary policy (stocks in euro millions, weekly data 2007/8/6–2023/8/7) (*MRO* base money injected through Main Refinancing Operations; *LTRO* base money injected through Longer-Term Refinancing Operations [including T-LTROs]; *Securities* base money injected through asset purchases [Securities held for monetary policy purposes]. *Source of data* Ecb, Statistical Data Warehouse)

hoarding of liquidity was a consequence of the uncertainty created by the malfunctioning of financial markets. Those measures were accompanied by the announcement that the Ecb was ready to provide all the liquidity needed for the smooth functioning of the banking system. This accommodating behavior of the central bank is part of the liquidity management that we have discussed in Chapter 3 (see Fig. 3.8 and the related comment) and it was not intended to expand the stance of monetary policy, according to the above-mentioned "separation principle". Nevertheless, those measures complemented the reduction of the policy rate and they amplified its impact on the money market: between October 2008 and May 2009 the rate on the MROs was lowered by 325 b.p., while the Eonia rate decreased by almost 400 b.p., dropping into the lower region of the interest rate corridor (see Fig. 4.4).

4.5 The Sovereign Debt Crisis and "Whatever It Takes"

The second wave of unconventional measures have been taken by the Ecb to overcome the sovereign debt crisis hitting the euro area between 2010 and 2012. Although in a different context than under the 2007/2008 crisis, these measures still respond to the need of preserving the correct transmission of monetary policy in presence of a high volatility of financial markets. More specifically, the purpose of the new tools introduced in this period was twofold. I) Curb the cross-country interest rate spreads, by eliminating the redenomination risk, i.e. the possibility that some member countries might be induced to leave the EMU and denominate its outstanding public debt in a (devaluated) national currency. II) Preserve the liquidity of the banking system, particularly in those (high-debt) countries where banks were facing significant funding strains. The first target has been achieved by adopting two programs of intervention in the sovereign debt market: the Securities Market Programme (SMP) and the Outright Monetary Transactions (OMT). The second one by further extending the maturity (up to three years) and the size of the LTROs. Fig. 4.5

a. Securities Market Programme (SMP). For institutional and political reasons, the purchase of government bonds by the Ecb has been a controversial issue in the euro area, causing hot policy debates and

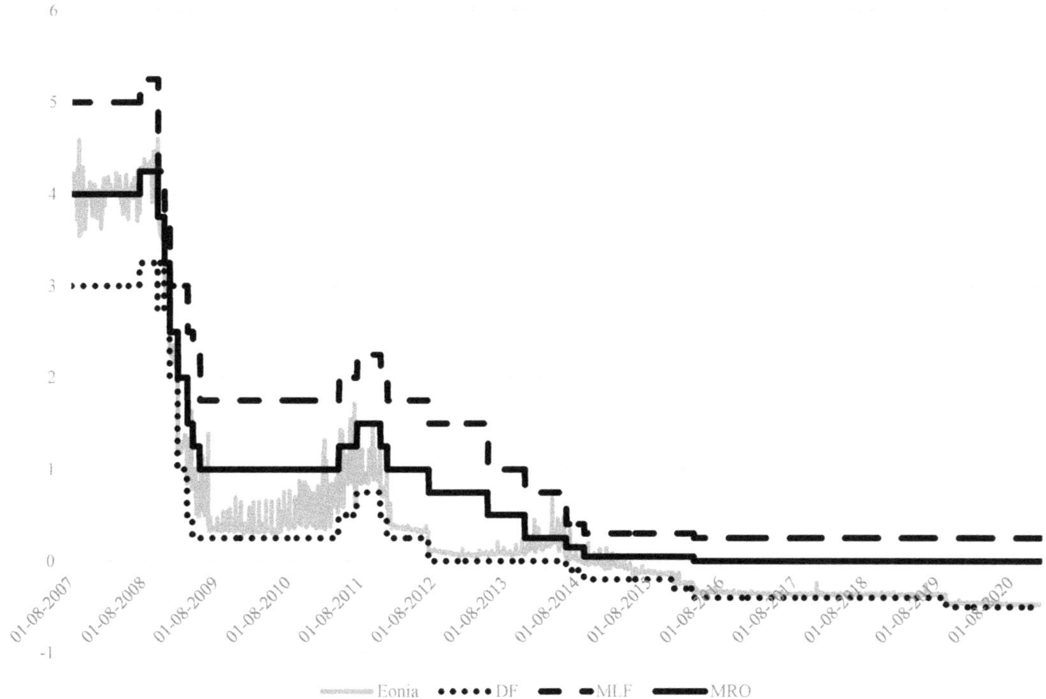

Fig. 4.4 From the corridor system to the floor system in the euro area (percentage points, daily data 2007/8/1–2020/12/28) (*EONIA* [Euro OverNight Index Average]: interest rate in the interbank O/N market, computed as an 8.5 b.p. spread over the €STR [euro short-term rate] since 2019/10/1; *MRO* interest rate applied to the Main Refinancing Operations [minimum bid rate until 2008/10/8, fixed rate afterwards]; *DF* interest rate applied to the deposit facility; *MLF* interest rate applied to the marginal lending facility. *Source of data* Ecb, Statistical Data Warehouse)

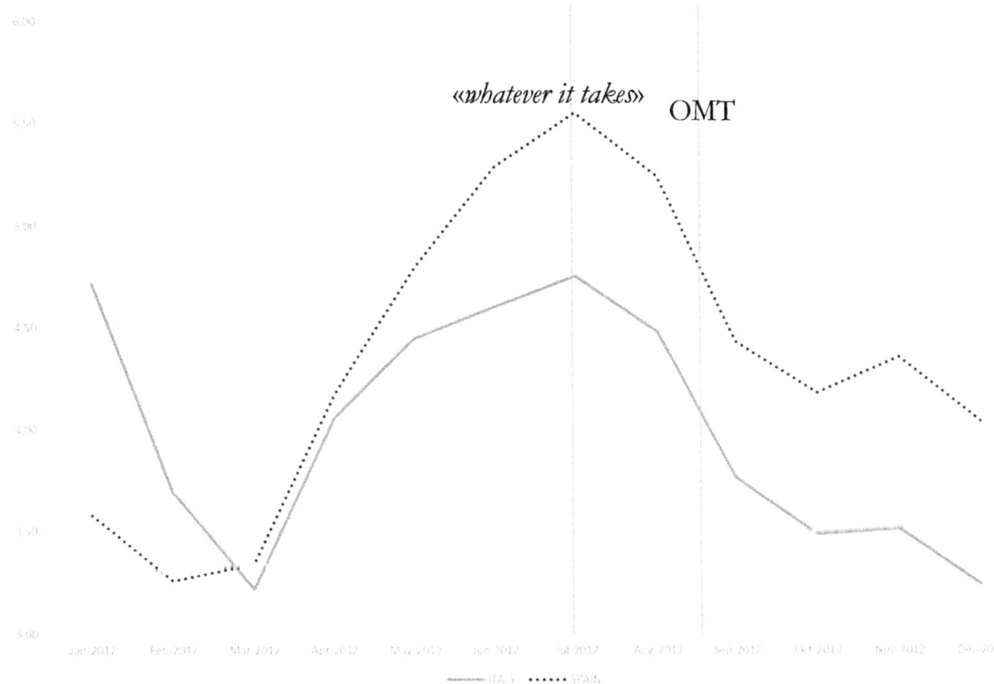

Fig. 4.5 BTP-BUND and BONOS-BUND spreads: the impact of OMT program (percentage points—monthly data 2012/1–2012/12) (*ITALY* interest rate spread between 10Y Italian and German government bonds; *SPAIN* interest rate spread between 10Y Spanish and German government bonds. *Data source* OECD.Stat)

legal disputes. This is the reason why the first program of sovereign debt purchase introduced by the Ecb (in 2010), the SMP, was accompanied by a communication policy signaling that the program was going to be limited in size and timing.[13] In addition, the base money created with the SMP has been sterilized through weekly liquidity-absorbing operations. The rationale behind this sterilization seems to be more political than technical: as we have discussed above, since monetary policy operations are implemented with a full allotment procedure, the amount of base money created by such operations is completely endogenous and potentially unlimited.

b. Outright Monetary Transactions (OMT). The OMT program, introduced in the summer of 2012 and preceded by the famous sentence of President Draghi ("we will do whatever it takes to preserve the euro area"), was accompanied by a completely different communication policy, stating that the program was intended to be potentially unlimited.[14] This policy was very effective: it had a great impact on financial market participants' expectations and it made the cross-country spreads on sovereign bonds to decline sharply in a few months, despite the fact that no operation has ever been made under this program: see Fig. 4.5. With the adoption of the OMT, the Ecb has de facto become the lender of last resort for the Governments of the euro area.

c. LTROs with 3 years maturity. Between December 2011 and February 2012, the Ecb implemented a couple of LTROs with two exceptional features: unprecedented size (500 billion euro altogether) and maturity (three years). Their purpose was to avoid a liquidity crisis in the banking system, given the high exposition of some banks to the sovereign risk and the dry up of trades in the interbank market. A technicality of these operations is worth mentioning: the prepayment option, enabling banks to repay the loans received from the central bank after one year. This option was exercised in 2013–2014 by many banks, implementing a deleveraging process and reducing the flow of credit to the economy, in a period where the business cycle in the euro area was weak and

[13] See the Introductory statement to the press conference of 10 June 2010, where President Trichet said that the SMP was "temporary in nature".

[14] See the press conference following the Governing Council meeting of 6 September 2012.

> the inflation rate was well below the 2% target. This unintended outcome was due to the prepayment option, leaving the size the LTROs in the hands of the banking system, so partially endogenous: the reduction of the size of the LTROs is visible in Fig. 4.3, and it is mirrored in the downsizing of the Ecb balance sheet (see Fig. 4.8).

The huge amounts of liquidity injected into the money market, first through the MROs with full allotment and later with the large size LTROs, created an excess liquidity able to drive the market interest rates close to the lower bound of the "corridor": the rate applied to the DF (see Fig. 4.4). Since then, this has become a permanent feature of the money market in the euro area. However, during this transition from the corridor to the floor system, the Ecb was still following the separation principle: the level of the policy rate (that applied to the MROs) was the only tool used to signal the stance of its policy, with the management of liquidity playing a technical role and being used to preserve the correct transmission of monetary policy through the banking channel. Only with the adoption of the QE policy in 2015 the Ecb began to target the size of its balance sheet and to use it as a way to signal the stance of its policy.

4.6 Quantitative Easing and Negative Interest Rates

In 2012–2013 the euro area economy was in recession and the inflation rate was well below target. After several cuts, the policy rates reached the ZLB by the end of 2014 (see Fig. 4.4). The Ecb decided to address this critical situation by using two main tools: a new generation of LTROs and a large asset purchase program. The introduction of these innovations marks the beginning of the QE policy in the euro area. They have been complemented by the forward guidance (FG) and by the Negative Interest Rate Policy (NIRP). While the previous rounds of unconventional measures taken by the Ecb (between 2008 and 2012) responded to the need of preserving the correct transmission of monetary policy in a context of financial instability (either due to the international financial crisis or to the sovereign debt crisis in the euro area) the new round of innovations, introduced in 2014–2015, responded to the need of expanding the stance of monetary policy to support the recovery of the euro area economy from the ongoing recession, in presence of a level of interest rates reaching the ZLB. A new wave of QE measures was taken in 2020 to address the pandemic crisis. Let me briefly summarize all these measures.

a. T-LTROs. The Targeted Longer-Term Refinancing Operations are loans (with a maturity of 3–4 years) offered by the central bank to the banking system, structured in a way to create an incentive for banks to increase their supply of loans to firms and households (excluding mortgage loans). Since September 2014, there have been three generations of T-LTROs with different features. However, the basic framework is the same for all of them. For each bank, the dynamic of the loans volume over an observation period is confronted with a pre-determined benchmark. A bank showing a loan dynamic above (below) the benchmark enjoys better (worse) funding conditions: either in terms of the amount it can borrow (the so-called "borrowing allowance") or in terms of the interest rate applied. The latter has sometimes been set at levels below the other policy rates,[15] to encourage banks to apply for those loans. Actually, some of the first operations were disappointing for their low take-up ratio (the ratio between the amount taken up by the banking system and the total amount made available by the central bank). It remains true that this kind of operations does not allow the central bank to take full control of the size of its own balance sheet, since their amounts depend on the behavior of banks, relative initially to the take-up ratio and eventually to the exercise of the prepayment option.
b. APP and PEPP. To take full control of the size of its own balance sheet, the Ecb introduced a large-scale Asset Purchase Program (APP) in January 2015. The APP actually included two pre-existing programs: the CBPP (Covered Bonds) and the ABSPP (Asset Backed Securities). Two new programs were added: the PSPP (Public Sector) and the CSPP (Corporate Sector). Among these four programs, the PSPP is by far the largest one for its size. Between 2015 and 2018, the Ecb accumulated assets for a total amount

[15] For example, the rate applied to the T-LTROs III (2020–2022) could be as low as −1%, compared with the zero rate applied at that time to the MROs and to −0.50% applied to the deposit facility.

of 2,600 billion euros. After a suspension in 2019, the program has been re-activated and coupled with the Pandemic Emergency Purchase Program (PEPP) in March 2020. The latter, introduced to address the Covid-19 crisis, has been endowed with a huge envelope: 1850 billions, spent (actually not entirely) during the two years up to March 2022. The pattern of the whole securities portfolio held by the Ecb, together with the size of the LTROs, can be seen in Fig. 4.3. The dynamics and composition of the different asset purchase programs can be seen in Figs. 4.6 and 4.7.

c. The NIRP has been introduced in the euro area in 2014, when the interest rate applied to the DF has been lowered to −0.10%. This rate has been later reduced down to −0.50% in several steps: see Fig. 4.4.[16] At the same time, the rate applied to the MROs has been lowered to zero. The NIRP has driven below zero the level of interest rates not only in the money market (as it can be seen in Fig. 4.4) but also on medium-long-term bonds, through the portfolio rebalancing channel, thus contributing significantly, together with the other unconventional measures taken at the same time, to expand the stance of monetary policy in the euro area. Keeping the interest rate on the excess liquidity (deposited on the current accounts and on the DF) at negative levels for a long time would imply a relevant cost for the banking system. This is the reason why, in October 2019, the Ecb decided to apply a two-tier remuneration scheme on bank reserves. Up to a threshold level, equal to six times the reserve requirement, the balances held on current accounts were exempted from the application of the negative rate: they were paid a zero rate. The balances exceeding this allowance were applied the negative DF rate.

d. Like other central banks, the Ecb has introduced the FG into its "toolbox" when the level of interest rates was approaching the ZLB. In July 2013, the Governing Council declared to expect the policy rates to remain "at current or lower levels for an extended period of time". Since then, similar indications have been provided several times. Through time, the focus of the FG has shifted from the interest rate policy to the QE policies, providing information about

[16] The interest rate applied to the current account balances, exceeding the reserve requirement, was set in that period at the same negative level as that applied to the DF, to prevent banks from arbitraging between the two instruments.

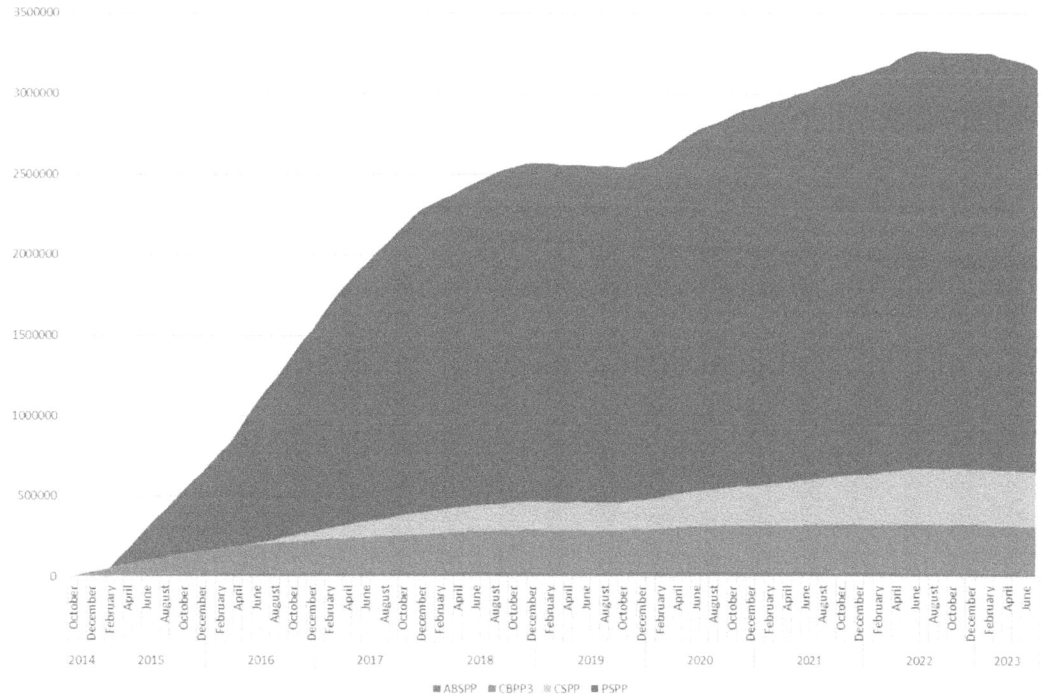

Fig. 4.6 Eurosystem: securities holdings under APP (million euro, stocks—monthly data 2014/10–2023/7) (*PSPP* Public Sector Purchase Programme; *CSPP* Corporate Sector Purchase Program; *CBPP3* Covered Bond Purchase Programme 3; *ABSPP* Asset Backed Securities Purchase Programme. *Data source* Ecb, Statistical Data Warehouse)

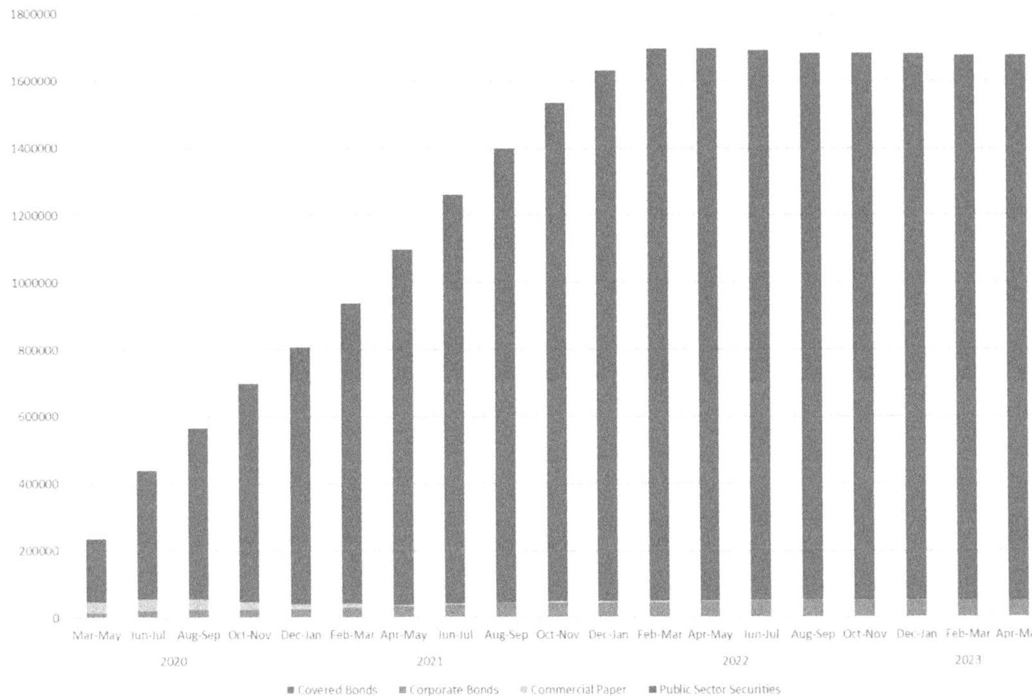

Fig. 4.7 Eurosystem: securities holdings under PEPP (million euro, stocks—bimonthly data 2020/3–2023/5) (*Data source* Ecb, Statistical Data Warehouse)

Fig. 4.8 Size of the Eurosystem balance sheet (stocks in euro millions, annual data 1999–2023) (End-of-year, except for 2023 (mid-year). *Data source* Ecb, Statistical Data Warehouse)

the features of the asset purchase programs and of the different rounds of LTROs, like: the size and length of the programs, the range of assets under purchase, the terms and conditions for accessing loans through LTROs, and the exit strategy.[17]

By taking all the above-mentioned innovations, the Ecb has completed the transition from the traditional interest rate steering approach (corridor system) to the new approach, based on QE measures and on the floor system of monetary policy implementation, modeled in Sect. 3.3. The separation principle was de facto abandoned. The injection of liquidity through the unconventional measures did not play a pure technical role anymore: instead, it started to give a crucial contribution to implement the stance of the policy decided by the Governing Council, together with the level of interest rates. In November 2014, the Council set for the first time a quantitative target for the size of the Ecb balance sheet.[18] In a three-year time (2015–2017) the size of the balance sheet has been doubled (see Fig. 4.8); a further huge expansion has been implemented as a reaction to the Covid-19 crisis (2020–2021).

Figure 4.9 shows the huge expansion of the excess liquidity (defined as the sum of the balances held by the banking system on current accounts and deposit facility, exceeding the reserve requirement) starting from early 2015, due to the several rounds of T-LTROs and asset purchase programs (APP and PEPP). As we know from the previous chapter, this structural excess supply of reserves is an essential feature of the floor system, leading the level of money market interest rates to stick to the lower bound, provided by the (negative) rate on the DF, as it can be seen in Fig. 4.4. A closer look at Fig. 4.9 shows that the excess of liquidity actually started in 2008, due to the Enhanced Credit Support measures, and it was eventually increased by the 3-year LTROs between 2011 and 2012. In those years, the rate applied to the DF was positive while that applied to the current account balances (exceeding the reserve requirement) was zero: this is why banks used to keep all their excess liquidity

[17] The evolution of the communication policy of the Ecb over time is analyzed in the report Ecb (2021c).

[18] In the Introductory Statement to the press conference, following the meeting of 6 November 2014, the Governing Council communicated its intention to increase the size of the Ecb balance sheet up to the level of early 2012 (after two years of reduction, mainly due to the prepayment of the above-mentioned LTROs).

on the DF. Starting in July 2012 the two instruments, DF and current accounts, were applied the same interest rate (zero up to June 2014 and negative afterwards): therefore, banks were indifferent between keeping their excess liquidity either on their current accounts or on the DF. The introduction (October 2019) of the above-mentioned two-tier remuneration scheme for bank reserves determined a preference for keeping the excess liquidity on current accounts.[19]

The transition from an operational framework based on the shortage of bank reserves to one based on a structural excess of reserves has made the reserve requirement, still present in the euro area, de facto redundant: it does not play any significant role in shaping the demand for reserves, which is perfectly elastic in the range of values relevant for the market equilibrium (see Fig. 3.10). On the supply side, the MROs have become insignificant as a channel of base money creation, which is injected into the system through asset purchases and LTROs (see Fig. 4.3).

At this point, it may be worthwhile to sum up the unconventional monetary policy measures taken by the ECB since 2008: see Table 4.2.

4.7 Exit Strategy and New Normal

4.7.1 The Exit from QE Policies

In Sect. 3.4 we have identified the different steps of a gradual exit strategy from QE policies: (1) tapering, (2) roll-over, (3) interest rate tightening, and (4) roll-off. This kind of exit strategy has indeed been followed by the Ecb in two circumstances. The first was in 2018, when the size of the monthly net asset purchases, made under the APP, was reduced (in a few steps) from 60 billion euro to zero by the end of the year. The Governing Council announced that the roll-over of the securities held in its portfolio would continue for a long time after the increase of policy rates. Due to the weakening of the business cycle in the euro area in 2019, steps 3 and 4 were not actually taken: the APP was re-activated in November of that year and the policy rates were not increased. In March 2020, the Covid-19 crisis induced the Ecb to restart the QE policy by launching the Pandemic Emergency Purchase Program (PEPP) and new rounds of

[19] This preference has been reversed after September 2023, for the reason that we are going to see in the next section.

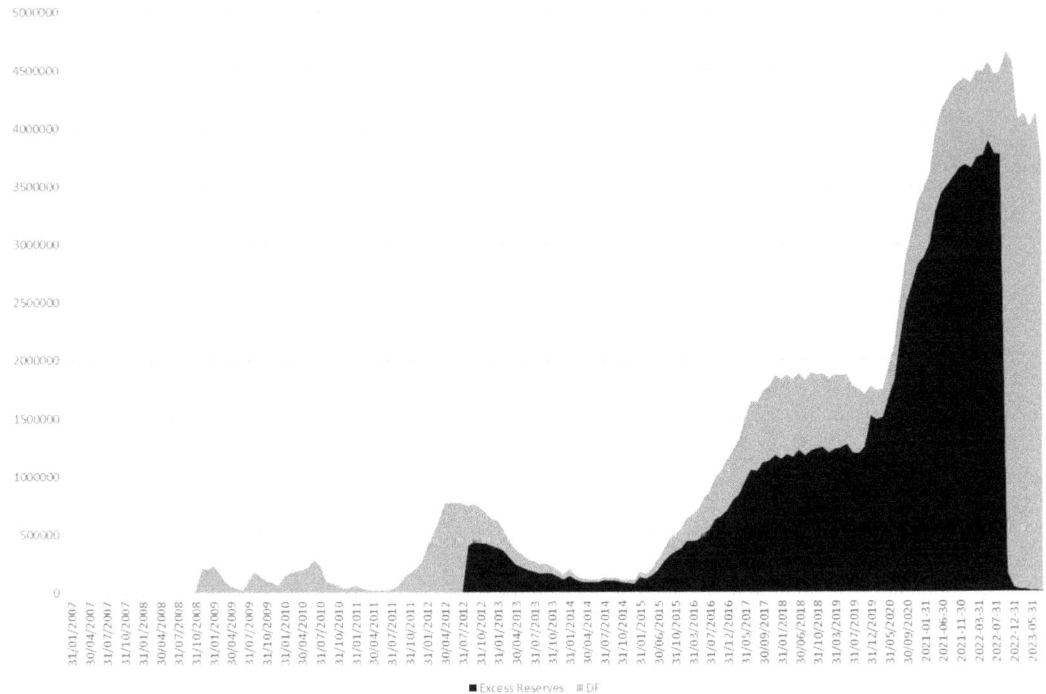

Fig. 4.9 Excess liquidity in the euro area (stocks in euro millions, monthly data Jan. 2007–Aug. 2023) (*Excess reserves* balances held by euro area banks on their current accounts at the Eurosystem, exceeding the reserve requirement. *DF* balances held by the euro area banking system on the deposit facility. Excess liquidity is defined as the sum of Excess reserves and DF (i.e. the sum of the two areas in the picture). *Source of data* Ecb, Statistical Data Warehouse)

Table 4.2 Unconventional monetary policy measures in the euro area

Financial crisis: Enhanced Credit Support	MROs with fixed rate full allotment	Since 2008 up to present
	LTRO with maturity up to one year	2008–2009
	Widening the range of assets eligible as collateral	Since 2008 up to present
	Covered Bond Purchase Programme (CBPP)	2008–2022
	Currency Swaps	Since 2008 up to present
Sovereign debt crisis	Securities Market Programme (SMP)	2010–2012
	LTRO with 3 year maturity	2011–2012
	Outright Monetary Transactions (OMT)	Since 2012 to present
Fighting recession: QE and NIRP	Forward guidance	2013–2022
	T-LTRO I and II	2014–2020
	Negative Interest Rate Policy (NIRP)	2014–2022
	Asset Purchase Programme (APP): PSPP, CSPP, CBPP, ABSPP	2015–2022 (suspended in Jan.–Oct. 2019)
Covid-19 crisis: a new wave of QE	Pandemic Emergency Purchase Programme (PEPP)	2020–2022
	Strengthening T-LTRO III	2020–2021 (program initiated in Sept. 2019)
	Pandemic Emergency—LTROs (PELTROs)	2020–2021

long-term loans at favorable conditions to the banking sector (T-LTROs III and PELTROs).

The same path has been followed by the Ecb in its exit strategy from those exceptional measures taken during the pandemic crisis. The net asset purchases under PEPP have been reduced and finally discontinued in March 2022; at the same time, the Ecb announced that the roll-over of securities purchased under PEPP would continue until (at least) the end of 2024: see in Fig. 4.7 the constant pattern of the stock of securities held under PEPP since March 2022. The net asset purchases under APP has been downsized and finally discontinued in July 2022. Starting on this date, the official policy rates have been increased (in several steps) by more than four percentage points: see Fig. 4.10. Finally, in 2023 the Ecb started the roll-off of the securities purchased under APP, by limiting and eventually discontinuing the reinvestment of the proceeds from maturing securities: this added a "Quantitative Tightening" (QT) dimension to the monetary restriction implemented through the interest rate tightening. Actually, the degree of QT has been rather low, since the amount of non-reinvested APP redemptions has been small compared to the size of the securities portfolio (including both APP and PEPP). It is also true that the repayment of the different tranches of long-term loans (T-LTRO III) by banks has endogenously determined a consistent downsizing of the Eurosystem's balance sheet, adding a relevant component to the QT: see Figs. 4.3 and 4.8.

The ability to implement the exit strategy from QE policies through several steps, and in particular to delay the roll-off of the securities portfolio well after the increase of policy rates, derives from the decoupling principle. This possibility turns out to be particularly useful in the euro area, where the Ecb has purchased large amounts of sovereign bonds issued by member countries, including high-debt countries. A rapid roll-off of those securities (by stopping the reinvestment of principal payments or by selling those securities) might be destabilizing for the government bond market in the euro area, possibly leading to wide cross-country spreads and impairing the transmission of monetary policy throughout the euro area. The decoupling principle enables the Ecb to tighten the stance of its policy, if it needs to do so, by raising its policy rates and, at the same time, to delay and implement in a gradual manner the roll-off of its portfolio of government bonds.

The exit from QE policies and the increase of the policy rates came together with a change of the communication policy of the Ecb. The forward guidance has been replaced by a meeting-by-meeting approach, in which the Governing Council retains the freedom to decide in each meeting, based on the incoming information, without making any pre-commitment. This new approach enables the Governing Council to enjoy a much higher degree of discretion than it used to do under the forward guidance approach. On one side, this change can be appropriate in the transition from a balance sheet policy to an interest rate policy[20] On the

[20] See Lane (2022).

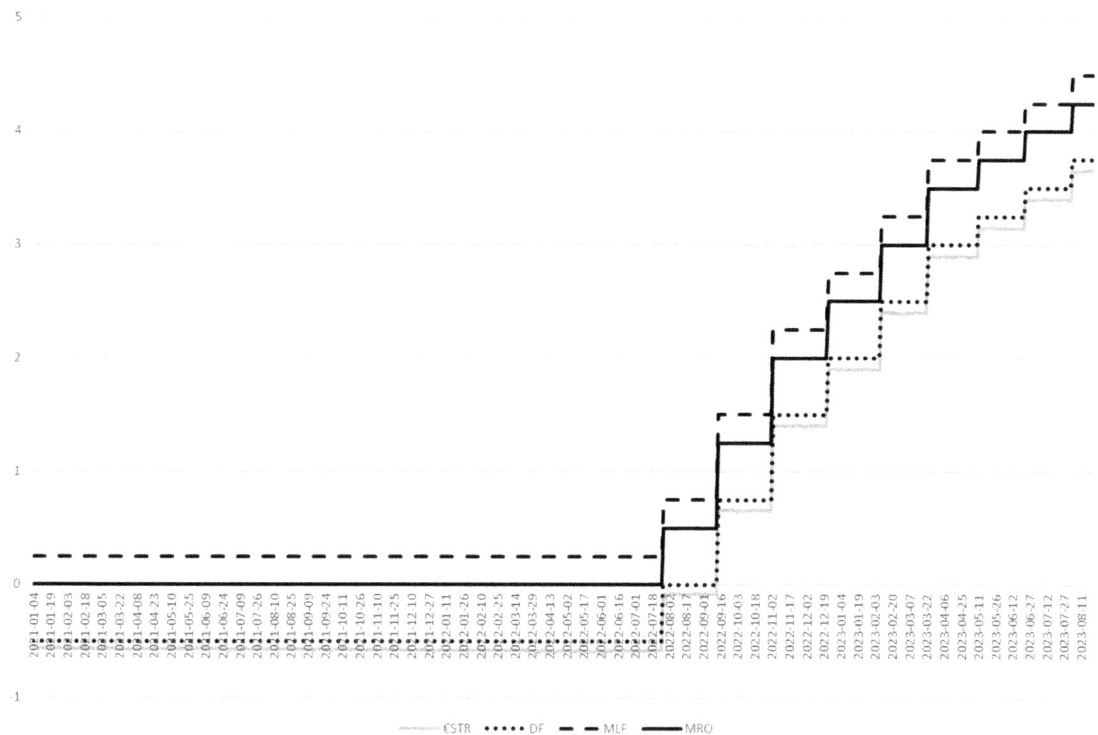

Fig. 4.10 Interest rate tightening in the euro area (percentage points, daily data 2021/1/4–2023/8/21) (*€STR* euro short-term rate; *MRO* interest rate applied to the Main Refinancing Operations [fixed rate]; *DF* interest rate applied to the deposit facility; *MLF* interest rate applied to the marginal lending facility. *Source of data* Ecb Data Portal)

other side (as it is well-known in monetary policy theory[21]) a higher degree of discretion reduces the ability of central banks to "anchor" inflationary expectations.

4.7.2 *The New Normal*

How is the "new normal" in monetary policy implementation, once the QE policies have been abandoned? In principle, the features of the new normal can be identified as follows (see Sect. 3.4): (1) The level of interest rates is the primary operational target of monetary policy. (2) This target is implemented in a floor system, where the relevant policy rate is the interest rate on bank reserves. To this aim, the central bank should maintain an excess liquidity in the money market (see Fig. 3.11). (3) The new tools (AP, LTLO and FG) remain in the toolkit of monetary policy (they should not be labeled as "unconventional measures" anymore).

Within its strategy review,[22] in July 2021 the Ecb announced that its new normal exhibits features (1) and (3). As far as (2) is concerned, through time the floor system has de facto become the operational framework of the Ecb and the rate applied to the deposit facility has become the key policy rate, taking up the role that used to be played by the rate applied to the MROs in the past. This has been acknowledged in several documents and speeches by top ECB representatives, including President Lagarde: "In the current conditions of ample liquidity and full allotment in our main refinancing operations, the interest paid on the reserves that banks hold in the ECB's deposit facility is the Governing Council's main instrument for setting the monetary policy stance".[23]

Figure 4.10 shows that the O/N market rate in the euro area (€STR) has been in line with the DF rate (the floor of the system) throughout the whole normalization process. Actually, the Euro short-term rate keeps at a level slightly below the DF rate: the reason is that some non-bank financial intermediaries (such as investment funds), which cannot hold accounts with the Eurosystem, trade in the money market. These intermediaries, which have accumulated large amounts of liquidity by selling

[21] See Barro and Gordon (1983) and the literature building on this seminal contribution.

[22] See ECB (2021a, 2021b).

[23] Letter from President C. Lagarde to some members of the European Parliament, 22 September 2023.

securities to the central bank during the QE years, are willing to lend their liquidity at rates below the DF rate to banks, which in turn can deposit that money with the Eurosystem and earn the DF rate.[24] Despite the QT policy started in 2023 and the repayment of the T-LTRO III loans by banks, the level of excess liquidity remains very high by historical standards, as it can be observed in Fig. 4.9. The allocation of this excess liquidity has rapidly shifted from the current accounts to the DF since September 2022, and the reason is simple: since then, the interest rate applied to the DF has become positive, while the current account balances are not remunerated (the two-tier scheme has been suspended).

Looking ahead, the balance sheet of the Eurosystem is expected to shrink further in the coming years, and the level of excess liquidity to decline accordingly, due to the repayments of the third series of long-term refinancing operations (T-LTRO III) and the reduction of the stock of securities held for monetary policy purposes. This process will continue until "the optimal long-run size and composition of the Eurosystem's balance sheet, and by implication the adequate level of excess liquidity"[25] will be reached. Further details about the operational framework of the ECB in the steady state are expected to be released in 2024 as an outcome of the ongoing (as of end-2023) comprehensive review.

4.8 Institutional Issues Specific to the Euro Area

The transfer of monetary sovereignty to a supranational institution, such as the Ecb, while at the same time maintaining a fragmentation of fiscal sovereignty, assigned to individual member states, represents a fundamental institutional anomaly of the eurozone, which has conditioned the timing and manner in which QE has been adopted. In other countries, such as the US, the UK, and Japan, the central bank can freely decide to proceed with the purchase of government debt securities, without encountering the obstacles that the Ecb has encountered on its way. In those countries, there is no problem of which securities to buy: there is a national (federal in the case of the US) public debt, which is the natural

[24] See Corsi and Mudde (2022) for more details.

[25] Speech by President C. Lagarde at the Hearing of the Committee on Economic and Monetary Affairs of the European Parliament, 25 September 2023.

target of securities purchases under a QE program, in addition to private debt (but private debt is not a problem in the eurozone either). Nor is there a prohibition of monetary financing of public debt: the central bank, in its autonomy and in accordance with its final objectives, decides whether and to what extent to buy public bonds and whether to guarantee their roll-over at maturity. In those countries, the central bank acts as a guarantor of the liquidity of the government bond market, preventing speculative attacks from generating yield increases that are not justified by fundamental factors; in other words, it acts as a "lender of last resort" (LLR) for governments, as well as for credit institutions.

This is not possible, or is very problematic, in the European Monetary Union. First of all, there is the problem of which securities to buy within the framework of a QE program. Due to the absence of federal debt, the Ecb can only buy securities of the public debt of the individual member states of the monetary union. In what proportion? This problem was solved, when the PSPP was introduced, by using the principle of "capital keys": in practice, by allocating the purchases of government bonds according to the size of the euro area member countries. More precisely, the capital keys are the shares held by each national central bank of the euro area in the capital of the Ecb; they are computed upon the relative sizes of GDP and population of member countries: see Table 4.3. However, this principle can lead to an excessive rigidity of the program in some circumstances, in particular when action is needed to contain interest rate spreads between one country and another, in order to safeguard the proper transmission of monetary policy throughout the euro area. For this very reason, the Governing Council of the Ecb decided to introduce some flexibility in the application of this principle when it adopted the PEPP.

In this section, we are going to address some issues related to the peculiar institutional framework of the euro area. First, the necessity to adopt specific measures to preserve the correct transmission of monetary policy across the member countries of the monetary union. Second, the implications of the prohibition of monetary financing of the public sector. Third, the legal controversies raised by the purchases of Government bonds by the Ecb (under the PSPP). Finally, the controversial issue known as "TARGET balances".

Table 4.3 Capital keys (euro area NCBs' percentage shares in Ecb's paid up capital)

Belgium	3.6139
Germany	26.1494
Estonia	0.2794
Ireland	1.6798
Greece	2.4536
Spain	11.8287
France	20.2600
Croatia	0.8044
Italy	16.8518
Cyprus	0.2134
Latvia	0.3865
Lithuania	0.5741
Luxembourg	0.3268
Malta	0.1040
Netherlands	5.8133
Austria	2.9033
Portugal	2.3217
Slovenia	0.4776
Slovakia	1.1360
Finland	1.8221
Total	100

4.8.1 *The Need to Preserve the Smooth Transmission of Monetary Policy*

The normalization of monetary policy, implemented by exiting QE policies and lifting the level of interest rates well above the ZLB, can potentially produce tensions in the cross-country interest rates spreads in the euro area. The reason is that the asset purchase programs and the zero-rate policy used to provide a strong support to the sustainability of public debts in some high-debt countries, like Italy, Greece, and Spain. Without such support, the risk of wide cross-country spreads on government securities, preventing uniform monetary conditions across the euro area, is material. This is the reason why, when the Ecb decided to start the increase of its policy rates (in July 2022), it also decided to introduce a new instrument to preserve the correct transmission of monetary policy across the euro area: the *Transmission Protection Instrument* (TPI).

The TPI is an instrument to avoid the fragmentation of monetary conditions between a member country and another. It is not an instrument to provide support to a specific country, which is conducting unsustainable public finance management. The TPI allows the Ecb to initiate purchases of a country's public debt securities on the basis of an assessment comprising several criteria. (1) The country concerned must not be subject to an excessive deficit procedure under the European fiscal framework. (2) The country must not be subject to an excessive macroeconomic imbalance procedure. (3) The country's public debt must be on a sustainable path, according to a sustainability assessment made by the Ecb itself, together with the European Commission, the European Stability Mechanism (ESM) and the International Monetary Fund. 4) The Government must comply with the commitments made under the national Recovery and Resilience Plan and with the European Commission in the context of the European Semester. These are strict conditions, which do not allow a country deviating from the European fiscal framework to benefit from the "anti-spread shield". The third condition, in particular, seems very demanding and subject to wide margins of discretion: predicting the trajectory of the debt/GDP ratio in the long run and assessing its sustainability is an exercise whose outcome depends crucially on the underlying assumptions.

Two other tools to prevent an excessive widening of cross-country spreads, that have been introduced before the TPI, remain in the toolkit of the Ecb. One is the OMT (Outright Monetary Transactions) program, adopted by the Ecb in 2012 (see Sect. 4.5). However, the activation of this instrument requires the Government of the interested country to sign a financial assistance agreement with the ESM, together with an associated fiscal and macroeconomic adjustment program. This heavy conditionality is the reason why the OMT has never been used so far and it seems unlikely to be used in the future: presumably it could be used if the Governing Council intended to induce a country's Government to agree on a fiscal consolidation plan with the ESM.

The other instrument, designed to prevent an excessive widening of the cross-country spreads on government bonds, is the flexibility in the rollover of maturing bonds purchased with the pandemic program (PEPP). Flexibility in the geographic distribution of purchases was used in the initial phase of the pandemic crisis (spring 2020) to contain the spreads of high-debt countries that had come under strain. In the following months, purchases tended to converge towards the country distribution derived from the principle of capital keys. Subsequently, a return towards a flexible use of purchases, made when maturing bonds are rolled-over, has been observed; however, the amounts at stake have been quite small so far (mid-2023). Whether the Ecb will be willing to use this flexibility to a greater extent, and how effective it will be in the face of a possible speculative attack on a member country's debt, remains an open question.

4.8.2 The Prohibition of Monetary Financing of the Public Sector

Article 123 of the Treaty of the European Union prohibits the Ecb and the national central banks (NCBs) from directly financing governments and local public bodies by extending credit lines and directly purchasing securities. The latter expression has always been interpreted as a ban on the purchase of public debt securities in the primary market, i.e. in the issuing phase. Instead, the prohibition does not apply to the purchase of securities in the secondary market: this is explicitly included among the instruments available to the ECB (Art. 18 of the Statute). However, secondary market purchases should not be such as to produce effects equivalent to those that would be produced by direct purchases: as we shall see, this subtle distinction can give rise to legal disputes.

The prohibition of monetary financing, in addition to the aforementioned anomaly of the European Monetary Union (centralization of monetary policy and decentralization of fiscal policy), produces a situation in which, when the governments of member countries issue debts in euros, it is in fact as if they were issuing debts denominated in a foreign currency. The euro is in fact a currency issued by a supranational institution, the ECB, which is beyond the jurisdiction of the national governments of the member countries. In addition, the prohibition of monetary financing prevents it from acting as a "Lender of Last Resort" (LLR) like other central banks.

This prohibition has a precise origin. It was introduced to prevent any monetary financing of national public deficits from becoming a way around another rule of the union: the "no-bail out clause" (Art. 125 of the EU Treaty). This states that an EU member country is not liable for the financial liabilities of another member. If the ECB suffered some losses as a result of the insolvency of a government whose securities it had previously purchased, those losses would be borne by the other governments, which would be called upon to restore the ECB's capital. Beyond the legal issue of the "no-bail out clause", the prohibition of monetary financing stems from mutual mistrust between governments, particularly those of countries with high public debt: it is feared that monetary financing could be a way of easing the budgetary discipline that financial markets normally exert on governments by raising the cost of funding for countries that are "undisciplined" in the management of public finances ("moral hazard" effect).

Whatever its justification, the prohibition of monetary financing has the consequence that the ECB cannot explicitly exercise the role of LLR for euro area governments. An important improvement has been made in 2012, when the adoption of the OMT program (followed later by PSPP and PEPP) created a situation in which the ECB has de facto assumed the role of LLR. However, this took place in an institutional framework that remains unclear, generating controversies and forcing the ECB to justify its interventions in the public securities market as responding and proportional to the ultimate objective of price stability.

The need for a lender of last resort stems from the fact that it represents a fundamental stabilizing mechanism for the public debt market, given the possibility of multiple equilibria: a "good" equilibrium (solvent government) and a "bad" equilibrium (insolvent government). A crucial variable, in determining which equilibrium prevails, is the cost of debt, together with the fundamental public finance variables: primary deficit (net of interest expenditure) and evolution of the debt/GDP ratio. In turn, the cost of debt depends on the expectations of market participants: hence the "self-fulfilling prophecy" nature of a liquidity crisis, which can lead to the insolvency of a State.[26] In this respect, the market for government debt is no different from the market for bank deposits, which are subject to "bank runs".[27] In both cases, the central bank, with its guarantee of intervention as LLR, plays a crucial role in coordinating economic agents' expectations towards the "good" equilibrium. The fragility of the Eurozone became evident during the sovereign debt crisis of 2010–2012: at that time, doubts about the sustainability of the public debt of some countries, together with the risk of redenomination (i.e. break-up of the monetary union), led to a strong volatility of interest rates on public bonds, jeopardizing the resilience of the Union and the solvency of some governments. The communication ("whatever it takes") and the introduction of the OMT program in summer 2012 were crucial in preventing the situation from getting out of hand.

[26] See Calvo (1988). More recent contributions, specifically focused on the eurozone, are: De Grauwe (2011), De Grauwe and Ji (2013), Gros (2012), and Corsetti and Dedola (2013).

[27] See Diamond and Dybvig (1983) and the extensive literature that grew out of this fundamental contribution.

In addition to the problems just outlined, the prohibition of monetary financing of the public sector has an undesirable side effect: it places the burden of stabilizing the government bond market on the banking system, in the absence of a central bank exercising the role of LLR. This is what happened in the euro area during the sovereign debt crisis, when the portfolio of domestic government bonds held by the banking system grew significantly. It only decreased when the PSPP was initiated: this highlights the role that banks had played in the meantime in supporting the government bond market.[28] The fact that the banking system can be called upon, even by means of moral suasion, to exercise that role is not without consequences. It leads to a strong concentration of risk in credit institutions, given the clear predominance of domestic securities in the portfolio of government bonds generally held by a bank (home bias). Although mitigated compared to the years of the sovereign debt crisis, the problem of excessive risk concentration in favor of domestic governments is still acute.

Solving these problems is a complex matter. The removal of the prohibition of monetary financing of the public sector faces such political obstacles as to be unrealistic. A more feasible solution could be the introduction of a European-level public bond (Eurobond or European safe asset), allowing the ECB to exercise the LLR function limited to this bond.[29] In this perspective, a significant step forward is the issuance of debt securities by the EU Commission, initiated in the course of 2020 to finance the European programs, introduced as a response to the economic crisis generated by the Covid-19 pandemic. Correcting the home bias in the banks' holdings of sovereign bonds would require a relevant innovation in the prudential regulation of the banking system, revising the current exemption of sovereign bonds from capital requirements on credit risk and introducing penalties for risk concentration in sovereign exposures.[30]

[28] For a systematic analysis of the role of the banking system in ensuring the liquidity of the government bond market, see Manna and Nobili (2018).

[29] Both solutions are discussed in Baglioni and Bordignon (2018).

[30] For an analysis of the different options for reforming the prudential treatment of government bonds, see Baglioni and Cefalà (2021).

4.8.3 The Legal Controversy over the PSPP

The purchase of government bonds by the central bank is, as has been said, a controversial issue: so delicate as to give rise, in the European context, to legal battles. To go into the merits of the legal issues is not the purpose of this book (nor would the author have the competence to do so). However, it is worth briefly summarizing the terms of the issue raised by some German citizens, on which the European Court of Justice (ECJ) has been called upon to give an opinion. The ruling issued by the ECJ on 11 December 2018 is very interesting, as it clarifies well some controversial points regarding the PSPP program. The ruling had been requested by the German Constitutional Court (CC) to which citizens of that country had addressed, contesting the fact that some ECB decisions were not applicable in Germany as they were contrary to the German Constitution, thus questioning the application of those decisions by the Bundesbank. The German CC, before giving its final ruling, asked for a ruling from the ECJ.

The appeal of the German citizens essentially concerned two questions: (1) whether the PSPP was compatible with the ECB's mandate (as defined in Article 127 of the EU Treaty); (2) whether the PSPP did not constitute a form of monetary financing of the member states' public debt, thus violating Article 123 of the EU Treaty. On both questions, the ECJ came out clearly in support of the decisions taken by the Governing Council of the ECB, rejecting the doubts raised by the German citizens' appeal.

On the first issue, the ECJ first recalls that the EU Treaty gives the ECB the responsibility to manage monetary policy in full autonomy. The ultimate objective of price stability itself is defined by the Treaty in a general way: it is up to the ECB to define it exactly and decide how to pursue it. Within this room for maneuver, the ECB considered that the traditional tools (i.e. changes in policy interest rates) were no longer an appropriate instrument for pursuing its ultimate goal (inflation below but close to 2%) given the risk of deflation in the euro area at the beginning of 2015. The ECB therefore decided (as like as other central banks) to initiate a purchase program of financial assets including government bonds, giving transparent reasons for its decision. The ECJ also recalls that the outright purchase of securities, including sovereign bonds, is one of the instruments available to the European System of Central Banks (ESCB) to implement monetary policy (Article 18 of the Statute). The PSPP therefore falls within the scope of monetary policy.

A specific issue, still pertaining to the alleged breach of the mandate given to the ECB, is that deriving from the principle of proportionality: this requires that EU institutions pursue their objectives through acts that do not go beyond what is strictly required to achieve those objectives. On this point, the ECJ acknowledges that the ECB has fully argued the technical reasons underlying its decision to launch the PSPP, exercising its legitimate discretion: the ECJ therefore does not consider that the ECB's decision to launch the PSPP, in order to pursue the ultimate objective of price stability, is vitiated by a "manifest error of assessment". The program therefore clearly does not go beyond what is necessary to achieve its objective, not least because of a number of features. First, the fact that the PSPP is aimed at influencing the general financial conditions of the euro area ensures that it is not intended to meet the specific financing needs of certain member states. The program is temporary in nature: it is intended to be implemented for the period necessary to reach the final target (although the term of the program has been revised over time to respond to changing economic conditions). In terms of quantity, the program is also limited, both through the schedule of monthly amounts to be purchased and by the limit of 33% per issuer and per issue.[31] Finally, the potential losses on securities holdings are shared within the Eurosystem only up to 20% of the program.

The last point deserves an explanation, with the aid of Fig. 4.11. The risk allocation rule agreed upon for the PSPP (and applied later to the PEPP as well) is the following. Risk-sharing within the Eurosystem is applied to 20% of the asset purchases: national government bonds purchased by the ECB (10% of the programs) and securities issued by European supranational institutions (another 10% of the programs). The remaining share of the asset purchases (80%) is made by the national central banks, buying domestic government bonds: the risk related to this share of the securities under purchase remains on the books of the NCBs.

On the second issue, that of monetary financing of government debt, we recall that Article 123 of the EU Treaty prohibits direct financing, in particular the purchase of securities in the primary market. The question posed by the German citizens is whether secondary market purchases, as

[31] This is a limit self-imposed by the Ecb: under the PSPP, the Eurosystem did not buy an amount of securities exceeding the 33% of each issue and the 33% of the total outstanding bonds issued by a government.

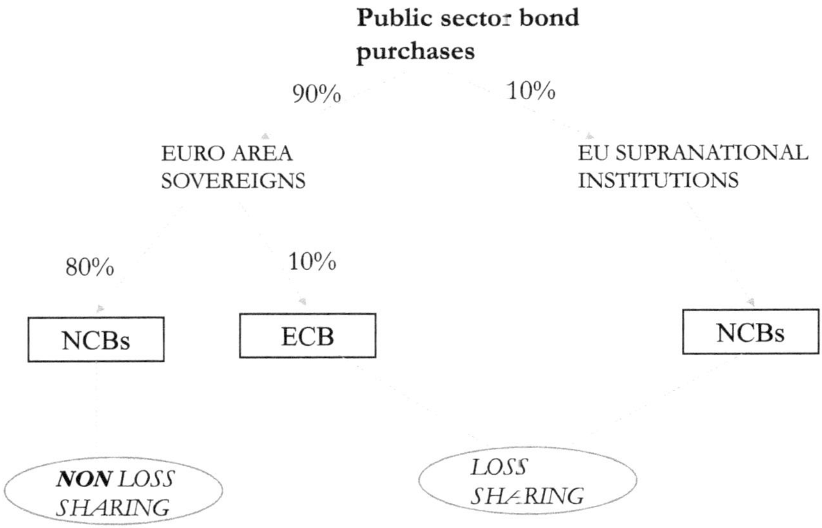

Fig. 4.11 Public sector bonds: distribution of purchases and risk allocation within the Eurosystem

envisaged under the PSPP, can be considered a way around this prohibition: they would be so if they produced effects equivalent to those of hypothetical primary market purchases. What effects and for whom? Here a distinction must be made between private agents and the public sector.

For the private sector, equivalence would occur if buyers of government bonds in the primary market were certain that the central bank would purchase those bonds in the secondary market within a timeframe and on terms that would allow them to act, de facto, as central bank's intermediaries for the direct purchase of bonds from the public sector. According to the ECJ, this eventuality is to be ruled out due to the following features of the PSPP. First, the "black-out" period: the ECB has committed to allow a few days to elapse between the issuance of a bond and its purchase by the central bank itself. Second, financial agents do not know in advance which specific securities will be purchased by the Eurosystem, for several reasons: there are some (limited) operational margins of flexibility in the application of the capital keys criterion; the 33% limit (per issue and per issuer) prevents an operator from being certain that a specific bond, purchased in the primary market, can be fully sold to the Eurosystem in the secondary market; detailed public information on individual securities held by the Eurosystem, as a result of the PSPP, is not available, as only aggregate statistics are released.

For the public sector, the problem stems from the fact that the certainty of central bank intervention could distort market conditions and reduce the incentive of governments to conduct sound fiscal policy. This is the classic argument of moral hazard, which would result from a lack of market discipline. In this regard, the ECJ observes that monetary policy generally involves interventions in interest rates and banks' refinancing conditions, thereby influencing the funding conditions for government deficits: the open market operations envisaged under the PSPP are no exception in this respect. On the other hand, it is necessary that the program for the purchase of government bonds does not give governments the certainty that, thanks to the central bank's guarantee, they will be relieved of the need to seek funding in the market to cover a public sector deficit. Even this eventuality seems to be ruled out due to the characteristics of the PSPP. The temporary nature of the program requires governments to take into account that, sooner or later, they will have to find in the market the resources needed to finance their deficits. The principle of capital keys ensures that, if one country accumulates more debt than the others, the share of that country's securities purchased by the Eurosystem, out of the total securities eligible for the program, is reduced. The 33% limit obviously forces governments to apply to the market to cover the bulk of their funding needs. An irresponsible fiscal policy exposes a government to the risk that, following a downgrade of its debt by the rating agencies, its securities will be excluded from the PSPP. Finally, the fact that the Eurosystem holds the securities, purchased under the PSPP, until maturity does not imply a violation of the prohibition on monetary financing, for several reasons: first, the governments issuing those securities will still have to repay their debts at maturity; second, the ECB retains the right to sell those securities in the market before maturity; and of course there is no obligation on the part of the ECB to purchase additional sovereign securities (either net purchases or roll-over of securities holdings), particularly those issued by a government that does not observe budgetary discipline.

In conclusion, the ECJ ruled in its December 2018 judgment that the ECB, by adopting and implementing the PSPP, did not go beyond the limits of its institutional mandate, nor did it violate or circumvent the prohibition of direct monetary financing of public debt. It should be stressed that this conclusion was also possible thanks to certain program features and limits self-imposed by the ECB, including: the program was temporary; the size of the purchases was limited (by the monthly amounts and the 33% limit); the purchase of national government bonds was mostly carried out by the NCBs without sharing any losses within the Eurosystem; the distribution of purchases per country respected the capital keys principle. It is interesting to note that, when adopting the PEPP, the ECB did not self-impose the 33% limit and decided to deviate to some extent from the capital keys principle.

4.8.4 *TARGET Balances and Monetary Policy Operations*

The massive purchases of financial assets, mainly government bonds, by the Eurosystem under the APP program had a strong impact on the interbank payment system of the euro area: TARGET2. In particular, it led to a significant increase in the balances that each National central bank has in this system, known as "TARGET balances". This has caused a controversy in the policy debate, as negative balances have sometimes been interpreted as a debt position accumulated by some countries against others, i.e. those whose central bank has a positive balance.[32] Such debit/credit positions might have fiscal implications, due to possible wealth transfers from one (creditor) country to another (debtor). Is this really the case? To answer this question, it is necessary to take a step back and understand what TARGET2 is and what determines the TARGET balances.

Since the beginning of its operations (1 January 1999), the Eurosystem has adopted a real-time gross settlement system for large-value interbank payments: TARGET (Trans-European Automated Real-time Gross Settlement Express Transfer System). In practice, this means that when bank X sends a payment message to bank Y, the actual transfer of money (settlement) takes place in real time (within one minute) via the central bank, using the current accounts that the two banks hold with the Eurosystem: bank X's account is debited and bank Y's account is credited with the amount of the payment. In other words, the payment is settled by transferring reserves from bank X to bank Y: let us remember that bank

[32] See Sinn and Wollmershauer (2012). To get an idea of the controversy generated by TARGET balances, it may be useful to see the numerous articles that have appeared on the topic on the *vox.eu* website. The ECB has also devoted numerous insights to it in its publications: *Working Papers* and *Economic Bulletin*.

reserves are the balances held by banks on their accounts with the central bank. This way of transferring money is particularly safe for two reasons. First, settlement takes place "in central bank money": Bank Y receives a credit from the central bank, not from other financial institutions as in other payment systems (e.g. the traditional current accounts at correspondent banks). Second, each payment is settled immediately, with no delay between the payment message and the actual transfer of funds. Hence the term "real-time gross settlement" (RTGS), to distinguish this type of payment system from the "end-of-day net settlement" systems, in which the balance of all incoming and outgoing payments for each bank is settled at the end of the business day, allowing the accumulation of potentially large intra-day debit positions.[33] The TARGET system was in fact a network between national gross settlement systems, operated locally by each NCB. In order to increase its efficiency, through more centralized management, TARGET was replaced in 2008 by TARGET2: a single technological platform managed by three NCBs (Bank of Italy, Bank of France and Bundesbank) but with the same basic features as TARGET.

The mechanism just described, concerning the settlement of payments through TARGET2, does not only apply to payments within a country, but also to payments involving two banks located in different countries of the euro area, with one important difference: each cross-border payment involves a transfer of bank reserves from one country to another of the euro area, and consequently a change in the balances that the two NCBs of those countries hold in the system, called "TARGET balances". Let us continue with the previous example, imagining that bank X is Italian and bank Y is German. The payment from the former to the latter results in a debit to bank X's account at Bank of Italy and a credit to bank Y's account at the Bundesbank: bank reserves have been transferred from Italy to Germany. In the TARGET system, this flow is recorded as an outgoing flow for the Bank of Italy and an incoming flow for the Bundesbank. At the end of the day, the daily net position is calculated for each central bank: the sum of all incoming flows, received from all the other central banks in the system, minus the sum of all outgoing flows. The TARGET balance of each NCB is the cumulated sum of all its daily net positions,

[33] This increased security comes at a cost: the amount of liquidity needed to make a real-time gross settlement system work is much greater than that needed in a system relying on end-of-day netting. For an analysis of the trade-off between safety and liquidity cost in payment systems, see Baglioni (2006).

from the beginning of TARGET (4 January 1999) until a certain date: if positive, it represents a claim against the ECB; if negative, it represents a debt to the ECB. To conclude our example, the payment from bank X to bank Y has a negative impact on the TARGET balance of Bank of Italy and a positive impact on that of the Bundesbank.

It is worth using our example once again to clarify a point. As we have just seen, the settlement of the payment from an Italian bank X to a German bank Y involves a transfer of bank reserves from the former to the latter. This implies that a liability of the Eurosystem towards the banking system is transferred from the Bank of Italy to the Bundesbank. In principle, this should give rise to a liability of the Italian central bank towards the German central bank (remember that the Eurosystem is a federal system of central banks, each with an autonomous balance sheet). In the TARGET2 system, it has been decided that these bilateral debits/credits between BCNs are replaced by debits/credits to the ECB, which in fact acts as a clearing house. That is why TARGET balances are debits/credits of the NCBs vis-à-vis the ECB.

Small digression: how does the US system work? It is natural to compare the Eurosystem to the Federal Reserve System, since the latter is also a federal system: the territory of the USA has been divided into twelve districts, each of which has its own Federal Reserve Bank with its own balance sheet. Together they form the Federal Reserve System, which takes care of the settlement of interbank payments, both within each district and across districts, similarly to what happens in the euro area. Inter-district payments give rise to flows between the *Inter-District Settlement Accounts* (ISAs) of the Feds involved. The balances on these accounts, the ISA balances, play an entirely similar role in the US system to the European TARGET balances, with one difference. The US system does not rely on a central counterparty, so the ISA balances are bilateral positions: they represent the credits (if positive) and debits (if negative) accumulated by each Fed towards every other Fed.[34]

Which payments are settled through TARGET2? All interbank payments and those related to monetary policy operations. In turn, interbank payments can have two origins: either commercial or financial. Continuing with our example, the payment may be originated by an

[34] On other technical features of TARGET, also in comparison to the US system, and on the relationship between the APP and TARGET balances, see Eisenschmidt et al. (2017). On the latter point, see also ECB (2017).

export of goods from Germany to Italy: X is the bank of the Italian importer and Y is the bank of the German exporter. In this case, the payment reflects a transaction which is recorded with a minus sign on the Italian trade balance and with a plus sign on the German trade balance. In principle, therefore, a negative TARGET balance of the Bank of Italy and a positive TARGET balance of the Bundesbank could mirror a negative and positive current account balance of the respective countries: in this case, the TARGET balances would indeed reflect the accumulation of a debt position of Italy vis-à-vis Germany. However, the payment could also be financial in nature, reflecting a capital flow from Italy to Germany: e.g. because an Italian entity (financial or non-financial) repays a debt to a German entity, or because it purchases a financial asset issued in Germany. In aggregate, a worsening of the Bank of Italy's TARGET balance and an improvement in the Bundesbank's TARGET balance could therefore mirror a reduction in Italy's liabilities and/or an increase in Italy's financial claims against Germany.

The settlement of monetary policy operations also takes place in TARGET2, possibly affecting the balances of the NCBs in the system. Refinancing operations are carried out in a decentralized manner: each NCB makes loans to domestic banks by crediting their current accounts with the same NCB. If, for example, the Bank of Italy makes a loan to an Italian bank as part of a monetary policy operation, this will have an equal impact on the asset side of the Bank of Italy itself (the loan granted) and on the liability side (the increase in bank reserves). At first, a refinancing operation has no impact on TARGET balances: this is why it is said to be "TARGET-neutral". However, the story may not end there. The Italian bank, which received the loan, could use it to repay foreign liabilities or purchase financial assets abroad. In such a case, we would see a capital outflow, which would have a negative impact on the TARGET balance of the Bank of Italy. On the latter's balance sheet, against the increase in assets (the loan disbursed) there would be a worsening of its TARGET balance (instead of an increase in bank reserves, which have been transferred abroad).

This is precisely what happened during the sovereign debt crisis, when the abundant liquidity injected by the Eurosystem through its refinancing operations (especially the two large-size operations with three-year maturity made between December 2011 and February 2012) was used by many Italian and Spanish banks to compensate for the drop of funding in the international financial markets. The confidence crisis in those markets forced many banks in the "peripheral" countries to repay previously issued liabilities (interbank debt and bank bonds), creating capital flows from these countries to the "core" countries, primarily Germany. Figure 4.12 shows the widening, in 2011–2012, of the negative TARGET balances of the three main peripheral countries (Italy, Spain, Portugal) and of the positive TARGET balances of the three countries where capital flows were directed (Germany, the Netherlands, Luxembourg).[35]

Figure 4.12 shows a new widening of TARGET balances since the beginning of 2015, coinciding with the start of QE policies in the euro area. Although this widening looks quite similar to the previous one, it is somewhat different. It is true that TARGET balances also widened from 2015 onwards as a result of monetary policy operations. In this case, however, the impact is more direct and it stems from cross-border purchases of financial assets, mainly government bonds, by some NCBs in execution of the APP program: a large part of the financial assets purchased by central banks were sold by foreign counterparties. In particular, many Italian government bonds purchased by the Bank of Italy, and Spanish bonds purchased by the Bank of Spain, were sold by financial intermediaries located in Germany (and to a lesser extent in the Netherlands) or by London-based intermediaries via their subsidiaries located in Germany, the Netherlands and Luxembourg. If Bank of Italy buys an Italian government bond from a German bank, it will pay for it by sending a TARGET payment: this will directly have a negative impact on its TARGET balance (increase in liabilities) against the increase in assets due to the bond added to its balance sheet. At the same time, the reserves of the German bank, receiving the payment, at the Bundesbank will increase and the TARGET balance of the German central bank will increase by the same amount. The final part of Fig. 4.12 shows, after a decline in 2019, a new widening of the TARGET balances in 2020 as a result of the introduction of the pandemic asset purchase program (PEPP).

Let us close this in-depth discussion on TARGET by trying to answer the initial question: do TARGET balances represent debts/credits between euro area member countries? If we look within the Eurosystem, the answer is yes. If we look at a member country as a whole, the answer depends on the nature of the payments underlying the TARGET balances.

[35] For a more detailed analysis of these events, see Rostagno et al. (2019).

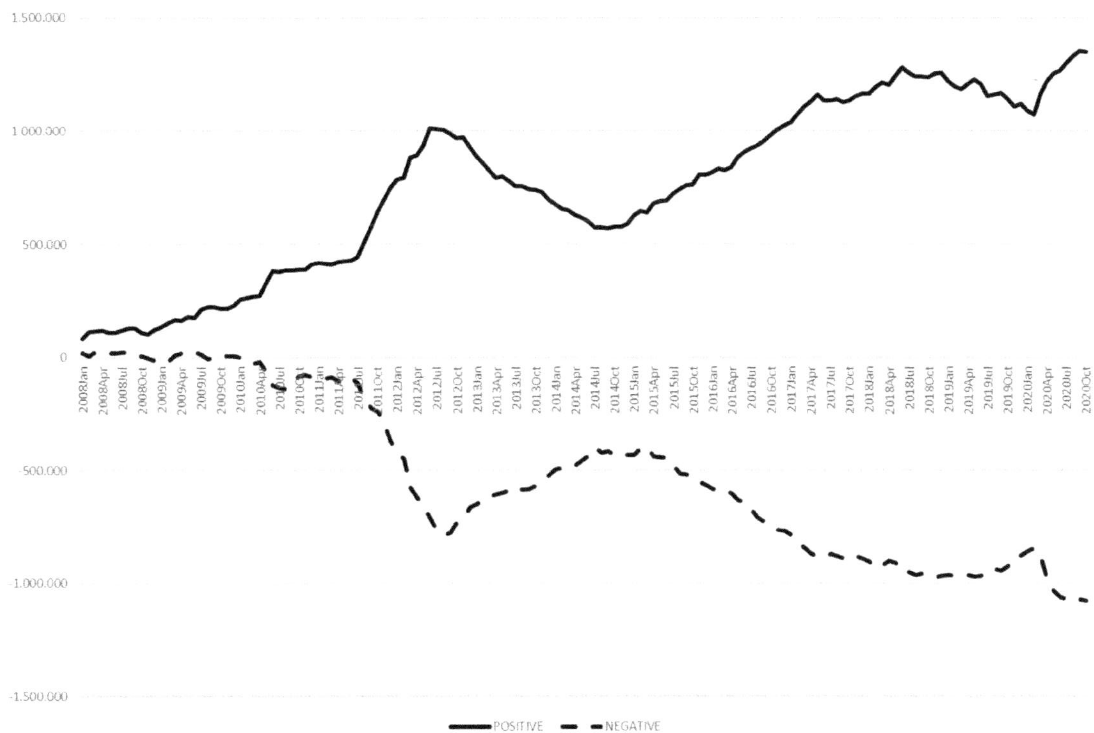

Fig. 4.12 TARGET *balances* (EUR millions, stocks—monthly data 2008/1–2020/10) (POSITIVE. Sum of the TARGET balances of the three national central banks with the largest positive balances: Germany, the Netherlands, Luxembourg. NEGATIVE. Sum of the TARGET balances of the three national central banks with the largest negative balances: Italy, Spain, Portugal. *Data source* ECB, *Statistical Data Warehouse*)

Conceptually, as we have seen, the settlement of a cross-border payment generates a liability of the sending central bank towards the receiving central bank, although in the Eurosystem it has been decided to account for these reciprocal exposures as debts/claims towards a central counterparty: the ECB. For a country as a whole, however, the nature of the payments that generate TARGET balances must be taken into account. If a negative TARGET balance were generated by an accumulation of negative trade balances of a country vis-à-vis other euro area members, it would indeed represent a debt of that country to the rest of the euro area. If instead it reflects some capital outflows from a country to other euro area members, the negative balance of the central bank on TARGET is offset by the acquisition of external financial assets (or reduction of liabilities): in this case, it cannot be considered as a worsening of the country's net financial position. This is the case for capital flows generated by the redistribution of liquidity injected with refinancing operations. This also applies to cross-border purchases of securities made in the execution of asset purchase programs: if a central bank buys sovereign securities of its own country from a foreign intermediary, on the one hand this worsens its TARGET balance, on the other hand it reduces a foreign liability of the country.

References

Altavilla C., Lemke, W., Linzert, T., Tapking, J., & von Landesberger, J. (2021). *Assessing the efficacy, efficiency, and potential side effects of the ECB's monetary policy instruments since 2014* (ECB Occasional Paper no. 278).

Baglioni, A. (2006). The organization of interbank settlement systems: Current trends and implications for central banking. In S. Schmitz & G. Wood (Eds.), *Institutional change in the payments system and monetary policy*. Routledge.

Baglioni, A., & Bordignon, M. (2018, July). *Sovereign debt restructuring: Rules versus discretion* (LUISS Policy Brief).

Baglioni, A., & Cefalà, F. (2021). Banks' sovereign exposures: In search of new rules. *Journal of Financial Regulation, 7*, 100–148.

Barro, R., & Gordon, D. (1983). Rules, discretion, and reputation in a model of monetary policy. *Journal of Monetary Economics, 12*(1), 101–121.

Calvo, G. (1988). Servicing the public debt: The role of expectations. *American Economic Review, 78*(4), 647–661.

Corsetti, G., & Dedola, L. (2013). *The mystery of the printing press: Self-fulfilling debt crises and monetary sovereignty* (CEPR Discussion Paper no. 9358).

Corsi, M., & Mudde, Y. (2022). *The use of the Eurosystem's monetary policy instruments and its monetary policy implementation framework in 2020 and 2021* (ECB Occasional Paper no. 304).

De Grauwe, P. (2011). *The governance of a fragile Eurozone* (CEPS Working Document no. 346).

De Grauwe, P., & Ji, Y. (2013). Self-fulfilling crises in the Eurozone: An empirical test. *Journal of International Money and Finance, 34*, 15–36.

Diamond, D., & Dybvig, P. (1983). Bank runs, deposit insurance, and liquidity. *Journal of Political Economy, 91*, 401–419.

ECB. (2017). *The ECB's asset purchase programme and TARGET balances: Monetary policy implementation and beyond* (ECB Economic Bulletin, no. 3/2017).

ECB. (2021a, July). *The ECB's monetary policy strategy statement*. European Central Bank.

ECB (2021b, July). *An overview of the ECB's monetary policy strategy* (European Central Bank).

ECB (2021c). *Clear, consistent and engaging: ECB monetary policy communication in a changing world* (ECB Occasional Paper no. 274).

Eisenschmidt, J., Kedan, D., Schmitz, M., Adalid, R., & Papsdor, P. (2017). *The Eurosystem's asset purchase programme and TARGET balances* (ECB Occasional Paper no. 196).

Gros, D. (2012). *A simple model of multiple equilibria and default* (CEPS Working Document no. 366).

Lane, P. (2022, August 29). *Monetary policy in the euro area: The next phase*. Speech at annual meeting of the Central Bank Research Association, Barcelona.

Manna, M., & Nobili, S. (2018). *Banks' holdings of and trading in government bonds* (Working Paper no. 1166). Bank of Italy.

Neri, S., & Siviero, S. (2018). The non-standard monetary policy measures of the ECB: Motivations, effectiveness, and risks. *Kredit und Capital, 51*(4), 513–560.

Rostagno, M., Altavilla, C., Carboni, G., Lemke, W., Motto, R., Guilhem, A. S., & Yiangou, J. (2019). *A tale of two decades: The ECB's monetary policy at 20* (ECB Working Paper no. 2346).

Sinn, H.-W., & Wollmershauer, T. (2012). TARGET loans, current account balances and capital flows: The ECB's rescue facility. *International Tax and Public Finance, 19*(14), 468–508.

Schnabel, I. (2023, September 25). *Money and inflation*. Lecture at the annual conference of the Verein fur Socialpolitic, Regensburg.

CHAPTER 5

The Federal Reserve System from the Traditional Operating Framework to the *New Normal*

Abstract This chapter starts by showing that the organization (both governance and operations) of the Fed System is more centralized than that of the Eurosystem. It then discusses the strategy of the Fed, including the 2020 review. The main focus is on the Fed's implementation framework, which used to be the interest rate steering with an active management of scarce liquidity until the 2007/2008 financial crisis. Once the interest rates hit the ZLB, the Fed introduced credit and quantitative easing policies, creating a large excess of liquidity and making the operational framework shift to a floor system (with two floors, due to the segmentation of the US money market between banks and non-banks). The normalization process, started in 2014, led to a framework where the policy stance is signaled by communicating a target range for the federal funds rate, and the open market operations are aimed at keeping the level of excess reserves sufficiently ample. This supply-driven two-floor system is still in place, after the exceptional measures adopted to address the pandemic crisis and a new round of normalization. The latter had some negative side effects on financial stability, which are discussed in the final section.

Keywords Strategy review · Federal funds market · Two-floor system · Credit and quantitative easing · Ample reserves regime · Balance sheet normalization · Banking crisis

A. Baglioni, *Monetary Policy Implementation*,
https://doi.org/10.1007/978-3-031-53885-8_5

5.1 Introduction

Before the financial crisis of 2007/2008, the Fed used to follow the *interest rate steering* approach to monetary policy implementation, along the lines of the model presented in Sect. 3.2. The Fed announced a target value for the overnight interbank rate (federal funds target) and adjusted the supply of bank reserves accordingly, so as to keep the effective money market rate in line with that target. To this end, the New York Fed intervened daily with open market operations. That scheme was based on the shortage of bank reserves, in presence of a reserve requirement, and on the central bank's monopoly in issuing base money.

Beginning with the financial crisis, the management of US monetary policy underwent profound transformations that were bound to remain in the Fed's new operational framework. Once the policy interest rates had reached the zero lower bound (ZLB), the Fed introduced *credit easing* and *quantitative easing* policies: exceptional lending operations to both the financial and non-financial sectors, and large-scale purchase programs of securities (government bonds and mortgage-backed securities). These policies had a considerable effect on the size of the Fed's balance sheet, which increased fivefold over a seven-year period: 2007–2014. The injection of base money via financial asset purchases created a structural excess of bank reserves, pushing money market rates towards the lower bound: this led to a shift to a *floor-system* type of operational scheme, which corresponds to the model introduced in Sect. 3.3. However, certain institutional features of the US money market introduce a special property into this scheme: that of having two floors. The effective US money market rate fluctuates between these two floors, which generally coincide with the limits announced by the Fed for its federal fund target range.

In 2014, the Fed started its exit process from QE policies. However, the exit from QE and the "normalization" of US monetary policy did not imply a return to the old interest rate steering approach, but rather a transition to a "new normal" characterized by some of the innovations introduced in previous years. The Fed's operational framework is characterized today by the following elements. (1) The monetary policy stance is signaled to the market by indicating a target range for the federal funds rate. This operational target is realized through the two "administered rates": the one on bank reserves and the one on deposit transactions (reverse repos) of non-bank intermediaries. (2) The Fed's securities portfolio is managed, through open market operations, so as to maintain an excess of bank reserves ("ample supply of reserves") sufficient to guarantee the functioning of the money market according to a *supply-driven two-floor system*, without need for the daily active management of the monetary base typical of the old interest rate steering framework. (3) The extraordinary and innovative policies, involving changes in the size and/or composition of the central bank's balance sheet, remain in the Fed's "toolbox", ready to be used if interest rate management is not sufficient to address the ongoing economic conditions. This is what actually happened during the crisis triggered by the Covid-19 pandemic, in which the Fed resorted both to operations previously implemented (during the years of credit and quantitative easing) and to new instruments aimed at supporting credit flows to the economy, going so far as to directly finance a wide range of entities: companies, households, local (non-federal) governments, and non-profit organizations. The end of the pandemic and the surge of inflation led the Fed to implement a new round of normalization in 2021–2023.

The Fed preceded the ECB in moving to a QE policy. There are other differences between the two sides of the Atlantic. The long-term lending programs to the banking sector (T-LTROs) represent—in terms of their size, maturity, and technical features—an instrument with far greater relevance in the euro area than in the US. Moreover, the Fed has never resorted to a negative interest rate policy, which has instead entered the ECB's "toolbox". Other important differences are related to the organization and to the strategies of the two central banks: these are the items that we are going to address in the first two sections of this chapter. Then we will move to the operational framework of the Fed and illustrate its evolution over time. Finally, we will discuss the 2023 banking crisis: an illustrative example of how the normalization of monetary policy, after a long period of QE policies, may have some undesired side effects on the financial sector.[1]

[1] For a historical view of the US monetary policy, covering its evolution from the sixties to the Covid-19 crisis, see Bernanke (2022). Several issues related to the management of monetary policy in recent years, including the Fed's late reaction to the inflationary pressures of 2021–2022, are discussed in Bordo et al. (2023).

5.2 The Organization of the Federal Reserve System

Let us begin with the organization of the Federal Reserve System. When it was established (by the Federal Reserve Act of 1913), the territory of the United States was divided into twelve Districts (each comprising several States): each of them has been assigned a Federal Reserve Bank, which is part of the Fed System. Until the 1930s, each Federal Reserve Bank retained considerable autonomy: the discount rate, which was applied to lending operations to the banking system, could differ from one District to another. It was only with the reforms to the Federal Reserve Act in 1933 and 1935 that the responsibility for taking monetary policy decisions was centralized with the Federal Open Market Committee (FOMC), which has been the Fed's top decision-making body ever since. The twelve Federal Reserve Banks have retained other important tasks: the prudential supervision of banks, the management of the payments system, the provision of loans to ensure the liquidity of local banks, and the supervision of compliance with the rules protecting the consumers of financial services. In addition, each Fed retains its budgetary autonomy. Only one of them, the New York Fed, has retained a federal-level operational role: that of conducting Open Market Operations (OMOs) on behalf of the entire Fed System.

The system formed by the twelve federal banks is coordinated by a Washington-based body: the Board of Governors. This consists of seven members, including the President, appointed by the US President with the approval of the Senate. The Board sets the guidelines and oversees all the system's activity, ensuring continuity in the direction and coordination of the actions taken by the twelve federal banks. We can say that it plays a similar role to that played for the Eurosystem by the Executive Board of the ECB, based in Frankfurt.

All the monetary policy decisions are taken by the FOMC, which meets periodically: usually eight times a year. The FOMC consists of twelve members, each with one vote: seven are members of the Board of Governors and one is the President of the New York Fed. The other four votes are assigned in rotation to the Presidents of the other eleven federal banks. It can be seen that the governance of the Federal Reserve System is more centralized than that of the Eurosystem (see Fig. 5.1). In the latter, the body analogous to the FOMC is the Governing Council, composed of the six members of the Executive Board and the twenty Governors of the national central banks (NCBs) of the euro area countries, who hold (with a rotating mechanism) fifteen votes. The Governing Council of the Eurosystem is thus more exposed to the risk of national instances prevailing over a unified vision, looking at the eurozone economy as a whole. In the US, the votes allocated to local representatives are fewer than those held by the "center" of the system, formed by the Board of Governors and the New York Fed: these, due to the role they play, are more likely to have a vision extended to the whole economy of the US.

The US system is also more centralized than the European one from an operational perspective. Although the local Feds retain the important functions mentioned above, they have no operational role in the conduct of monetary policy. In the euro area, by contrast, the NCBs contribute to the implementation of monetary policy by maintaining operational relationships with domestic banks. Monetary policy decisions taken by the FOMC are implemented through open market operations: OMOs are executed by the Open Market Desk of the New York Fed, according to the instructions received from the FOMC. At the end of each meeting, the FOMC issues not only a statement announcing its monetary policy

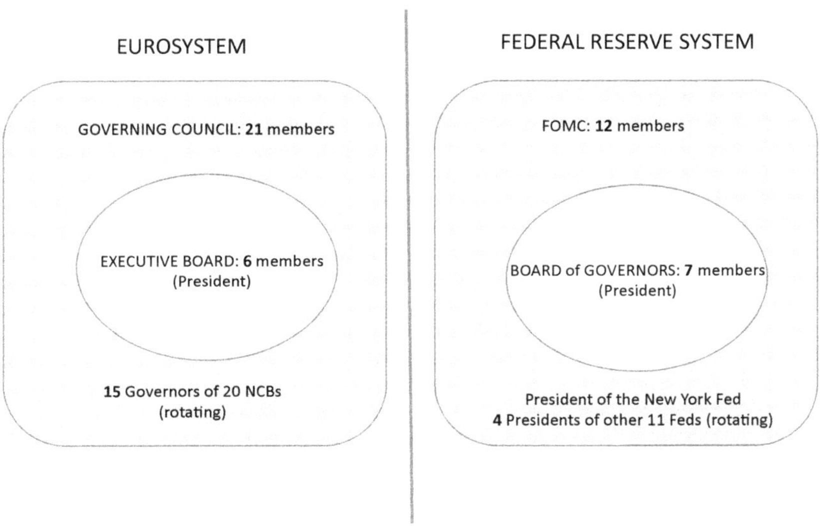

Fig. 5.1 ECB and Fed governance compared

decisions and the underlying rationale, but also a set of detailed guidelines ("Decisions regarding monetary policy implementation") on the operations to be carried out by the Desk to implement the monetary policy stance decided at that meeting. The securities used in OMOs are deposited in a portfolio known as the System Open Market Account (SOMA) in which the twelve central banks in the system participate; however, the New York Fed holds more than half of them, while each of the other Feds holds a small share.[2]

5.3 Dual Mandate and Strategy Review

The dual mandate, assigned by the US Congress to the Fed, establishes the final targets of US monetary policy: full employment and price stability. To be precise, the Federal Reserve Act assigns three objectives to monetary policy: "maximum employment, stable prices, and moderate long-term interest rates". However, the third objective can be seen to a large extent an implication of the first two: in an economy where full employment and price stability prevail, the conditions are in place for interest rates to be at moderate levels. In official Fed statements and in the policy debate, reference is commonly made to the dual mandate: to pursue full employment within a framework of price stability.

Over time, the Fed has developed its own strategy and specified its ultimate objectives, within the mandate received from the Congress. Since 2012, the FOMC has made its monetary policy strategy public in the annual "Statement on Longer-run Goals and Monetary Policy Strategy" (henceforth the "Statement"). In 2019, the Fed initiated a review of its strategy, which was completed in August 2020. It is good to take a step back from the current situation, and examine what the strategic lines of US monetary policy were up to 2020, and then go on to illustrate the important innovations introduced in that year.

[2] For details on how the securities deposited in the SOMA are traded in OMOs, see Ihrig et al. (2017).

5.3.1 The Fed's Strategy Until 2020

In the last Statement before the revision of its strategy, issued in 2019, the FOMC confirmed what has been the Fed's strategy for years: a balanced approach in pursuing its two final targets.[3] The aim of US monetary policy is to minimize the deviations of the inflation rate from its long-run target value and the deviations of employment from what can be considered its maximum level, according to the FOMC's own assessment. The two targets are explicitly placed on an equal footing.

This approach can be traced back to the Taylor rule: J. Taylor's (1993) article was inspired precisely by observing the policy followed by the Fed over the years. The Taylor rule can be written as follows:

$$r_t = r_L + \delta_\pi(\pi_t - \pi^*) + \delta_y(y_t - y_L)$$

where r_t and r_L are the current and natural real rates of interest respectively, π_t and y_t are the current inflation rate and output level respectively. Using this formalization, the Fed reacts to deviations of the inflation rate from the target value (π^*) and to deviations of the output level from its long-run potential (y_L), corresponding to the estimated maximum level of employment. Moreover, the two parameters, which assign the relative weights to the inflation gap and the output gap, assume the same values: $\delta_\pi = \delta_y = 0.5$.

However, when interest rates were at the ZLB, an *instrument rule* such as the Taylor rule, which provides for a direct link between the policy rate and the final targets, was not quite adequate to describe the Fed's dual mandate. In presence of a Federal Funds rate close to zero for a long time, the Fed's strategy was better described by a *targeting rule*: the central bank minimizes a quadratic loss function, whose arguments are the inflation gap and the output gap, where they assume the same weight.[4] In any case, the Fed's approach can be seen as a special kind of "flexible inflation targeting", in which the objectives of price stability and full employment are perfectly balanced and neither prevails over the other.[5] It is thus a different strategy from that followed by the ECB, whose Statute assigns a

[3] See Fed (2019).

[4] See Svensson (2020) and English et al. (2015).

[5] To be precise, we should say "inflation-forecast targeting": the Fed tries to keep the *expected* values of the two strategic variables, inflation and employment, in line with their targets.

hierarchy of objectives to monetary policy: price stability takes precedence over support for economic activity and employment.

What are the values assigned by the FOMC to the two final targets? Under this regard, there is a conceptual difference between them. Inflation is considered a monetary phenomenon: in the long run, it is mainly determined by monetary policy. Therefore, the FOMC can assign a numerical target value to the inflation rate: a 2% annual change in the consumer price index. This is a long-term symmetrical target: the Fed reacts to persistent positive and negative deviations of the inflation rate from 2%. The communication of a symmetrical target has the explicit aim of anchoring inflationary expectations, convincing economic agents that in the long run inflation is bound to be around 2%, although temporary deviations are possible. In this respect, too, the Fed's strategy differs from that followed by the ECB until 2021, which instead used to define the price stability target asymmetrically: an inflation rate "below but close to 2%".

On the contrary, the maximum level of employment, and with it the potential level of output, is largely determined by non-monetary factors related to the structure and developments in the labor market. For this reason, the FOMC refrains from formulating and publishing a quantitative target for the level of employment. The fact remains that its decisions are made on the basis of assessments that are formed within the FOMC and are made public in the name of transparency: every quarter, the FOMC members' forecasts of "normal long-term" unemployment and GDP growth rates are published in a report called the "FOMC's Summary of Economic Projections".

The US central bank's monetary policy decisions result from a comparison between its targets and the outlook for the economy. On the basis of several indicators, the "balance of risks" is assessed: in addition to the macroeconomic variables, the risks to the financial system enter into this assessment. Financial stability is not an objective of the FOMC: it is a matter for prudential supervision, exercised by the Fed together with other authorities. However, the instability of markets and financial intermediaries represents a source of risk, which could threaten the achievement of monetary policy objectives. We can find here a legacy of the 2007/2008 financial crisis, which had so many consequences for the American and global economic system.

5.3.2 The Strategy Review

At the beginning of 2019, the Fed initiated a review of its strategy, which led to some major innovations, introduced with the Statement issued by the FOMC on 27 August 2020.[6] At the origin of this revision are some important developments of the US economy taking place in the previous decade.[7] Of course, these developments took place before the sharp rise in inflation experienced in the US (as well as in other countries) from 2021 onwards: therefore, the strategy review reflects an economic scenario still characterized by very low levels of inflation and interest rates. Despite the changes experienced by the US economy since 2021, the Fed has reaffirmed in 2023 the strategy outlined in its 2020 review.[8]

The first development is the decline in the general level of interest rates. The natural rate of interest (defined as the level of the real interest rate corresponding to the potential level of output) has gradually declined, bringing with it a reduction in nominal rates. The FOMC estimates that the nominal money market rate has almost halved between 2012 and 2020, from 4.25% to 2.5%.[9] This secular decline, together with the crises that led the Fed to repeatedly lower the policy rate (the target on the federal funds rate), led monetary policy to reach the ZLB for interest rates. With nominal rates close to zero, the weapon of a policy rate cut is not available, generating an asymmetry: interest rate steering can be used in a restrictive direction but not in the opposite one. The Fed, like other central banks, reacted to this situation by introducing several "unconventional" monetary policy measures, which can be summarized along two lines of action: quantitative easing (QE) programs and a more sophisticated communication strategy explicitly aimed at guiding agents' expectations (forward guidance—FG). These measures changed the Fed's operational framework, as we shall see later in this chapter.

The second trend is the progressive flattening of the Phillips curve, which implies that the labor market can remain in full employment for a long time, without this having a major impact on the inflation rate. For

6 See Fed (2020).

7 The reasons that led the Fed to revise its strategy are explained in the two speeches by R. Clarida (2019) and J. Powell (2020), at that time Vice-Chairman and Chairman of the Fed respectively.

8 See Fed (2023a).

9 See Powell (2020).

example, in early 2020 (before the outbreak of the coronavirus crisis), the US unemployment rate had been at historically low levels for two years without generating any inflationary pressure. The flattening of the Phillips curve has two consequences, one positive and the other negative. The positive one is that the inflation-unemployment trade-off becomes very favorable for the central bank, which can exploit it in the short term: compressing the unemployment rate below its structural level, by "overheating" the economy, entails very little, if any, cost in terms of higher inflation. The negative side is that the persistence of the inflation rate at levels below the central bank's target makes it difficult for the central bank to anchor expectations at 2%.

In its Statement of August 2020, the FOMC has reaffirmed that the primary instrument of monetary policy is the indication of a target range for the federal funds rate. However, noting the decline of the natural interest rate and the constraint set by the ZLB, the FOMC affirmed its willingness to use the full range of available tools to achieve its objectives of maximum employment and price stability. It thus acknowledged the changes that had already taken place in the implementation of US monetary policy: since then, the unconventional measures are a permanent component of the Fed's "toolbox".

The other two innovations included in the 2020 Statement relate more specifically to monetary policy strategy: they introduce a revision of the two final targets. As regards full employment, the revised strategy envisages that the Fed will react to *shortfalls* in employment from the maximum level estimated by the FOMC. In this respect, the Fed's reaction function is no longer symmetrical: it does not aim to minimize employment deviations from its maximum level, but only negative ones. In other words, the Fed intends to react with a more accommodative policy stance, if the unemployment rate rises above its long-term structural level. Otherwise, it does not intend to react with a more restrictive policy stance unless there are clear signs of an undesirable rise in inflation. The Taylor rule should be modified accordingly, with the central bank reacting only in the face of a negative output gap ($y_t < y_L$) and no reaction in the opposite case, unless inflationary tensions emerge at the same time.

This important change in the reaction function, which introduces an asymmetry in US monetary policy, is closely linked to the abovementioned flattening of the Phillips curve in particular, to the fact that the inflation-unemployment trade-off has become more favorable. When this relationship was steeper, the Fed reacted to the "overheating" of the economy (positive output gap) with monetary tightening, as that was seen as a risk to price stability. This is no longer the case: not only because this relationship is flatter, but also because estimates of the structural level of unemployment are considered less reliable, due to changes in the labor market. The FOMC estimates indicate a decline of the structural level of unemployment for the US from 5.5% in 2012 to 4.1% in 2020.[10] With uncertain and varying estimates of the potential levels of employment and output, the Fed does not believe it must act promptly to "cool" the economy in the face of a positive output gap. On the contrary, it believes it must act promptly to support the economy if it observes a negative output gap. This bias, in favor of an expansionary monetary policy stance, stems from a long period of low inflation, below the 2% target: from 2012 through 2020, and before then in 2008–2009.

As mentioned above, the flattening of the Phillips curve and the persistence of inflation at very low levels (as of 2020) had another consequence: it was more difficult for the central bank to provide an anchor for expectations by communicating a target level for inflation. Hence the other change introduced by the strategy review: the inflation target (2%) has been defined as a long-term *average* target, with the explicit clarification that, following a period in which the inflation rate is persistently below 2%, monetary policy will aim to bring inflation moderately above 2% for a certain period. This was not the case before the strategy review: if inflation was below 2%, the Fed used to try to bring it back to that level, not above. This actually used to introduce an asymmetry in the conduct of monetary policy, although the Fed's reaction function was formulated symmetrically, by assigning monetary policy the objective of minimizing deviations (both negative and positive) of inflation from the 2% target. The revised Fed's strategy can be labeled as "flexible average inflation targeting": not only is price stability balanced with the full employment target (hence the qualification *flexible*), but it is pursued as an *average*: any periods with a negative inflation gap ($\pi < \pi^*$) should be offset by others in which there is a positive inflation gap ($\pi > \pi^*$). The purpose of this clarification was to make the Fed's strategy truly symmetrical in relation to the inflation target and thus to make the 2% target value more credible, providing a more effective anchor to expectations. Figure 5.2

[10] See Powell (2020) again.

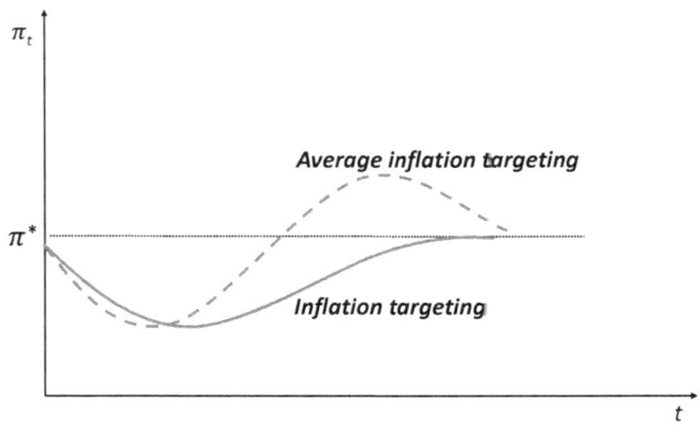

Fig. 5.2 Average inflation targeting

shows the evolution of inflation over time, following a hypothetical shock pushing the inflation rate below its target value for a certain period, and it compares the two strategies: inflation targeting (solid line) and average inflation targeting (dashed line).

5.4 The Operational Framework Before the Financial Crisis

The financial crisis of 2007/2008 represented a turning point in US monetary policy management, which led to important innovations in the Fed's operational framework, similarly to the ECB and other central banks. Prior to that crisis, the US central bank used to follow an *interest rate steering* (IRS) approach to the implementation of monetary policy, along the lines of the model introduced in Sect. 3.2. The Fed used to announce a target value for the overnight interbank rate and adjust the supply of bank reserves accordingly, so that the effective rate in the interbank market was as close to that target as possible. This scheme is based on a relative shortage of reserves, determined by two elements: a reserve requirement, which helps to shape the demand curve for reserves; a monopoly position of the central bank in the issuance of bank reserves. It is an operational framework that has many features in common with that used by the ECB, which we analyzed in the previous chapter, but also some significant differences.

The operational target of US monetary policy is the *Federal Funds rate* (FF rate): the interest rate at which banks trade, on the O/N maturity, their deposits at the Federal Reserve System. The FOMC determines the monetary policy stance by announcing a target value for this rate: the *Federal Funds target* (FF target). Following this decision, it delegates the Open Market Desk of the Federal Reserve Bank of New York to conduct the necessary operations for the implementation of that target. Based on a projection of the banking system's need for reserves, formulated at the beginning of each business day, the New York Fed's Desk intervenes in the market on a daily basis to adjust the amount of existing reserves through Open Market Operations (OMOs). These can be either outright or temporary. On the basis of the guidelines received from the FOMC, the New York Fed can decide to permanently increase/decrease the quantity of reserves by buying/selling securities in the market: since the transactions are settled through the banking system, the corresponding amount is credited/debited to the current accounts that the banks hold with the Fed System. The Fed can also opt for a temporary creation of reserves through a repurchase agreement (*repo*): spot purchase and forward sale of securities. Or it can temporarily drain liquidity from the system through a *reverse repo*: spot sale and forward purchase of securities. Repos and reverse repos are, respectively, central bank loans to banks and deposits of excess bank liquidity at the central bank. The interest paid on these transactions is generated by the price difference between the spot purchase and the forward resale of bonds.

In contrast to the euro area, where the entire Eurosystem is involved in monetary policy operations, in the US the operational management of monetary policy is centralized: operations are conducted only by the New York Fed. Moreover, while the Eurosystem's operations are potentially addressed to all banks in the euro area, those of the New York Fed normally take place with a limited number of counterparties: the *primary dealers*, which include some leading commercial and investment banks. Finally, the Fed has always made outright transactions in the securities market, whereas the Eurosystem has only recently started to use this instrument as part of its unconventional measures.

In addition to the policy interest rate, the FF target, the US operational framework relies on another interest rate: the *primary credit* rate. This instrument is part of the *discount window*, through which banks can borrow funds from the Fed. Since the beginning of 2003, primary credit has been granted at a penalizing rate, significantly higher than the FF target, which is the pivot for all money market interest rates. Overnight loans, granted by the Fed through primary credit, are available to all banks that meet some financial and solvency criteria. Since most of the US banking system is able to access this funding facility, the rate on primary credit provides the upper limit of the interbank interest rate "corridor": only exceptionally will a bank borrow in the market at a higher rate, should it fear to incur a negative reputational effect (*stigma effect*) in case of request for central bank's financial assistance. Primary credit plays the same role as the marginal lending facility in the euro area. By contrast, the US implementation framework did not include an instrument equivalent to the deposit facility (before the introduction of the interest paid on excess reserves in October 2008): there was therefore no lower limit to the "corridor" of money market rates, other than zero.

The reserve requirement has always played a less important role in the US than in the euro area, even when the reserve coefficient used to be higher.[11] The US system, like the European one, relies on an averaging facility: the reserve requirement refers to the average of daily balances during a maintenance period. Banks can therefore engage in inter-temporal arbitrage transactions, substituting one day's reserves for those of another business day within the same period. However, the stabilization effect on money market rates is weaker in the US than in the euro area: this is the reason why the Fed intervenes in the market on a daily basis to stabilize the overnight rate around the FF target, while the ECB intervenes weekly with its main refinancing operations. There are several reasons for this difference.

A first reason is related to the length of the maintenance period, which in the US is two weeks, compared to about six weeks in the euro area: the room for inter-temporal arbitrage is by definition more limited in the US. Second, the reserve requirement applies to demand/checking accounts only. Banks have the possibility (via *sweep programs*) to temporarily switch funds from checking accounts to exempted savings accounts. The increasing use of these programs has led over time to a significant reduction of the actual incidence of the reserve requirement. Finally, US banks can also meet the reserve requirement with vault cash,

[11] Above a certain exemption threshold, the reserve coefficient in the US used to be 3% or 10% depending on the amount of deposits, compared to a ratio of 1% (2% until 2011) in the euro area. In March 2020, the reserve coefficient has been set to zero in the US.

which is used to provide payment services to customers: this reduces the need to hold reserves in the form of deposits at the central bank.

Banks hold current account balances at the central bank not only to meet the reserve requirement, but also for their operational needs related to the settlement of interbank payments. The demand for bank reserves therefore has two components. The first, due to the reserve requirement, is elastic with respect to deviations of the current interbank rate from the expected rate for the remainder of the maintenance period. The second, being determined by the technical features of the payment system, is rather rigid. The sum of the two components results in an aggregate demand for bank reserves such as that (R^D) depicted in Fig. 5.3: it is decreasing with respect to the O/N market rate, although the elasticity of the demand function is lower in the US than in the euro area, for the above reasons.

The money market equilibrium is depicted in Fig. 5.3, where *R* denotes the quantity of bank reserves and *i* the interest rate in the O/N interbank market: the FF rate. The vertical line represents the supply of bank reserves at a certain date: this is adjusted by the Fed, through its open market operations (OMOs), so that it intersects the demand curve at the FF target i^*. In calibrating the daily supply of reserves, the

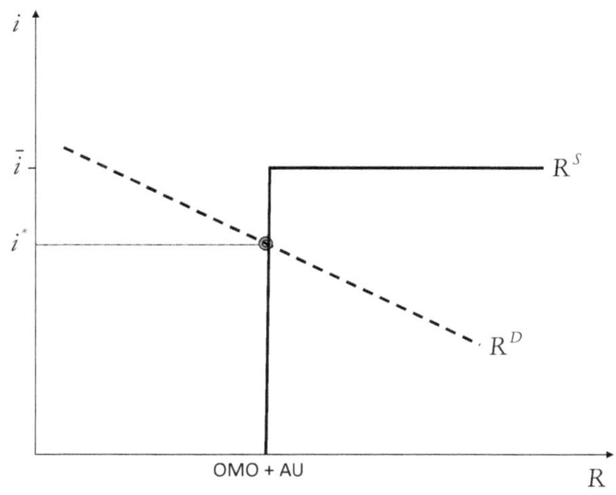

Fig. 5.3 Money market equilibrium: the traditional IRS framework

Fed must offset any fluctuations in the stock of available reserves due to autonomous factors (AU: see Chapter 3). The main autonomous factors are the public sector and cash. In particular, the US federal government holds an account with the Fed to settle its payments (Treasury General Account - TGA): each time the government receives a payment, e.g. a tax payment, this causes a reduction in the reserves held by the bank making the payment to the Treasury. The rate $\bar{i}$ is that on primary credit, which places a "cap" on market rates (which is actually reached quite rarely). When activated, the primary credit creates bank reserves to the extent required by banks themselves: hence the horizontal segment of the reserve supply schedule R^S. The absence of a deposit facility introduces a difference between this framework and the standard corridor system shown in Fig. 3.4: the only lower bound to the level of market rates is the zero lower bound (ZLB), which in fact was never relevant in the years before the financial crisis.

Figure 5.4 shows the evolution of the policy and market rates in the US (up to mid-December 2008). The market equilibrium, represented in theory in Fig. 5.3, is the one prevailing until the beginning of August 2007. The effective FF rate is maintained throughout this period very close to the level desired and communicated to the market by the Fed: the FF target. Fluctuations of the market rate around the policy rate are limited to a few basis points, reflecting the central bank's ability to exert control over the market price of bank reserves and, by this means, over the short-term yield curve. The rate on primary credit is set by the Fed at a penalizing level: one percentage point above the FF target, so as to limit the use of this instrument to exceptional situations concerning individual credit institutions, without any relevant impact on the aggregate market for liquidity. This picture was bound to change substantially with the outbreak of the financial crisis in August 2007, as we shall see in the next section.

5.5 QE and Interests on Reserves: The Two-Floor System

The historical 2007/2008 financial crisis started in the US banking sector, more specifically in the business of real estate loans to people with low creditworthiness (*subprime* mortgages), and it quickly became the most serious economic crisis since the 1930s. From the mortgage sector it spread to other segments of the financial system, not only in the US but

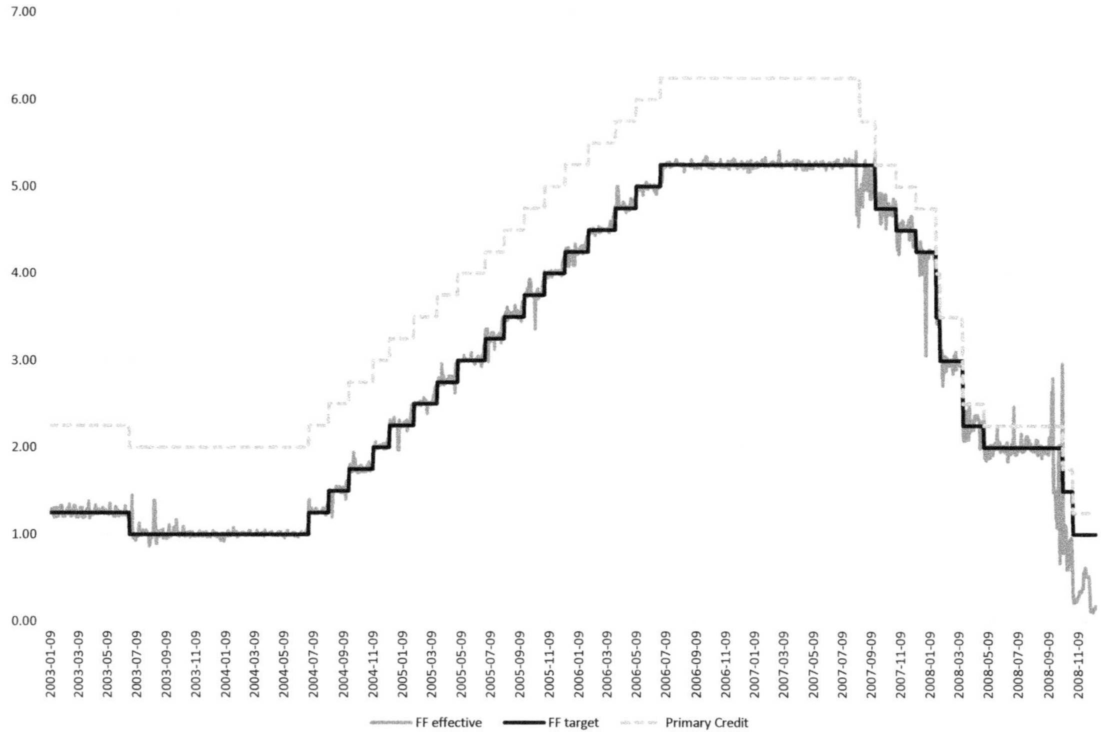

Fig. 5.4 USA: Policy and market interest rates up to 2008 (percentage points, daily data 2003/1/9–2008/12/15) (*Data source* Federal Reserve Economic Data [FRED], Federal Reserve Bank of St. Louis)

also in other parts of the world. The detonating event was the suspension of redemptions on three investment funds by the French bank BNP Paribas on 9 August 2007. This fact shows that the crisis already had an international dimension from its inception, due to the spread of investment instruments and derivative products originated and distributed by the US financial sector. The epicenter of the crisis, with a chain of events culminating in the bankruptcy of Lehman Brothers in September 2008, was in the US. The crisis had a strong negative impact on the liquidity of markets and financial intermediaries. Entire segments of the financial market suffered what is called a "dry-up": a drastic drop in trading, due to a shortage of buyers, in the presence of strong flows of "fire sale" orders.[12] In such circumstances, recourse to the usual sources of funding, such as the bond and interbank markets, became difficult for both banks and non-financial companies. Through time, the difficulties of the financial sector were transferred to the real sector of the economy, generating a deep and widespread recession.

The Fed's reaction to the financial crisis was twofold. (1) *Interest rate policy*: the FF target rate was reduced by five percentage points in a bit more than one year: from 5.25% in August 2007 to the ZLB in December 2008 (see Figs. 5.4 and 5.5). (2) *Credit easing and quantitative easing policies*: the central bank introduced some measures to provide liquidity to financial intermediaries and some large-scale asset purchase programs (which will be described in the next section). As a consequence, the size of the Fed balance sheet increased by five times between August 2007 and December 2014 (from 869 to 4509 billion dollars) mainly due to the expansion of its securities portfolio (from 791 to 4247 billion dollars). This expansion was matched, on the liability side, by the huge increase of excess reserves held by the banking system on Fed's accounts: from 14 to 2610 billion dollars.

The peak of the financial crisis marks an important innovation in the operational framework of the Fed. Since October 2008, the balances held by banks on their current accounts at the central bank, exceeding the reserve requirement, are paid an interest: *Interest on Excess Reserves* (IER, equal to that paid on required reserves). At the same time (more precisely in December 2008) the Fed started announcing a range (25 basis points) for its policy rate: the *FF target range*, delimited by a Lower

[12] See Brunnermeier (2009) and Duffie (2011).

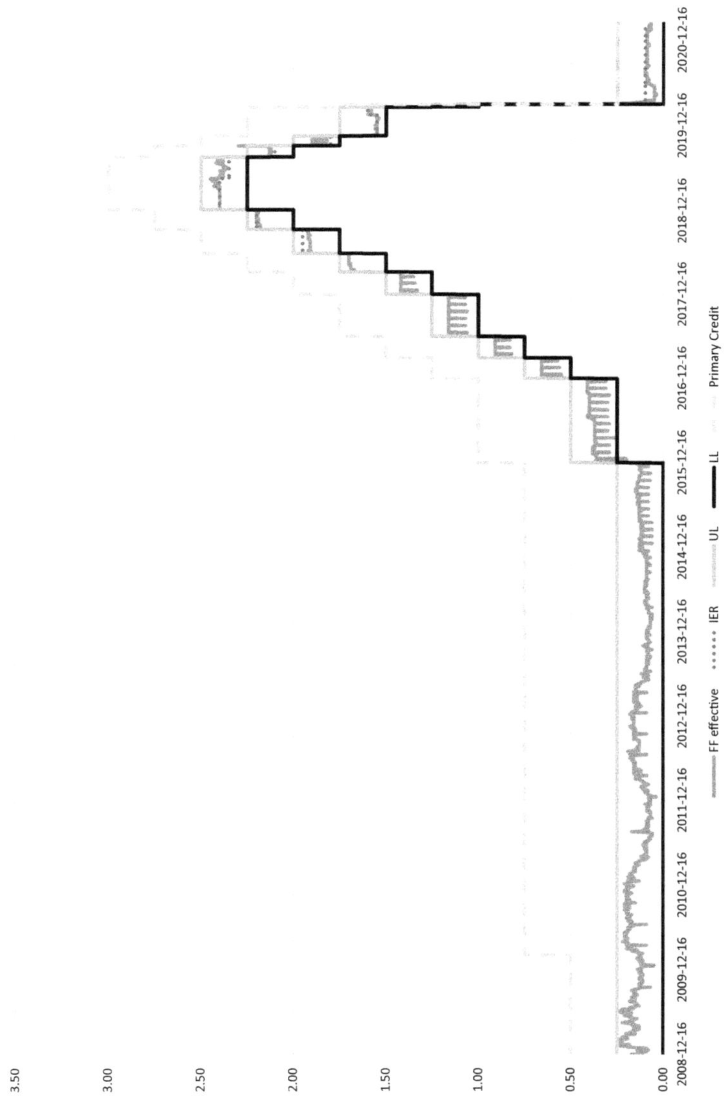

Fig. 5.5 USA: policy and market rates after 2008 (percentage points, daily data 2008/12/16–2021/2/24) (*Data source* Federal Reserve Economic Data [FRED], Federal Reserve Bank of St. Louis)

Limit (LL) and an Upper Limit (UL). As it can be seen in Fig. 5.5, for seven years (from December 2008 to December 2015) the target range was kept between 0 (LL) and 0.25% (UL). The IER coincides with UL, and enables the Fed to keep the effective FF rate oscillating within those two limits. If, to the contrary, excess reserves were not remunerated, the huge abundance of liquidity, created by credit easing and QE policies, would drive the effective FF rate to zero.

To understand how this monetary control framework works, we have to consider that there are important financial institutions, the Government Sponsored Enterprises (GSEs),[13] which are not entitled to receive an interest on their current accounts at the Fed: therefore, they are ready to lend money in the federal funds market at rates below IER. In addition, there are non-bank intermediaries trading in the money market, like securities dealers. Banks can make profitable arbitrage trades by borrowing money from those institutions at rates below IER and depositing that money on their current accounts at the Fed, which are remunerated at the IER rate. These arbitrage trades, which are the largest share of trade volumes in the FF market, keep the effective FF rate above zero and in general close to IER.[14]

This institutional feature of the US money market explains a remarkable difference between the operational framework of the Fed and that of the ECB. As we have seen in the previous chapter, the rate applied by the ECB on the deposit facility provides a floor to the interbank market rate, playing the role of a *reservation price*: no bank is willing to lend money at a rate lower than that. The IER rate paid by the Fed plays a similar role, but it sets the upper limit (UL) to the FF target range: this is due to the presence of other intermediaries, trading in the money market, for which the reservation rate is zero. As a consequence, the operational framework, introduced in the USA when the Fed adopted the QE policy, is a *floor system with two floors*: see Fig. 5.6. This "two-floor system" relies on a structural excess of liquidity, created by the asset purchase programs, pushing the effective FF rate to its lower bound. The supply of reserves (vertical line) intersects the horizontal segment of the demand for reserves, where the demand is infinitely elastic because the market rate

[13] The main GSEs are: Fannie Mae, Freddie Mac, and the Federal Home Loan Banks (FHLBs).

[14] See Ihrig et al. (2015).

coincides with the reservation rate, so the opportunity cost of holding reserves is zero. The above-mentioned segmentation of the money market explains why we observe two different horizontal segments of the demand for reserves: the reservation rate for banks is the rate (IER) paid on their reserve balances held at the Fed (i_R in Fig. 5.6), while it coincides with the ZLB for other intermediaries trading in the FF market. The arbitrage trades keep the effective FF rate between those two boundaries.

The innovations, introduced in US monetary policy management since 2007/2008, have led to a shift from the traditional operational framework, based on the shortage of reserves and frequent open market operations to calibrate the supply of reserves (active management), to the typical implementation scheme of unconventional monetary policy. This is characterized by a structural excess of reserves, injected through QE operations, which pushes money market rates towards the lower limit: the floor system, actually the "two-floor system" in the US, for the reasons explained above. This is bound to become a permanent feature of the Fed's operational framework, as we shall see below (Sect. 5.7): the innovation, which will be introduced in 2015, is that the ZLB will be replaced by the positive interest rate applied to reverse repo transactions made by the Fed with non-bank financial intermediaries.

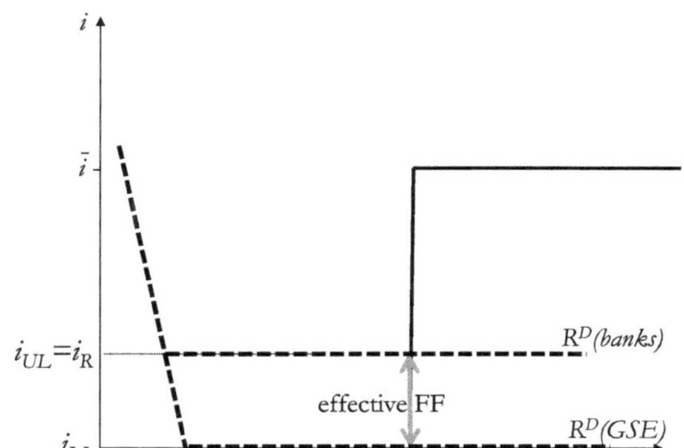

Fig. 5.6 USA: the two-floor system

5.6 The Fed's Unconventional Measures: 2007–2014

The financial crisis of 2007/2008 and the ensuing recessionary phase of the US economy were addressed by the Fed with several unconventional monetary policy instruments, in addition to the aggressive interest rate policy that quickly brought the policy rate to the ZLB. The first is the exceptional lending operations to the financial and non-financial sectors, introduced to fix-up the liquidity crisis in financial markets: these measures go under the name of "credit easing". The second is the quantitative easing policy: between 2008 and 2012, the Fed adopted several large-scale asset purchase programs, which led to a major expansion in the size of its balance sheet. The third is the so-called "twist policy": some operations designed to change the composition of the Fed's balance sheet, rather than its size. Finally, the Fed has made extensive use of communication policy, which has been substantially renewed: forward guidance has thus become part of its toolbox, as it has for other central banks.

5.6.1 Credit Easing

In the face of the liquidity crisis that began in August 2007 and precipitated with the bankruptcy of Lehman Brothers in September 2008, the Fed's discount window was no longer sufficient. This is a source of short-term funding, which US banks rarely resort to, for fear of incurring a negative "stigma effect": recourse to the discount window could signal to markets' participants that a bank is in trouble, especially if this happens within a crisis hitting the whole financial sector. For this reason, the Fed introduced several extraordinary financing programs starting in December 2007, directed primarily at banks but not only. One was the *Term Auction Facility*: a series of loans to the banking system, with a maturity of three months. Another was the *Term Asset-backed Securities Loan Facility* (TALF): a series of loans available to financial intermediaries, including non-banks, for them to invest in non-residential asset-backed securities. The purpose of this facility was to stimulate lending to consumers and businesses: these loans are the underlying financial assets of ABS. The *Commercial Paper Funding Facility* (CPFF) was a program for the Fed's direct purchase of commercial paper: a form of short-term debt issued in the money market by both financial intermediaries and non-financial firms. In this way, the Fed was directly providing funds not only to banks, but to non-banks as well. All these programs were abandoned in the course of 2010, as the US left the most acute phase of the financial crisis behind.

At an early stage, these programs were sterilized. Until September 2008, the Fed did not intend to expand the size of its balance sheet. For this reason, to compensate for the liquidity created through the exceptional lending programs, it sold government bonds for USD 315 billion: this explains the reduction in the stock of Treasury securities held by the central bank, which can be observed in the initial period shown in Fig. 5.7. Subsequently, the Fed stopped sterilizing its funding programs, allowing them to have an impact on the size of its balance sheet, which doubled within a few months (between September and November 2008): from less than USD 1,000 billion to more than USD 2,000 billion. Since then, the US banking system started accumulating a huge amount of excess reserves, as it can be seen in Fig. 5.8. This phase of US monetary policy, during which the expansion of the central bank's balance sheet was due to lending operations to the financial sector (and to a lesser extent to the non-financial sector) has been named "credit easing", to distinguish it from the subsequent phase of "quantitative easing", in which it was the purchases of securities that had a strong impact on the Fed's balance sheet.[15]

The *credit easing* policy led to a drastic increase in Fed lending in the autumn of 2008: from USD 260 billion to USD 1,400 billion. However, this instrument has played a more limited role in US monetary policy than the long-term refinancing operations made by the ECB since the same year. As we have seen in the previous chapter, in the euro area such operations have played an increasing role, not only because of their size, but also because of their maturity (up to four years) and their increasingly sophisticated technical features, aimed at creating incentives for banks to use the funds obtained from the central bank to make loans to businesses (*Targeted* LTROs). In the US, these programs were abandoned once the emergency of the financial crisis was over. These differences can be explained by observing that the aim of the Fed's credit easing policy was to avoid a liquidity crisis of financial intermediaries, with possible negative effects on the supply of funds to the economy. Some programs,

[15] It was Fed Chairman Ben Bernanke himself who coined the term "*credit easing*", according to Labonte (2014). Some other information reported in this section is taken from that article.

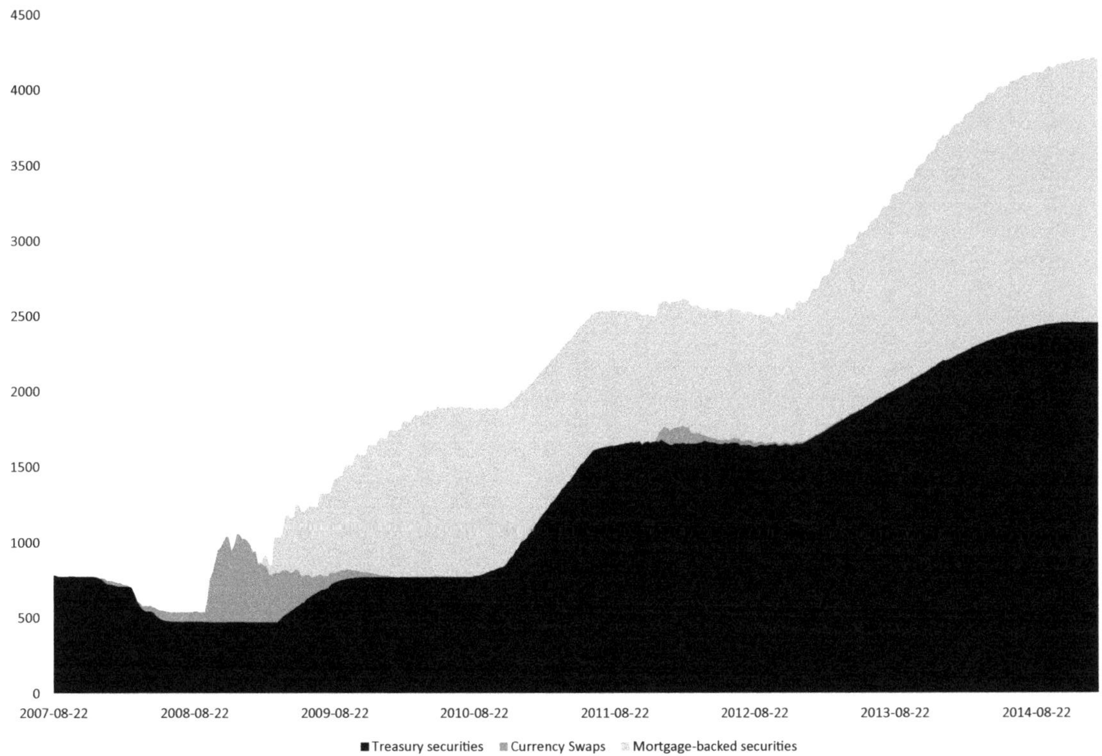

Fig. 5.7 Fed: cumulated asset purchases (USD billion—weekly data 2007/8/22–2015/1/28) (*Data source* Federal Reserve Economic Data [FRED], Federal Reserve Bank of St. Louis)

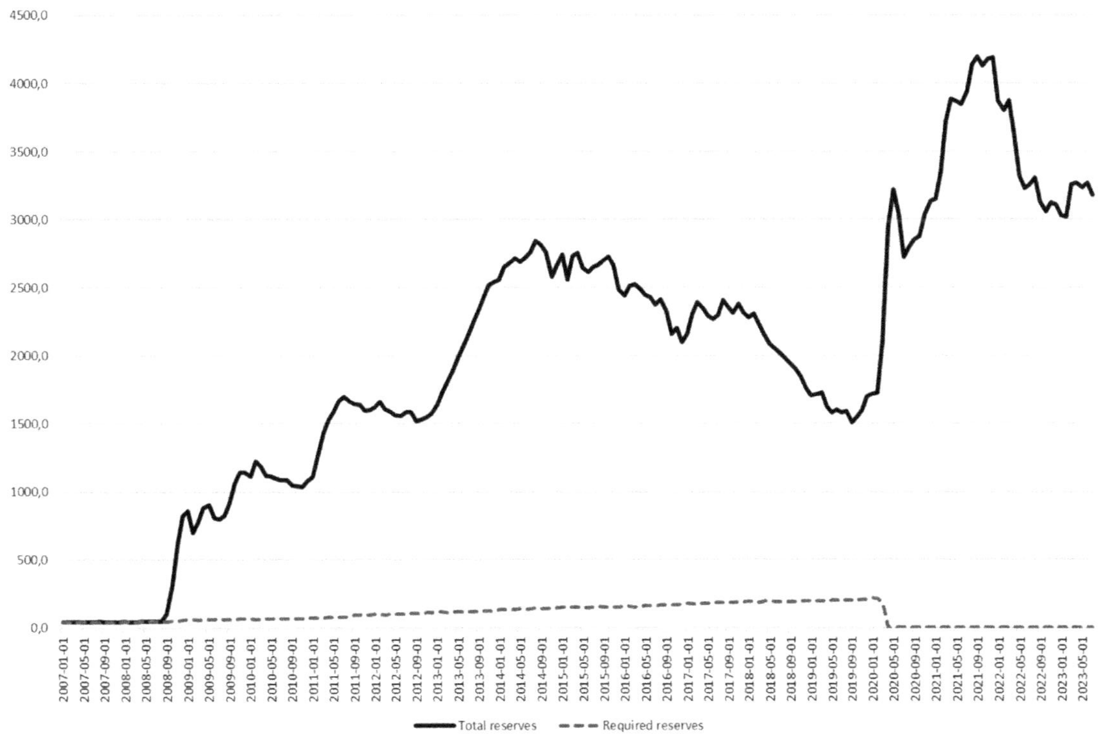

Fig. 5.8 Bank reserves in the US (USD billion—monthly data 2007/1–2023/7) (*Data source* Federal Reserve Economic Data [FRED], Federal Reserve Bank of St. Louis)

introduced at that time, were aimed at supporting specific segments of the financial market that had seen a sudden drop in trade and a collapse in prices: in particular, the MBS and ABS markets and the commercial paper market. In the ECB's approach, during the financial crisis and the sovereign debt crisis, the refinancing operations played a similar role as they did in the US: to provide a stable source of funding to the banking system, so as to protect the stability of intermediaries and preserve the transmission of monetary policy. However, they evolved later and became firmly established among the instruments used to expand the stance of monetary policy in the euro area, along with other QE measures.

Finally, the measures aimed at providing emergency liquidity to financial intermediaries include the *currency swaps* carried out by the Fed with some other central banks, including the ECB. This instrument was used in 2008–2009 to make a sufficient amount of US dollars available to those central banks so that they could in turn provide dollar funding to banks located in their own countries. When a swap line is activated, a foreign central bank makes a spot purchase of dollars, which are made available to it in an account with the New York Fed. The Fed in turn receives foreign currency: the corresponding increase in foreign currency reserves (recorded in official statistics) can be seen in Fig. 5.7. The swap agreement implies that at some future date an opposite transaction will take place, in which the foreign central bank buys back its own currency and returns the dollars (including an interest payment) to the Fed. The range of maturities of currency swaps goes from overnight to three-month.

5.6.2 Quantitative Easing

The Fed introduced its quantitative easing policy in November 2008, announcing the first round of Large-Scale Asset Purchases (LSAP). These, together with those launched in March 2009, constituted the first QE program adopted by the US central bank. Once the ZLB was reached, further easing of the monetary policy stance was implemented through an aggressive policy of expansion of the Fed's balance sheet. The first program was followed by two others, which became known as QE2 and QE3, launched in November 2010 and September 2012, respectively. The QE policy was thus introduced in the US well before than in the euro area. In the previous chapter we have already discussed the reasons, linked to the institutional set-up of the Eurosystem, why this policy was introduced later in the euro area than in other countries. Another important difference lies in the type of securities purchased.

While the purchases made by the Eurosystem (through the APP and PEPP programs) were largely concentrated on government bonds, the Fed's purchases also involved to large extent securities either guaranteed or issued by institutions operating in the market for real estate finance. They are predominantly MBS issued under the guarantee of the three agencies Fannie Mae, Freddie Mac, and Ginnie Mae. To a lesser extent, they are bonds directly issued by the GSEs: Fannie Mae, Freddie Mac, and FHLBs. It is evident, in this composition of the financial assets included in the QE programs, the US central bank's aim of supporting the mortgage sector and by this means the housing market, which is considered crucial for the US economy. Figure 5.7 shows the growth of the stock of MBS, together with Treasury bonds, accumulated by the Fed through the three QE programs altogether.

QE1. During 2009, the size of Fed's lending under the credit easing programs declined as the US gradually emerged from the most acute phase of the financial crisis. If the US central bank had done nothing to compensate for this decline, the size of its balance sheet would have contracted proportionally: the outcome of the loan repayments by banks would have been a drain of liquidity from the financial system. However, the still ongoing recession made it necessary to maintain an expansionary monetary policy stance. We have already noted this problem in the previous chapters: lending to the banking sector is a policy tool that does not allow a central bank to have complete control over the size of its balance sheet, since the actual amount of loans depends on the banks' behavior in taking up the offered funds and in exercising the prepayment option (when this is available, as it is for the LTROs made by the ECB).

For this reason, the Fed announced in March 2009 that the financial asset purchase program, which had already started in November 2008, would be significantly expanded to a total size of USD 1,725 billion. The bulk of the purchases was directed to MBS guaranteed by the three agencies operating in the real estate market: USD 1,250 billion. This was followed by US Treasury bonds (300 billion) and debt securities issued by the GSEs (175 billion). Unlike the previous credit easing policy, which was introduced to preserve the liquidity and stability of the financial sector, this QE program was aimed at keeping a sufficiently expansionary policy stance in the face of the weak economic cycle.

The program, later called QE1, was completed by early 2010. Once the net asset purchases were terminated, the Fed intended to prevent the size of its balance sheet from gradually shrinking as the securities purchased were reaching maturity. For this reason, the central bank announced in August of that year that maturing securities (of all types) would be replaced with Treasury securities. With this roll-over policy, the Fed was committed to keeping the size of its balance sheet constant for a long time, avoiding an unwanted tightening of its policy.

QE2. The weakness of the economic cycle led the Fed to further increase the monetary stimulus, by announcing in November 2010 an additional package of US Treasury bond purchases: USD 600 billion in total, to be implemented over the eight months ending June 2011. This program became known as QE2. The net purchases came in addition to the roll-over of securities in the Fed's portfolio, which was intended to continue. The maturity of the Treasury securities subject to the Fed's purchases ranged from two and a half to ten years.

QE3. In September 2012, the Fed declared that further monetary stimulus was needed, in presence of an economic growth still unable to generate substantial improvements in the labor market and a forecasted inflation below the 2% target. Therefore, it introduced a new MBS purchase program, with transactions amounting to 40 billion a month. In addition, a new round of Treasury bond purchases, amounting to USD 45 billion per month, started in December of the same year. The QE3 program was made up by all these operations together. Unlike its predecessors, this program was announced specifying the monthly pace of net purchases (85 billion in total) but not its overall size and duration, which remained open until further assessments and decisions by the central bank.

5.6.3 Operation Twist

In addition to the three rounds of QE, the Fed made use of another instrument: the so-called "Operation Twist". This consists of the purchase of long-term securities (e.g. 10-year) and the simultaneous sale of an equivalent amount of short-term securities (e.g. annual). The purpose of this operation is to exert a downward pressure on the general level of long-term interest rates, without altering the size of the central bank's balance sheet: in contrast to QE, a "Twist" policy only affects the composition of the central bank's balance sheet, in particular its securities portfolio. Of course, the sale of short-term securities may lead to a rise in short-term yields in the financial market, but this is not a serious problem in the presence of rates that are in any case very low, actually close to zero. The final effect of Operation Twist is to cause a flattening of the yield curve: in this way, monetary policy provides a stimulus to the economy,

Table 5.1 Unconventional monetary policy measures in the US

Credit Easing	Term Auction Facility Term Asset-Backed Securities Loan Facility Commercial Paper Funding Facility	2007–2010
Quantitative Easing (large-scale asset purchases)	QE1	2008–2010
	QE2	2010–2011
	QE3	2012–2014
	Asset purchases in Covid-19 crisis	2020–2022
Operation Twist	Maturity Extension Program	2011–2012
Lending programs (Covid-19 crisis)	Main Street Lending Program Primary and Secondary Market Corporate Credit Facilities Municipal Liquidity Facility	2020–2021

by reducing the cost of funding on longer maturities for companies and households.

The Fed (which had already used this instrument in 1961) introduced a twist program, called "Maturity Extension Program", in the time period between QE2 and QE3. In September 2011, it initiated purchases of long-term Treasury securities in the amount of USD 400 billion, combined with sales of short-term Treasury securities in the same amount. The program was then expanded in the middle of the following year by adding transactions for USD 267 billion, which ended by the end of 2012. A limit to this type of operations lies in the availability of a sufficient amount of short-term securities in the central bank's portfolio. The Fed actually came close to this limit towards the end of 2012, which is why it had to abandon this type of transactions. Given the need to prolong the monetary stimulus to the economy, it introduced the above-mentioned QE3 program.

Summing up, Table 5.1 provides a list of the unconventional measures taken by the Fed over the period 2007–2014 as well as during the Covid-19 crisis (the latter will be addressed in Sect. 5.8).

5.6.4 *Forward Guidance*

The Fed's communication policy, like that of other central banks, has undergone considerable changes over time. The traditional policy of providing very little disclosure about the central bank's orientations (President Alan Greespan's "constructive ambiguity" in the years 1987–2006) has been replaced by a policy of transparency and explicit guidance on the future course of monetary policy. The "forward guidance" (FG) has become a tool used by the Fed to drive the expectations of economic agents and financial market participants. It allowed the central bank to enhance the expansive stance of its interest rate policy, even in the presence of the ZLB: by lowering expectations of future short-term interest rates, it helped to contain the level of long-term rates.[16] With the advent of QE, the FG has been used to communicate the expected duration, as well as the size and characteristics, of the asset purchase programs. Depending on the circumstances, the Fed made use of both "calendar-based" and "outcome-based" FG (following the distinction introduced in Sect. 3.3).

Until 1994, the Fed did not make public its target level for the policy rate: the federal funds rate. Before that year, financial market participants had to identify the central bank's target by observing the money market rates, particularly the effective federal funds rate. From that year on, the Fed started to publish what has become the usual *FOMC Statement* at the end of each FOMC meeting, in which the *FF target* (which has become the *FF target range* since December 2008) is communicated, together with other information about the Fed's assessments and decisions. Since 2007, the *Summary of Economic Projections* (SEP) has been published every quarter, which summarizes the forecasts of the FOMC participants: both those regarding the main economic variables (GDP growth, unemployment rate, and inflation) and those regarding the "projected appropriate policy path", in particular the future trajectory of the FF target. Contributing to the transparency of monetary policy is also the publication of the minutes of the FOMC meetings, which are read by analysts to capture the Fed's orientations and the internal debate within the FOMC. As we mentioned above, since 2012 the US central bank has been communicating its monetary policy strategy by releasing the annual *Statement on Longer-run Goals and Monetary Policy Strategy*.

The *calendar-based* FG began in March 2009, when the Fed announced that the exceptionally low level reached by interest rates (ZLB) would remain for an "extended period of time". This announcement became more explicit in August 2011, when the Fed announced the

[16] In the words of Chairman Bernanke: "*forward guidance that lowers private-sector expectations regarding future short-term rates should cause longer-term rates to decline, leading to more accommodative financial conditions*". See Bernanke (2012, p. 9).

period for which it expected interest rates to remain at the exceptionally low level: until mid-2013 (a date that was postponed at subsequent FOMC meetings).

The *outcome-based* FG entered the Fed's communication policy in December 2012, when the time horizon in which to keep policy rates at the ZLB was identified with an economic event, rather than a future date: namely, until the unemployment rate had fallen to a level of 6.5%, provided the inflation forecast remained consistent with the 2% target (in fact, policy rates remained at the ZLB until the end of 2015, as shown in Fig. 5.5). The same type of announcement accompanied the introduction of QE3: on that occasion (September 2012), the Fed committed to continue its purchases of financial assets, as envisaged by that program, until labor market conditions had substantially improved, albeit in a context of price stability.

Transparency has become firmly established in the communication policy of the Fed (and other central banks as well). The exit process from the exceptional policies introduced during the financial crisis and the policy normalization (the subject of the next section) were accompanied by announcements explaining the Fed's exit strategy and the new normal towards which it was heading. With the outbreak of the Covid-19 crisis, the FG contributed to the stability of financial markets by supporting expectations of an accommodative monetary policy until the end of the crisis.

5.7 Exit Strategy and Policy Normalization

Towards the end of 2013, the Fed began a process of gradual exit from its quantitative easing policy. As we shall see, this process followed the same steps that we have identified in Sect. 3.4, and which we report here for convenience:

1. *Tapering*. The net asset purchases, made under QE programs, are gradually reduced and finally discontinued.
2. *Roll-over*. The size of the central bank's securities portfolio is kept unchanged, by reinvesting the proceeds from the redemption of maturing securities.
3. *Interest rate tightening*. Increase in policy interest rates.

4. *Quantitative tightening (roll-off)*. Gradual downsizing of the securities portfolio, by limiting the roll-over to a share of the securities holdings.

The design of the exit strategy along the above stages allows for a gradual exit from a monetary policy characterized by interest rates at the ZLB and large-scale purchases of financial assets by the central bank, leading to a huge increase in the size of its balance sheet. The exit process from such an accommodative monetary policy must be gradual and predictable in order to avoid a shock in financial markets, leading to a sharp rise in yields.

In setting up an exit strategy as described, central banks can exploit the theoretical principle of *decoupling*, which we examined in Chapter 3. Thanks to the excess liquidity accumulated by the banking system, the central bank can manage the supply of base money independently of interest rate steering. The downsizing of net asset purchases can precede the increase in policy rates. The drain of base money, which occurs when the quantitative tightening begins, can be postponed until later than the increase in rates.

The Fed's exit from QE policies did not imply a return to the traditional operational framework, based on reserve scarcity and interest rate steering through frequent open market operations by the New York Fed. On the contrary, the Fed initiated a "normalization" process, leading to a framework still characterized by an abundance of bank reserves: the "new normal" that we observe today. As can be seen in Fig. 5.8, the decline in reserves during the exit years from QE (2014–2019) did not go as far as eliminating altogether the previously created amount of excess reserves, which remained quite large. In the presence of a structural excess supply of reserves, the implementation of monetary policy relies on the indication of a maximum and a minimum level for the market interbank rate: the *FF target range*. The fact that money market rates remain within this range is ensured through the use of two instruments: the *administered rates*, namely the interest rate on excess reserves (IER) and the interest rate on reverse repos (IRR), which we will discuss shortly.

5.7.1 The Exit from QE

The first announcement concerning the exit from QE in the US was made by the Fed Chairman Bernanke in May 2013, in a hearing before the US Congress. That announcement (followed by a similar one made at a press conference in July of the same year) anticipated the first phase of the US exit strategy: the reduction of net asset purchases of financial assets (*tapering*). The announcement came as a surprise, and it created a turmoil in the financial markets, with large bond sales and a marked increase in volatility in the stock market. Some market participants feared an abrupt return to normality after years of very accommodative monetary policy. In the second half of the year, the tension in financial markets was reduced, as long as the Fed made clear that its exit from QE3 would be gradual, and that the interest rate policy would be kept separate from the balance sheet policy. This episode, known as "taper tantrum", had more negative effects on some emerging-market economies than on the US.[17]

Tapering actually began in January 2014, when the monthly size of asset purchases under the QE3 program was reduced from USD 85 billion first to USD 75 billion and then to USD 65 billion. Following further reductions, net purchases were terminated in October of the same year. This phase is clearly visible in Fig. 5.7: the growth of the two areas, representing the stock of government bonds and MBS held by the Fed, gradually declined during 2014 until it came to a standstill. Since then, the policy of rolling over securities in the Fed's portfolio kept the stock of securities held by the central bank constant until 2017.

Following the recovery of the business cycle and the improved outlook for the US economy, the Fed undertook a series of policy interest rate increases. Starting in December 2015, the FF target range was gradually raised from the bottom level of 0–0.25 percent to 2.25–2.50 percent in December 2018: see Fig. 5.5.

Finally, in October 2017, the Fed initiated the last step of its exit strategy: maturing securities were no longer rolled-over in full, resulting in a reduction of the stock and a corresponding drain of bank reserves (clearly visible in Fig. 5.8). At first, the amounts not rolled over were very small, then they were gradually increased (up to USD 50 billion per month). This *quantitative tightening* led to a reduction of more than 15

[17] For details about this episode, in particular on the problems related to communication between the Fed and financial market participants, see Bernanke (2022).

percent in the size of the Fed's balance sheet in less than two years: from USD 4.5 trillion (October 2017) to USD 3.8 trillion (August 2019). The contraction of the Fed's securities portfolio can be seen in Fig. 5.9.

5.7.2 *The New Normal*

Starting in September 2014, the FOMC adopted several decisions[18] in which it outlined the normalization of US monetary policy. It envisaged the gradual raising of policy interest rates and the reduction of the previously accumulated securities portfolio, bringing to completion the exit strategy just described. But in addition, the Fed was outlining the new implementation framework of US monetary policy, which was quite different from a simple return to that in place before the phase of exceptional measures taken in previous years. The Fed's *new normal* is characterized by the following elements.

a. *Interest rate steering* plays a central role. The indication of the range in which money market interest rates should be kept, the *FF target range*, becomes again the main instrument with which to signal the stance of monetary policy. In addition to the signaling role played by the announcement of the FF target range, the control of market interest rates relies on the two rates over which the Fed has direct control (*administered rates*): the interest rate on excess reserves (IER) and the interest rate on reverse repos (IRR). These two rates identify the so-called *two-floor system*. The structural excess of liquidity pushes money market rates steadily towards the *floor*, which is the rate at which bank reserves are remunerated. Intermediaries compete with each other in lending funds in the money market, but no one is willing to lend at a lower rate than they can receive from the central bank: this is their *reservation rate*. Actually, there are *two floors*, given the segmentation of the money market between banks, whose current account balances with the Fed are remunerated at the IER rate, and non-banks which are not entitled to this remuneration.

[18] Since the first document *Policy normalization principles and plans*, the Fed has released several decisions on the normalization and implementation of monetary policy. All these documents can be found in the *Policy normalization* section on the *Board of Governors'* website (www.federalreserve.gov).

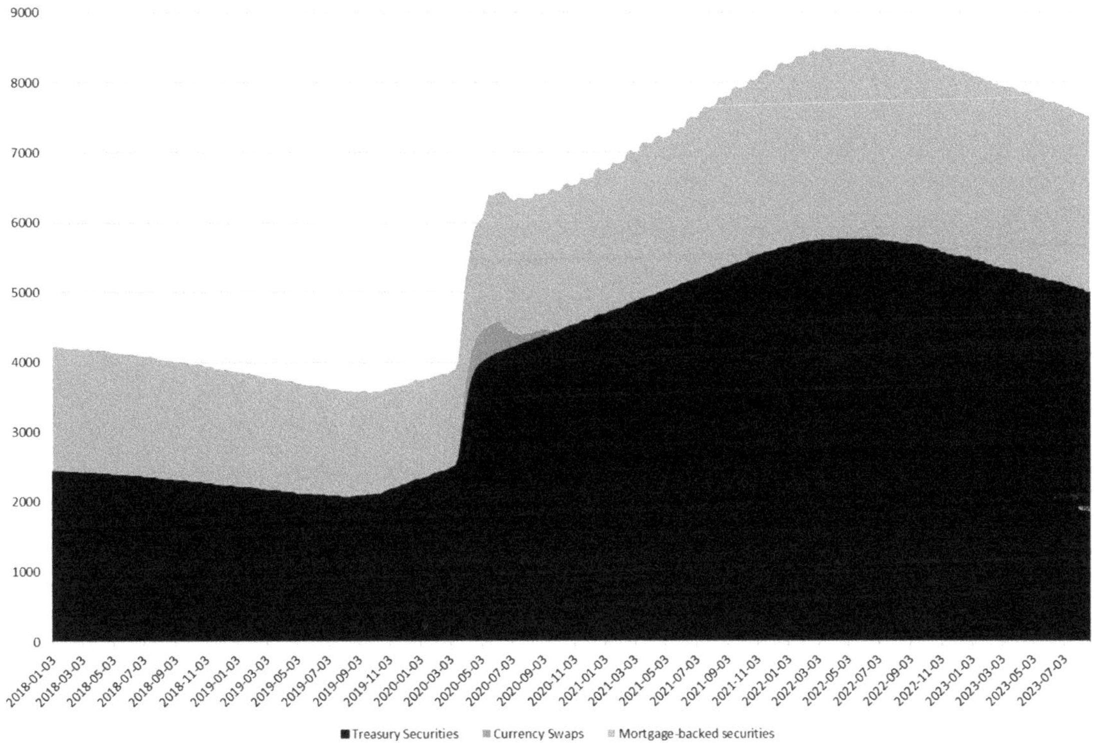

Fig. 5.9 Fed's securities holdings (stocks) (USD billion, weekly data 2018/1/3–2023/8/23) (*Data source* Federal Reserve Economic Data [FRED], Federal Reserve Bank of St. Louis)

The pivot rate for the US money market is the IER, which is considered by the Fed to be the main instrument for steering interest rates. As we know, US banks can arbitrage by borrowing at rates below IER from non-bank financial intermediaries and depositing the funds thus received on their accounts with the central bank. These transactions bring the market overnight rate (effective FF) close to the IER: this generally coincides with the upper limit (UL) to the FF target range (see Figure 5.5).[19]

An *overnight reverse repo* is a transaction in which the central bank sells today (spot) some securities to a financial intermediary and buys them back (forward) the next day. These operations enable those intermediaries, which either do not have current accounts with the Fed (money market funds) or do not receive a remuneration on their accounts (GSEs), to deposit money at the central bank and receive an interest: the *interest on reverse repos* (IRR). Therefore, these intermediaries are not willing to lend money in the market at rates below IRR. The Fed has made extensive use of this tool since December 2015, when it started to raise its policy rates above the ZLB: since then, the lower limit to the FF target range (LL) has come to coincide with the IRR.

b. The *excess supply of bank reserves* ("ample reserves regime") has become a structural feature of the operational framework. The "active management" of reserves, typical of the old interest rate steering framework, is no longer necessary. Once the downsizing of the securities portfolio came to an end (August 2019), the following securities transactions were aimed at maintaining bank reserves at a sufficiently high level, according to the FOMC's estimates: these transactions are technical in nature, and do not signal a change in monetary policy stance. Under this regard, the operational framework adopted by the Fed is a *supply-driven* floor system, where the stock of reserves is exogenously set by the central bank.[20] The securities purchases implemented between October 2019 and the first quarter of 2020, aimed at maintaining a level of reserves at

[19] Sometimes the Fed sets IER at a lower level than UL, to keep the market rates within a narrower band than that indicated by the FF target range. See, for example, the 2019–2020 interval in Fig. 5.5.

[20] Remember the distinction between *supply-driven* and *demand-driven* floor systems introduced in Sect. 3.4.3.

least equal to that prevailing in September 2019, should be read in this light. Part of these transactions were related to the roll-over of securities in the central bank's portfolio. The composition of the securities portfolio was changing over time: in order to gradually exit the MBS market, the Fed decided that each month 20 billion maturing bonds of this type would be replaced by investing the proceeds in Treasury securities. This process of first reducing and then maintaining an adequate size of the Fed's balance sheet goes under the name of "balance sheet normalization".

c. QE remains in the Fed's "toolbox". The Fed remains ready to use all the tools at its disposal, including changes in the size and composition of its balance sheet, to implement a monetary easing additional to that achievable through the interest rate policy.

Figure 5.10 visualizes the theoretical equilibrium of the US money market in the new two-floor system. For this purpose, we need to redefine what we mean by "bank reserves" to include not only the balances held by banks on their current accounts with the Fed, but also the overnight deposits of non-bank intermediaries made by activating the *overnight reverse repo* facility. For banks, the horizontal segment of the demand curve for reserves, R^D *(banks)*, lies at the IER rate, which is their reservation rate in the federal funds market. For other financial institutions (GSEs and money market funds), the horizontal segment of the demand curve for reserves, R^D *(non-banks)*, is at the level of the IRR rate: this is their reservation rate in the money market. The supply of reserves, determined by open market operations (OMOs) and autonomous factors (AUs), intersects the horizontal segment of the demand curves. The effective FF rate, and with it the short-term market rates, lie in the range between IRR (i_{RR} in the picture) and IER (i_R), which generally coincides with the FF target range indicated by the FOMC. The discount window remains among the Fed's available instruments, but it is hardly used: the interest rate applied to *primary credit* ($\bar{i}$) plays no role in controlling market rates.

The innovations, which have taken place in the implementation of US monetary policy since the financial crisis of 2007/2008, have altered the Fed's operational framework forever. Not only because the instruments, introduced with QE policies, remain in the central bank's toolkit. But

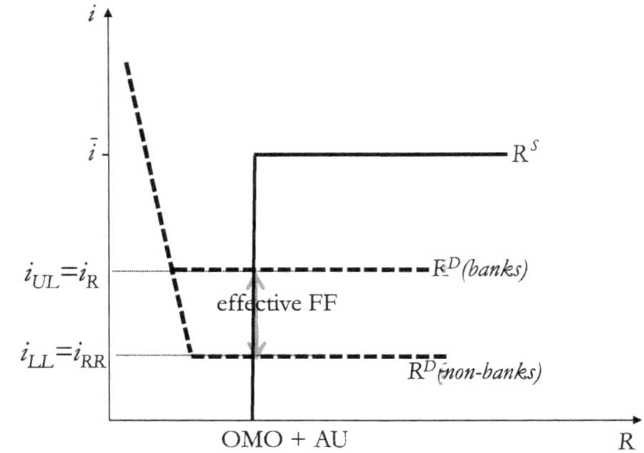

Fig. 5.10 USA: the *new normal*

also because the monetary control mechanism has changed: from the old interest rate steering to the new regime, based on "ample reserves" and the use of two floors to steer money market rates. In January 2019, the Fed made clear that this was going to be its approach to monetary policy implementation in the long run, thus ruling out a return to the old one, based on the active management of a scarce supply of bank reserves.[21] Since then, open market operations (OMOs) have been aimed at maintaining the market for bank reserves "satiated". To this purpose, it is necessary to maintain a level of excess reserves sufficient to absorb any temporary liquidity shock, represented by a shift of the vertical line in Fig. 5.10. However, this excess of reserves is normally lower than that prevailing during the years of QE.[22] The Fed's securities portfolio is adjusted to accommodate the changes in autonomous factors: the central bank's "non-reserve liabilities", in the Fed's terminology. Cash in circulation has shown a steady upward trend in recent years. The balance of the account held by the Treasury (TGA) has grown over time, showing wide

[21] See the press release of 2019/1/30: *Statement Regarding Monetary Policy Implementation and Balance Sheet Normalization*.

[22] The FOMC itself implied this, when stating that "*the Fed will, in the longer run, hold no more securities than necessary to implement monetary policy efficiently and effectively*".

fluctuations.[23] These factors absorb base money and have to be offset by securities purchases in the market by the Desk of the New York Fed: these purchases are technical in nature and do not imply an easier stance of monetary policy.

5.8 The Reaction to the Pandemic Crisis

The new normal of US monetary policy was severely tested by the pandemic crisis, which exploded in the US with at least as much violence as in other countries. The operational framework, based on the ample reserves approach, proved to be flexible and well-suited to meet the challenge posed by the abrupt slowdown in manufacturing activity and the turbulence experienced in the financial markets from March 2020 onwards. The Fed used all the tools already at its disposal, and introduced new ones, to support economic activity, to maintain orderly conditions in financial markets, and to ensure a sufficient flow of credit to businesses and households. The monetary policy stance was expanded by relying, as far as possible, on interest rate steering. In addition, financial asset purchase programs led to a significant quantitative easing, with a sharp increase in the size of the central bank's balance sheet. A wide range of programs, aimed at preserving market liquidity and credit flows, contributed to the smooth transmission of monetary policy. Finally, forward guidance was used to anchor the expectations of economic and financial agents, reassuring them of the FOMC's willingness to maintain an expansionary policy for as long as necessary, until the pandemic crisis had been overcome.

In March 2020, the FOMC quickly lowered the FF target range by 150 basis points, bringing it back to the ZLB: between 0 and 25 basis points. At the same time, the interest rate on reserves (IER) was lowered to an all-time low of 10 basis points. Thus, the effective federal funds rate was driven to a level close to 10 basis points (see Fig. 5.5), driving the short-term yield curve towards the ZLB. It should be noted that the rate applied to primary credit, which had traditionally been above the upper limit of the FF target range (UL), was lowered to the same level: 25 basis points. This, together with the communication policy and the lengthening of loan maturities (up to 90 days), was done to encourage banks to use

[23] For details about the autonomous factors affecting the stock of base money in the US, see Ihrig et al. (2020a).

the discount window, overcoming the fear of incurring an adverse *stigma* effect.

After an initial heavy reliance on temporary operations (repos), securities transactions focused on outright purchases of government bonds and MBS guaranteed by the GSEs. Between March and June 2020, the Fed purchased a total USD 2.5 trillion of these financial assets: the jump in the stock of securities held by the central bank is clearly visible in Fig. 5.9. Subsequently, purchases continued, albeit at a slower pace, bringing the size of the securities portfolio up to 8.5 trillion by March 2022: more than twice the pre-Covid-19 level. Also visible in the graph is the use of currency swaps to make US dollar liquidity available to other central banks during the most acute phase of the pandemic emergency.

Like the financial crisis of 2007/2008, the outbreak of the pandemic crisis caused similar effects on financial markets, although the origin of the crisis was quite different. Many companies were faced with a sudden drop in sales, due to lockdown measures, and therefore needed to find funding quickly. Faced with the uncertain economic landscape, many investors sold (risky) financial assets to hold more liquidity: bank deposits and short-term securities. The risk aversion of financial intermediaries increased, reducing their propensity to provide credit. Under these conditions, the Fed reactivated in 2020 some instruments already used in the 2007/2008 crisis, in order to preserve the liquidity of specific segments of the financial market. These include the *Term Asset-backed securities Loan Facility* (TALF): a program of loans to financial intermediaries so that they could invest in non-residential asset-backed securities. Another instrument was the *Commercial Paper Funding Facility* (CPFF): a program to purchase commercial paper, also issued by non-financial companies.

However, the most interesting element of the Fed's reaction to the pandemic crisis was the introduction of new instruments aimed at providing direct support for credit flows to the real economy, benefiting a wide range of players: businesses, households, local (non-federal) government authorities, and non-profit organizations. We report the main ones below.[24]

[24] For a full description of the programs introduced by the Fed to address the pandemic crisis, see the *Board of Governors'* website (www.federalreserve.gov). A summary is provided by Ihrig et al. (2020b).

The *Main Street Lending Program* (MSLP) was an instrument by which the US central bank, through a Special Purpose Vehicle (SPV) set up by the Boston Fed, acquired interests in loans originated by financial intermediaries. In the first phase of the program, the loans were intended to support small and medium-sized enterprises (SMEs) that met certain criteria: in brief, those that were in good shape before the outbreak of the pandemic crisis. At a later stage, the program was extended to non-profit organizations. The loan maturity was five years, and interest payments were suspended for the first year.

The *Primary Market Corporate Credit Facility* (PMCCF) and the *Secondary Market Corporate Credit Facility* (SMCCF) were tools with which the Fed could directly finance large companies with high creditworthiness (*investment grade*), by providing loans and purchasing corporate bonds in the primary and secondary markets, respectively. The securities portfolio acquired was large and diversified, able to replicate an index of the US corporate bond market. Financing was provided by an SPV created by the Fed, in which the Treasury also participated.

The Fed was also concerned about safeguarding the liquidity of local governments. These, unlike the federal government, are considered risky by financial market participants and potentially exposed to the risk of default, as they are not normally backed by the central bank acting as a lender of last resort. In the face of the pandemic crisis, which suddenly reduced or delayed the revenues and increased the expenditures of these local authorities, the danger arose that the debt market of these entities would suffer a liquidity crisis. For this reason, the Fed introduced a financial assistance program for them: the *Municipal Liquidity Facility* (MLF). This was a program for the direct purchase of short-term debt issued by states, counties (with a population of at least 500,000) and municipalities (with a population of at least 250,000), for a potential total funding up to USD 500 billion.

All of the measures introduced to cope with the pandemic crisis, both the asset purchases and the lending programs, have contributed to the expansion of bank reserves and the Fed's balance sheet. As we know, any additional financial asset entering the central bank's balance sheet is matched by an increase in its own liabilities, in particular in the balances held by banks on their accounts at the central bank. Indeed, Fig. 5.8 shows the jump in the level of bank reserves that occurred in spring 2020, at the same time when the above-mentioned measures were introduced. In the meantime, the reserve requirement ratio has been set to zero, thus de facto abolishing the reserve requirement from the end of March 2020. As of this date, all reserves held on banks' accounts with the Fed are *free reserves*. Actually, as we have already noted (Sect. 3.3.2), the reserve requirement has become redundant in an ample reserve regime, as the one prevailing from 2008 onwards (not only in the US but also in other countries).

Since the beginning of the pandemic crisis, the FOMC has accompanied its decisions with indications about the future course of monetary policy (*forward guidance*) to assure financial markets and economic agents that the central bank would continue to provide ample monetary stimulus to the economy until the crisis was over. When lowering rates to the ZLB (March 2020), the FOMC stated that it expected to keep the FF target range (0–25 b.p.) unchanged until it was "confident that the economy has weathered recent events and is on track to achieve its maximum employment and price stability goals". This statement has been reiterated in other communications following the FOMC meetings. In March 2021, the FOMC reinforced its forward guidance, indicating that the current FF target range would be maintained "until labor market conditions have reached levels consistent with Committee's assessments of maximum employment and inflation has risen to 2 percent and is on track to moderately exceed 2 percent for some time". In the last statement we can see the effect of the (2019–2020) strategy review, according to which the 2 percent inflation target is symmetric, and it should be pursued on average over the long term. This guidance on interest rate steering was complemented by information on open market operations and asset purchase programs. For example, the March 2021 FOMC statement indicated the intention to continue the purchases of Treasury securities and MBS at the pace of 80 billion and 40 billion per month, respectively, until substantial progress towards the final objectives of maximum employment and price stability had been achieved.

5.9 A New Round of Normalization

In 2021, the US economy was gradually overcoming the Covid-19 emergency. At the same time, several strong and unexpected inflationary shocks took place. The release of the restrictions, due to the pandemic, led to bottlenecks in several productive sectors. On the one hand, the demand for some goods and services was suddenly increasing, thanks also to the support provided by the fiscal policy. On the other hand, the (domestic and international) supply chains were not able to recover in a short time from the shutdowns imposed by the pandemic restrictions. This went together with an increase of raw material and energy prices, due (among other factors) to the geo-political tensions that exploded in 2022 with the Russian aggression to Ukraine. The outcome of all these developments was a sharp rise of inflation, due to a mix of demand and supply factors, in the US and in many other countries as well. The 12-month change of the Consumer Price Index raised, in the US, from 1.4% to 7.2% between January and December 2021, and it reached a peak of 8.9% by June 2022.

The Fed, like other central banks, initially supported the view that to the ongoing inflation was "largely reflecting transitory factors",[25] thus it did not justify a monetary restriction. Moreover, with inflation having run persistently below the 2% target, the FOMC was willing to achieve an inflation rate above 2% for some time: this was consistent with the *average inflation targeting* introduced with the recent strategy review (see Sect. 5.3.2). Through time, it became evident that the inflationary pressures were much more persistent than initially expected, and they deserved a reaction by the central bank. Indeed, the Fed decided to initiate an exit process from the extremely expansionary stance of its policy, that had been introduced at the outset of the pandemic crisis. The exit strategy from the unconventional measures taken during the pandemic has followed the same steps that had been followed in 2014–2019, when the Fed exited the QE policies previously introduced to face the financial crisis, although the more recent normalization process has been quite faster, mostly concentrated in 2022. These steps are the same that we have identified at a general level in Chapter 3 (and also followed by the ECB): (1) tapering, (2) *roll-over*, (3) *interest rate tightening*, (4) *quantitative tightening*. At the end of this process, the Fed's operational framework is back to the *new normal* reached before the pandemic crisis, characterized by *interest rate steering* within an *ample reserve regime*. Let me summarize these developments below.

The *tapering* phase started in November 2021, when the FOMC decided to begin reducing the monthly pace of net asset purchases: from 80 to 70 USD billion for Treasury securities, and from 40 to 35 USD billion for agency MBSs. Other reductions were decided in the following months, until the net asset purchases were terminated in March 2022.

[25] See the FOMC Statement of 22 September 2021.

At the same time, the FOMC communicated that "the Fed's ongoing purchases and holdings of securities will continue to foster smooth market functioning and accommodative financial conditions": in other words, the FOMC committed to a full *roll-over* of the securities portfolio for some time, "thereby supporting the flow of credit to households and businesses".[26]

The first step to *interest rate tightening* was taken in March 2022, when the FF target range was raised from 0–0.25% to 0.25–0.5%. This came together with the forward guidance: "the Committee anticipates that ongoing increases in the target range will be appropriate".[27] Indeed, several other decisions have been taken afterwards, leading to an overall increase of the Fed's policy rates by more than five percentage points (see Fig. 5.11[28]): quite an aggressive, albeit late, reaction to the inflation dynamics started in 2021.

Finally, the *quantitative tightening* started in June 2022, when the reinvestment of principal payments, received from maturing securities held by the Fed, began to be limited to the portion exceeding some monthly caps. For Treasury securities, the cap was initially set at USD 30 billion, and raised to 60 billion after three months. For agency debt and MBS, the cap was initially set at USD 17.5 billion, and raised to 35 billion after three months. Since then, the size of the Fed's securities portfolio, and of its balance sheet, shows a steady decline (see Fig. 5.9), adding a further monetary restriction to that implemented through the interest rate policy.

The normalization process has led the operational framework of the US monetary policy come back to the *new normal* introduced in the years before the pandemic crisis. The outcome of this process has been anticipated by the FOMC in a statement released in January 2022, communicating the *Principles for reducing the size of the Federal Reserve's balance sheet*. Among the others, two main principles are the following:

[26] See the FOMC Statement of January 26, 2022.

[27] See the FOMC Statement of March 16, 2022.

[28] In Fig. 5.11 the interest rate applied to Primary Credit is not reported, since it coincides with the upper limit of the FF target range (UL) over the whole time span considered.

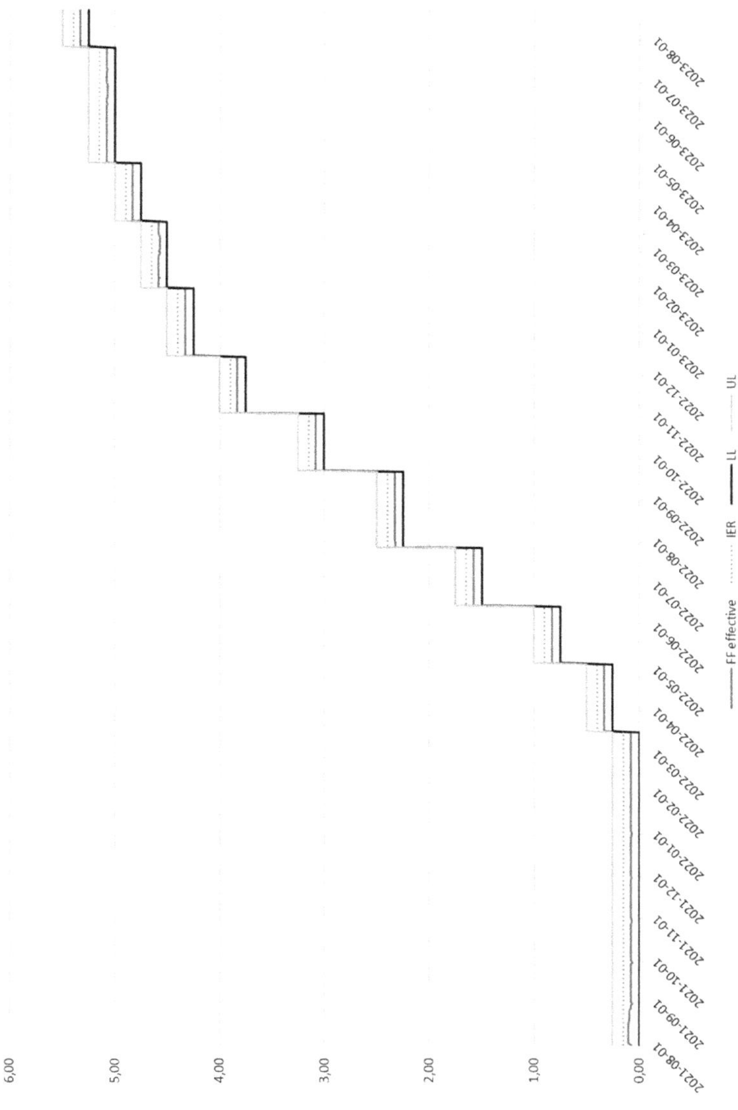

Fig. 5.11 The 2022–2023 interest rate tightening (percentage points, daily data 2021/8/1–2023/8/22) (*Data source* Federal Reserve Economic Data [FRED], Federal Reserve Bank of St. Louis)

- "The Committee views changes in the target range for the federal funds rate as its primary means of adjusting the stance of monetary policy".
- "Over time, the Committee intends to maintain securities holdings in amounts needed to implement monetary policy efficiently and effectively in its ample reserves regime".

Taken together, these two principles say that the US monetary policy is implemented by steering the level of interest rates (through the indication of the FF target range) and, at the same time, maintaining a sufficiently large excess supply of bank reserves, so that the money market rates stick to the lower limit provided by the two administered rates: the interest rate on bank reserves and the remuneration of the reverse repos, which delimit the band within which the effective FF rate is kept.[29] This *two-floor system* is visualized in Fig. 5.10.

The final steps of the transition to this ample reserve regime have been detailed in another statement released by the FOMC on 4 May 2022: *Plans for reducing the size of the Federal Reserve's balance sheet*. This statement provides the following indications:

- "To ensure a smooth transition, the Committee intends to slow and then stop the decline in the size of the balance sheet when reserve balances are somewhat *above* the level it judges to be consistent with ample reserves.
- Once balance sheet runoff has ceased, reserve balances will likely continue to decline for a time, reflecting growth in other Federal Reserve liabilities, until the Committee judges that reserve balances are at an ample level.
- Thereafter, the Committee will manage securities holdings as needed to maintain ample reserves over time".

These indications confirm that the FOMC is committed to maintain an ample reserve regime and to manage its portfolio of securities accordingly: this commitment responds to the design of a *supply-driven* floor system. To this aim, the central bank has to consider the impact of the autonomous factors ("other Federal Reserve liabilities") on the stock of

[29] Actually, this band can sometimes be narrower than the FF target range.

bank reserves. Once the target level for reserve balances has been reached, the management of the securities portfolio has a technical role: that of keeping the supply of reserves sufficiently "ample", offsetting the trends and volatility of the autonomous factors. It has no implication for the monetary policy stance.[30] Figure 5.8 shows that, after one year of quantitative tightening, the amount of excess reserves remains very ample by historical standards.

5.10 Normalization and Financial Stability: The 2023 Banking Crisis

At the beginning of March 2023, the Californian Silicon Valley Bank suffered a large outflow of deposits and went bankrupt on March 10. In the same days, the stock price of other US banks fell sharply and some of them experienced large withdrawals of money from depositors. On March 12, another bank failed: Signature Bank of New York. Concerns about tensions in the banking system led the authorities (Treasury Department, Federal Reserve and Federal Deposit Insurance Corporation) to intervene in order to preserve the stability of the sector. Deposit outflows subsequently slowed, but the underlying problems and stock market volatility remained. The third disruption, within a few weeks, was that of First Republic Bank, which was acquired by JP Morgan Chase (with government support) on May 1.

As we discussed in Chapter 3, these three cases highlighted the delicate relationship between monetary policy and financial stability. Many commentators have criticized the abrupt reversal of monetary policy introduced by the Fed at the beginning of 2022: according to them, the Fed failed to take due account of the repercussions of its policy on the financial system, which had become accustomed to a world with zero interest rates. However, this view seems to capture only one aspect of the problem: rising policy interest rates. On closer inspection, the banking crises of 2023 were mainly due to mismanagement problems and the very particular business model of the three failed banks. Moreover, the regulation and supervision of the US authorities showed some important shortcomings.

[30] In addition to managing its securities portfolio, the Fed conducts daily overnight repo operations, that serve as a backstop to maintain an ample supply of reserves. The *Standing Repo Facility* has been introduced in July 2021.

Let us start with the deregulation of the banking sector, introduced by the US Administration in 2018, and the resulting weaknesses in supervision. The global financial crisis of 2008–2009 had a profound impact on the US banking system and its regulatory and supervisory framework. To address the weaknesses in the banking sector that emerged at that time, the Fed established a set of "Enhanced Prudential Standards" (EPS) applicable to large banking groups. These standards implemented that part of the Dodd-Frank Act (Section 165) that required the US central bank to define EPS and apply them to bank holding companies and foreign banking institutions with total consolidated assets of USD 50 billion or more. The EPS cover capital and liquidity requirements, stress tests, and resolution plans. They were introduced to improve the resilience of large banking institutions and to reduce the impact of a possible failure of a large bank on the financial system and the US economy.

In May 2018, the US Congress passed the *Economic Growth, Regulatory Relief, and Consumer Protection Act* (EGRRCPA), which amended Section 165 of the Dodd-Frank Act by raising the minimum threshold for the general application of EPS from USD 50 billion to USD 250 billion: this was a very significant step of deregulation. At the same time, the EGRRCPA gave the Fed discretion to apply EPS to banks with total assets between USD 100 billion and USD 250 billion.

The Fed exercised the Congressional mandate by introducing the so-called "tailoring rule" in 2019. This established four categories of supervisory standards (Category I to IV) based on some indicators of supervised banks' riskiness, including: total assets, size of off-balance sheet exposures, and level of short-term wholesale funding. Based on these indicators, increasingly stringent prudential requirements were defined as the size and complexity of a financial intermediary increase.

The EGRRCPA and the tailoring rule resulted in a lowering of regulatory and supervisory standards for those banks that moved from a regional bank size (*Regional Banking Organization*, with total assets between USD 10 billion and USD 100 billion) to a large bank size (*Large Banking Organization*, with total assets over USD 100 billion). During the growth phase, the Fed used its discretion to grant long transition periods in the application of EPS, de facto exempting those banks for several years. Moreover, the Fed and the FDIC themselves admitted that they were late in alerting the management of the banks, that eventually failed in 2023, of their critical issues, and in taking steps to induce the management of those banks to take the necessary corrective actions.[31]

The three failed banks shared some characteristics, which we can summarize as follows. (1) They exhibited a remarkable growth within a few years, quickly reaching a medium-to-large size. This growth was mainly funded by collecting uninsured deposits from a few, often interconnected, entities. This aspect, together with new communication (especially social media) and payment technologies (with the possibility of moving large sums in real time through digital instruments), made the deposits of these banks particularly fragile, exposing them to rapid and massive bank runs. (2) The business model was highly concentrated on a few sectors: high-tech companies, crypto-asset intermediaries, real estate lending (both commercial and residential). This exposed such banks to idiosyncratic shocks that affected these sectors. (3) The management of those banks underestimated and mismanaged the liquidity and interest rate risks they were exposed to. During the normalization phase of US monetary policy, with an aggressive policy rate tightening starting in March 2022, the interest rate risk materialized with large losses in the value of securities holdings. Under pressure from the withdrawal of money by some large depositors, banks were forced to liquidate part of their securities portfolios at a loss, inducing other depositors to withdraw their deposits and thus starting a downward spiral.

It must be acknowledged that crisis management was swift. The FDIC promptly identified acquiring institutions for the troubled banks, in some cases after setting up a "bridge bank". However, the total cost of the three resolution operations for the FDIC was high (USD 35.5 billion), partly because of the full guarantee provided for deposits, including those in excess of the coverage limit (USD 250,000).[32] This cost should not be borne by taxpayers, but by the deposit insurance fund, which is funded by banks' contributions (as required by law); it is also true that the FDIC is ultimately guaranteed by the US government. The purpose of this blanket

[31] See Fed (2023b) and FDIC (2023).

[32] On 12 March 2023, the Secretary of the Treasury approved a *systemic risk exception*, whereby the FDIC was authorized to guarantee all the depositors of SVB and Signature Bank in the resolution procedures of the two banks. Unlike depositors, shareholders and some holders of unsecured debt were not protected. In addition, some managers of these banks were removed.

guarantee, extended to deposits that go far beyond the limit of the insurance coverage, is easily understood: to stabilize the funding of the banks in trouble, already stressed by a heavy drain of deposits, and to reassure the depositors of the other banks, thus avoiding a contagion effect. However, this measure can be criticized for (at least) one reason: intervening *ex-post* with a full guarantee, without having envisaged it *ex-ante*, is inefficient, as the cost of intervention is paid for without getting the benefit of stabilizing depositors' behavior.

To address the liquidity crisis, which from the three failed banks threatened to spread to other US banks, the Fed introduced (on 12 March 2023) the *Bank Term Funding Program* (BTFP). With this new instrument, the Fed offers loans, with a maturity of up to one year, to banks. The latter can pledge, as collateral for the loans, all types of securities normally used in the US central bank's open market operations, such as Treasury securities and mortgage-backed securities. These can be used as collateral for an amount equal to their face value, thus not considering the decline of their market value. Therefore those banks, that find themselves in a stressful situation as a result of the deposit drain, can obtain liquidity from the Fed without being forced to liquidate their securities holdings at a loss. This is quite a good measure, with which the Fed has strengthened its role as lender of last resort to the banking system. However, if it had been introduced earlier (before 12 March), it might have prevented the situation of SVB and Signature Bank from precipitating.

The BTFP has been added to the traditional refinancing instrument: the discount window. The liquidity stress affecting US banks at that time is evidenced by the extensive recourse to the two central bank refinancing tools, the discount window and the BTFP, since early March 2023. Recourse to the first instrument (in particular primary credit) jumped from USD 5 billion to over 150 billion and it eventually declined to around USD 70 billion. Recourse to BTFP showed several increases and it stabilized in April at a level between USD 70 and 80 billion: see Fig. 5.12.

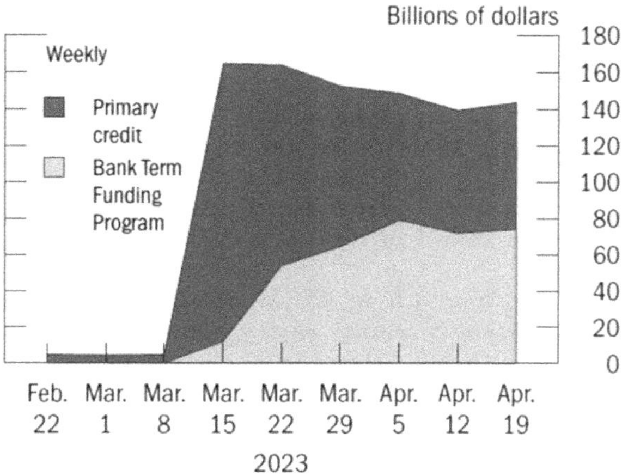

Fig. 5.12 Discount window and BTFP: outstanding balances (stocks, USD billions) (*Source* Federal Reserve Board, Statistical Release)

References

Bernanke, B. (2012, August 31). *Monetary policy since the onset of the crisis*, speech at the Jackson Hole (Wyoming) Annual Conference.

Bernanke, B. (2022). *21st century monetary policy*. Norton.

Bordo, M., Cochrane, J., & Taylor, J. (Eds.). (2023). *How monetary policy got behind the curve—And how to get back*. Hoover Institution Press.

Brunnermeier, M. (2009). Deciphering the liquidity and credit crunch 2007–2008. *Journal of Economic Perspectives, 23*, 77–100.

Clarida, R. (2019, February 22). *The Federal Reserve review of its monetary policy strategy, tools, and communication practices*, speech at the 2019 *US Monetary Policy Forum*, New York.

Duffie, D. (2011). *How big banks fail, and what to do about it*. Princeton University Press.

English, W., Lopez-Salido, D., & Tetlow, R. (2015). The Federal Reserve's framework for monetary policy: Recent changes and new questions. *IMF Economic Review, 63*, 22–70.

FDIC. (2023, April 28). *FDIC's supervision of Signature Bank*. Federal Deposit Insurance Corporation.

Fed. (2019, January 29). *Statement on longer-run goals and monetary policy strategy*. Federal Open Market Committee (FOMC) of the Federal Reserve System.

Fed. (2020, August 27). *Statement on longer-run goals and monetary policy strategy*. Federal Open Market Committee (FOMC) of the Federal Reserve System.

Fed. (2023a, January 31). *Statement on longer-run goals and monetary policy strategy*, Federal Open Market Committee (FOMC) of the Federal Reserve System.

Fed. (2023b). *Review of the Federal Reserve's Supervision and Regulation of Silicon Valley Bank*, Board of Governors of the Federal Reserve System, Washington, DC.

Ihrig, J., Meade, E., & Weinbach, G. (2015). *Monetary policy 101: A primer on the Fed's changing approach to policy implementation* (Finance and Economics Discussion Series 2015-047). Board of Governors of the Federal Reserve System, Washington, DC.

Ihrig, J., Mize, L., & Weinbach, G. (2017). *How does the Fed adjust its securities holdings and who is affected?* (Finance and Economics Discussion Series 2017-099). Board of Governors of the Federal Reserve System, Washington, DC.

Ihrigh, J., Senyuz, Z., & Weinbach, G. (2020a). *The Fed's "Ample-reserves" approach to implementing monetary policy* (Finance and Economics Discussion Series 2020-022). Board of Governors of the Federal Reserve System, Washington, DC.

Ihrigh, J., Senyuz, Z., & Weinbach, G. (2020b). *Implementing monetary policy in an 'ample-reserves' regime: When in crisis (Note 3 of 3)* (FEDS Notes). Board of Governors of the Federal Reserve System, Washington, DC.

Labonte, M. (2014). *Federal Reserve: Unconventional monetary policy options*. Report to the US Congress, Congressional Research Service, Washington, DC.

Powell, J. (2020, August 27). *New economic challenges and the Fed's monetary policy review*, speech at the Annual Meeting in Jackson Hole (Wyoming).

Svensson, L. (2020). Monetary policy strategies for the Federal Reserve. *International Journal of Central Banking, 16*, 133–193.

Taylor, J. (1993). Discretion versus policy rules in practice. *Carnegie-Rochester Conference Series on Public Policy, 39*, 195–214.

CHAPTER 6

Unconventional Monetary Policies in UK and Japan

Abstract Starting in 2009, the BoE has introduced large asset purchases and long-term lending operations. Since then, its operational framework relies on a structural excess of bank reserves. Money market rates are in line with the interest rate paid on reserves: Bank Rate, which is the policy rate. In 2022, the BoE started downsizing its securities portfolio within its exit strategy from QE policies. At the end of the normalization process, the stock of reserves will be determined by the demand made by banks applying to the STR facility: at the steady state, monetary policy will be implemented under a demand-driven floor system. The BoJ was the first central bank introducing a QE policy in 2001. The Comprehensive Monetary Easing program was introduced in 2010, under which the BoJ purchased a wide range of financial assets. The Quantitative and Qualitative Monetary Easing (QQE), introduced in 2013, gave a remarkable acceleration to the pace of asset purchases. Since 2016, a negative interest rate policy has been adopted. In the same year, the QQE with yield curve control has been introduced: the BoJ is committed to keep the yield of 10-year government bonds around zero through its bond purchases, thus making the size of the program unlimited.

Keywords Asset Purchase Facility · Bank rate · Short-Term Repo · Monetary Easing · Yield Curve Control · Inflation-overshooting commitment

A. Baglioni, *Monetary Policy Implementation*,
https://doi.org/10.1007/978-3-031-53885-8_6

6.1 Introduction

Since the financial crisis of 2007/2008, unconventional monetary policies have been adopted by several central banks around the world. They have left a durable legacy, as some innovative tools introduced in the last yeas have become part of the "new normal" in monetary policy implementation at the international level. As we have seen in the previous chapters, the instruments used can be grouped into four categories: (1) Asset Purchases (AP), (2) Long-Term Lending Operations (LTLO), (3) Negative Interest Rate Policy (NIRP), and (4) Forward Guidance (FG).

Over the years, the first instrument (AP) has become the main channel by which central banks pursue a quantitative target with regard to the size of their own balance sheet: the quantitative easing policy. With due differences, it has been used, for example, in the following countries: the US, Eurozone, the UK, Japan, Sweden, Switzerland, and Mexico. The second instrument (LTLO) has been used in Australia, Brazil, Canada, New Zealand, the Philippines, and Korea, in addition to the countries just mentioned. It too has contributed to the expansion of central banks' balance sheets. However, differently from AP, LTLOs do not allow central banks to take a complete control over their balance sheets, since the actual size of the loans disbursed depends in part on the behavior of banks (in taking up the offered loanable funds and in exercising the prepayment option). The third instrument (NIRP) is the least common: the ECB and the central banks of Japan, Sweden, Denmark, and Switzerland have pushed interest rates into negative territory for some time, but other major central banks, such as the Fed and the Bank of England, have not. Finally, almost all central banks pay far more attention to their communication policy nowadays than in the past: they are aware of the need to guide the expectations of financial market participants and economic agents in general.

Providing a systematic overview of the unconventional monetary policy instruments used by the different central banks around the world is not the purpose of this book. After having analyzed in detail the experiences of the ECB and the Fed in the previous two chapters, in this chapter I will briefly address the experiences of two other central banks: Bank of England and Bank of Japan.[1]

[1] For a systematic comparative analysis of unconventional monetary policies, see BIS (2019).

6.2 Bank of England: From QE to Normalization

The Bank of England (BoE) follows an *inflation targeting* strategy. Its mandate states that the primary objective of monetary policy is price stability, following the target set by the government. The latter has set a target of 2% for the annual growth rate of consumer prices. Subordinate to this target, the BoE contributes to pursuing the government's other economic policy objectives: economic growth and full employment. As is generally the case in an *inflation targeting* regime,[2] the BoE's institutional set-up provides for a high degree of transparency and accountability. Should the actual inflation rate deviate by more than one percentage point above or below its target, the BoE must account to the Minister of the Treasury (*Chancellor)* for the reasons why this has occurred and the actions the BoE intends to take to correct the deviation. The BoE is required to make its inflation forecasts public in a quarterly *Inflation Report*. At least three times a year the BoE has to account for its actions in parliamentary hearings. At the end of the meetings of the Monetary Policy Committee (MPC), which is its main decision-making body, the BoE makes its decisions public and explains them in a press release. After two weeks, the minutes of the meetings are released. The votes of the individual MPC members are made public.

Within the mandate thus defined, the BoE enjoys a high degree of operational autonomy. Starting in 2009, the BoE introduced *quantitative easing*, moving from a monetary control framework based on the active management of scarce liquidity through its open market operations to one based on a structural excess of reserves: the *floor system*, which we have already encountered in previous chapters. The lower limit to money market rates is the *Bank Rate*: this is the interest rate paid by the BoE on the reserves deposited by banks with the central bank itself. The abundance of reserves, created through the purchases of securities in the secondary market, keeps the interbank rate in line with the Bank

[2] For an overview of central banks following an *inflation targeting* strategy, see Hammond (2012).

Rate: see Fig. 6.1.[3] The latter is the *policy rate*, which drives the whole term structure of market rates.

As we know, in a QE regime the policy rate is rarely changed: it remains pegged at the ZLB (or at a level very close to it). In the British case, the *Bank Rate* remained for several years at the level of 0.5%: from 2009 to 2016. It then underwent a few changes and was lowered to an all-time low of 0.1% in 2020, at the outbreak of the pandemic. So far, the BoE has never adopted a negative interest rate policy.

Under these conditions, the stance of monetary policy is determined and communicated to the market mainly through the size and other features of the asset purchase programs. Over the years, purchase operations have led the BoE to hold in the *Asset Purchase Facility* (APF)[4] a stock of financial assets close to GBP 900 billion, with a clear predominance of government bonds (*gilts*): GBP 875 billion, against GBP 20 billion of corporate bonds (as of December 2021). The latter are issued by non-financial companies and are selected in proportion to the market portfolio, in accordance with the principle of "market neutrality".[5] Figure 6.2 shows the pattern of government bond holdings since the start of QE policy in 2009. Up to the end of 2021, the stock of bonds held in the APF has either increased (due to net asset purchases) or remained constant (due to the *roll-over of* maturing securities). The unwind of the APF has begun in early 2022, when the MPC has started its *quantitative tightening* (QT) policy to address the increasing inflationary pressures (see below).

The BoE has made extensive use of long-term lending operations to the banking system, the terms of which have been designed in such a way to provide an incentive for banks to lend the money received from the central bank to businesses and households: under this regard, the BoE's lending operations are similar to the *Targeted Longer-Term Refinancing Operations* (T-LTROs) implemented by the ECB. In 2012, the *Funding for Lending Scheme* (FLS) was introduced in the UK: a program

[3] If the overnight market rate falls significantly below Bank Rate, banks can borrow reserves cheaply in the wholesale money market and earn the Bank Rate by depositing them at the BoE. In doing so, they push the market rate upwards. However, because of the transaction costs related to these arbitrage trades, the money market rates often settle a little below Bank Rate: see Fig. 6.1. For further details, see Bank of England (2023a).

[4] APF is the BoE's subsidiary used to undertake purchases of gilts and corporate bonds.

[5] The principle of market neutrality will be discussed in the next chapter (Sect. 7.3.3).

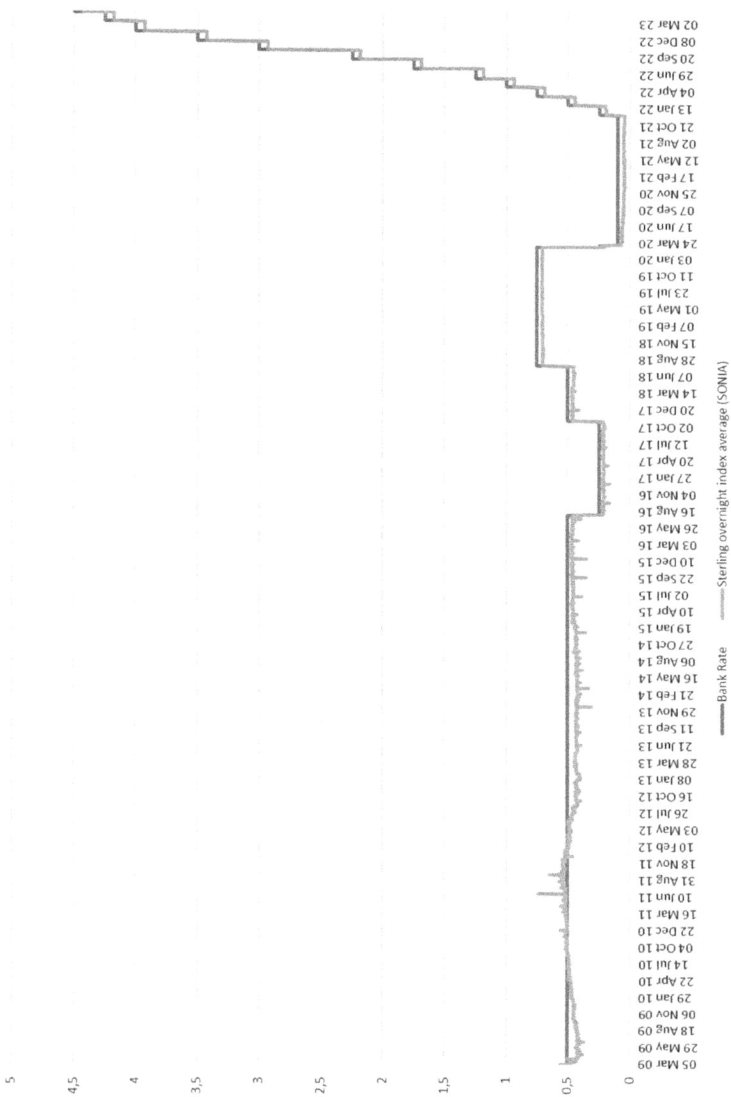

Fig. 6.1 UK: policy and market rates (percentage points—daily data 2009/3/5–2023/5/15) (*Data source* Bank of England database)

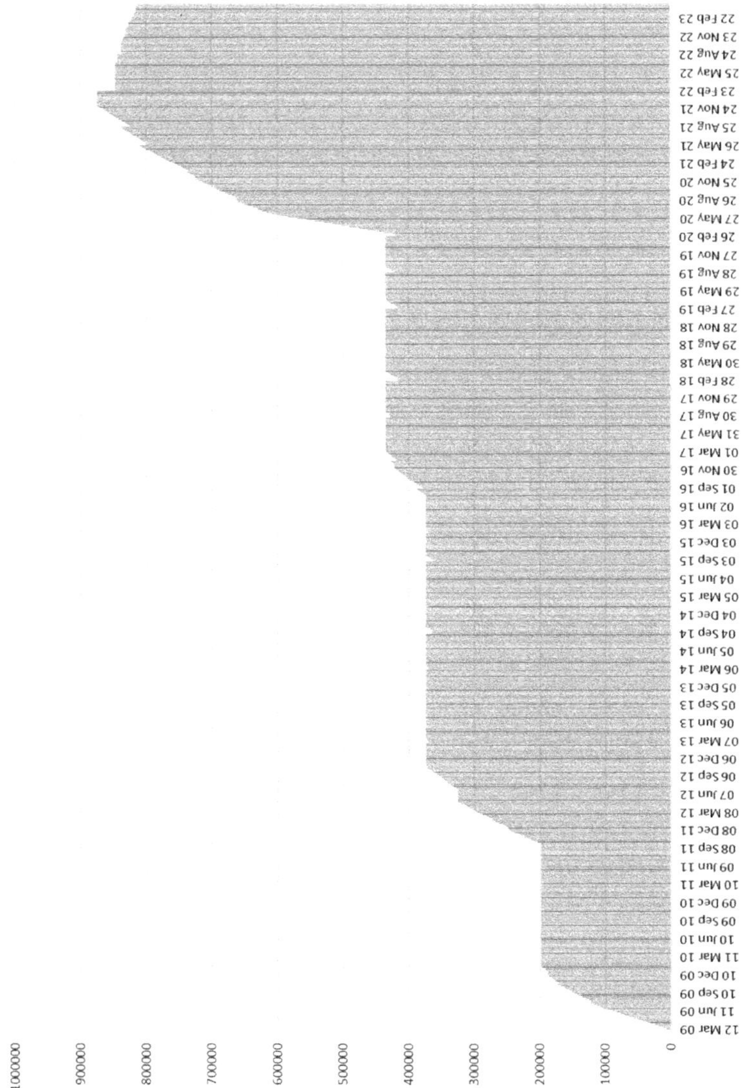

Fig. 6.2 Holdings of gilts by the Bank of England's APF (stocks—sterling millions—weekly data, March 2009–May 2023) (*Data source* Bank of England database)

of loans with four-year maturity and with interest rate and size linked to each bank's performance in lending to the economy. The program was maintained until the beginning of 2018 (the last loan expired in January 2022). It was joined in 2016 by another program with similar features, named *Term Funding Scheme* (TFS).

The latter, in turn, was replaced in March 2020, in the face of the Covid-19 crisis, by another program: *Term Funding Scheme with additional incentives for SMEs* (TFSME). As its name implies, this is a program designed specifically to facilitate credit access for *Small-Medium size Enterprises* (SMEs): the ones most affected by the drop of cashflows and the credit crunch during the pandemic crisis. The total amount of loans that each bank was entitled to receive (*borrowing allowance*) was the sum of two components: an *initial allowance* and an *additional allowance*. While the former was proportional to the amount of loans already outstanding, the latter was computed as follows: a multiple equal to five times the flow of loans to SMEs, observed during a given reference period, added to the flow of loans to other businesses and households (during the same reference period). The loans had a maturity of four years, with an option for early repayment. They were applied an interest rate equal or very close to the Bank Rate, with the purpose of reinforcing the pass through of the cuts in the Bank Rate to those rates faced by households and companies.[6]

The QE policy was in place until December 2021, when the net asset purchases were terminated. At the same time, the BoE started its policy of interest rate tightening (see Fig. 6.1). In February 2022, the MPC decided to start its QT policy, by no longer reinvesting maturing government and corporate bond holdings, and by adopting a program of corporate bond sales. In September 2022, the MPC agreed to downsize its portfolio of government bonds, by an amount of £80 billion over the next twelve months. As set out by the MPC, the exit strategy from the expansionary policy of previous years was designed so as not to disrupt the functioning of financial markets: to this aim, asset sales have been conducted in a gradual and predictable manner over a rather long period of time. Starting from this exit phase, the MPC's preference is to use the Bank Rate as its active tool when adjusting the stance of monetary policy.

[6] For further details, see Bank of England (2023b).

As for other central banks, the exit from QE has led the BoE to adopt an implementation framework where the stance of monetary policy is adjusted by steering the policy rate (Bank Rate) in an environment with an ample supply of bank reserves. The aggregate level of reserves is determined by the quantity of asset purchases/sales, and it exceeds by far the amount needed by banks to manage their day-to-day liquidity needs. This market condition keeps the wholesale market interest rates close to the Bank Rate, which is the reservation rate for financial intermediaries trading in the Sterling Money Market.

According to the BoE, this floor system "has proved successful in ensuring overnight rates in wholesale markets remain stable and close to Bank Rate. Overnight wholesale interest rates were closer to Bank Rate on average in the years following the introduction of the floor system than at any point in the preceding twenty years. .. The regime in place prior to the MPC launching its policy of QE, known as 'reserves averaging', was also successful at controlling interest rates when the stock of reserves was relatively stable. But it did not cope as well when demand for reserves spiked, so we injected large quantities of reserves for liquidity insurance purposes during the crisis".[7] These statements of the UK central bank support the view, taken in this book (see Chapter 3), that the floor system performs better than the corridor system in keeping the money market rates in line with the policy rates.

Looking ahead, the BoE plans to continue unwinding the asset purchases accumulated in previous years. This process, together with the repayment of the loans made under the TFSME, implies a decline in the supply of bank reserves, until the stock of reserves will eventually approach the minimum level needed by banks. At that point, banks might begin bidding for reserves at rates higher than Bank Rate, impairing the transmission of monetary policy. According to BoE's estimates, that point is presumably several years away, given the current (mid-2023) level of excess reserves and the pace of asset sales. To avoid any shortage of bank reserves at the steady state, the BoE has introduced a new open market operation, the *Short-Term Repo* (STR). This facility allows market participants to borrow central bank reserves for a one-week period in exchange for high-quality, highly liquid assets. It is priced at Bank Rate and the supply of reserves made available through this facility is unlimited. These

[7] See Bank of England (2023a), page 11.

features are aimed at keeping the money market rates in line with the Bank Rate, by ensuring banks have no need to bid for reserves at rates above the Bank Rate.

According to the BoE, "the STR will allow the MPC to focus solely on monetary policy considerations in setting its strategy for APF unwind, without concern for the Bank's ability to align short-term market interest rates close to Bank Rate. Without the STR, in order to maintain control of short-term market interest rates the MPC would have to reconsider APF unwind at the point that upwards pressure on market rates began to appear, whether or not that was optimal from a monetary policy perspective". At the steady state, "this framework will allow the Bank to retain the flexibility to expand or contract its balance sheet as needed to achieve its statutory policy objectives, while maintaining control of short-term interest rates".[8]

This statement highlights one important point. In the normalization process and in the "new normal", the Bank of England intends to use both the balance sheet and the interest rate policies to adjust the stance of monetary policy. In doing this, it will exploit the decoupling principle that we have introduced in Chapter 3, enabling the central bank to use balance sheet and interest rate policies as two independent instruments. This approach is quite different from that taken by the Fed. The latter (as we have seen in the previous chapter) has used both tools to tighten the stance of its policy during the normalization process started in 2022, but it has also announced that in the new normal (once the target level for bank reserves has been reached) the balance sheet policy will have a technical role only, namely to keep the amount of reserves sufficiently ample.

Figure 6.3 illustrates the normalization process of monetary policy in the UK. After the QE policy, leading to an expansion of the BoE's balance sheet, the QT policy implies a decline of the central bank's securities holdings and of bank reserves accordingly, until the supply of reserves approaches the minimum level needed by banks. Starting at this point, the stock of reserves will not be determined by the pace of asset sales anymore, but it will be endogenously determined by the demand for reserves made by the banking system: banks will be able to meet their demand through use of the STR. The outcome of the normalization

[8] See Bank of England (2022).

process will be a "demand-driven floor system", which differs considerably from the "supply-driven floor system" adopted by the Fed (see the discussion in Sect. 3.4.3).

A feature of the BoE's approach to the normalization of its policy is that banks are able to deposit and borrow money from the central bank *at the same rate*, while other central banks generally apply a penalizing rate to their lending facilities (e.g. the discount window in the US and the Marginal Lending Facility in the euro area).[9] By both supplying and remunerating reserves at Bank Rate, the BoE intends to ensure that banks have no need to pay up in money markets for reserves (since they can borrow additional reserves at Bank Rate through the STR facility) or to lend excess reserves below Bank Rate (since they can earn Bank Rate by holding reserves at the central bank). This framework should be able to

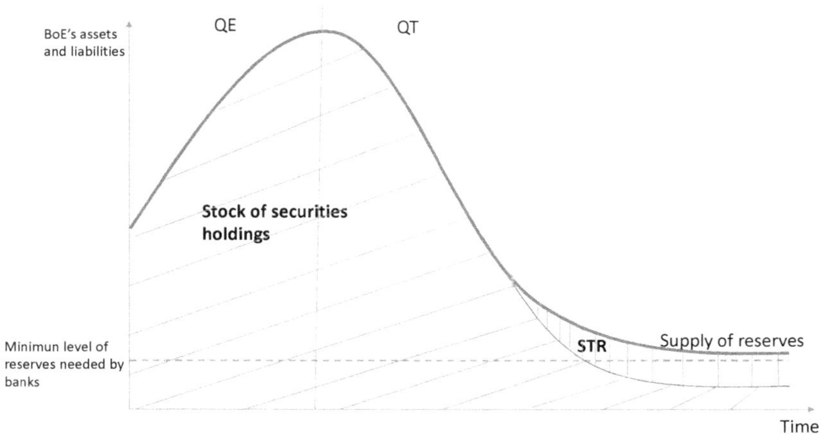

Fig. 6.3 UK: stylized supply of bank reserves during the normalization process

[9] Actually, the BoE's market operations include the *Operational Standing Facility*, enabling banks either to borrow or deposit money overnight at the central bank at penalizing rates: 25 basis points above and below the Bank Rate, respectively. However, the main purpose of this facility is helping banks to manage any unexpected payment shocks that could arise due to technical problems in payment and settlement infrastructures. So, it is more related to the financial stability objective than to monetary policy implementation. See Bank of England (2023b).

keep the money market rates in line with the Bank Rate, which remains the main tool to implement monetary policy in the UK.

6.3 Bank of Japan: QE with Yield Curve Control

In the history of monetary policy, the Bank of Japan (BoJ) occupies a special position. On the one hand, it is often remembered for being the first in the international scene to have adopted unconventional policies, in particular quantitative easing. On the other hand, it has been accused in the past of having acted late and weakly, thus having contributed to the great depression Japan experienced in the 1990s and which lasted into the following decade. Both claims have merit, as we shall see in this section.[10]

In the 1990s, the Japanese economy experienced a decade of stagnation after the boom of the 1980s: between 1992 and 2001, average GDP growth was 0.8% per year. A long period of deflation followed, with an average annual decline in consumer prices of 0.3% between 1999 and 2012. Despite this, until 2001 the BoJ limited itself to using the conventional monetary policy instrument, i.e. interest rate management: the target on the overnight interbank rate (*call rate*) was lowered from 8% to 0.5% over four years, from 1991 to 1995. In 1998, the BoJ inaugurated the *Zero Interest Rate Policy* (ZIRP), lowering the target on the call rate to 0.25% and implementing open market operations such as to inject abundant liquidity into the banking system, so as to push the effective interbank rate towards zero (see Fig. 6.4). The communication used at that time by the BoJ anticipated the forward guidance that would be adopted some years later by other central banks, announcing that the very expansionary stance of its policy would be maintained until the danger of deflation had vanished.[11]

The transition to quantitative easing took place in 2001, when the operational target of monetary policy became the overall size of the balances held by the banking system on current accounts with the BoJ. The target of monetary policy shifted from the interest rate to the size of bank reserves. The size of the BoJ's balance sheet increased as a result of the purchases of Japanese Government Bonds (JGBs) and, to a much

[10] For a more in-depth analysis of Japanese monetary policy from the 1980s until 2013, see Kuttner (2014).

[11] See the press release of April 1999.

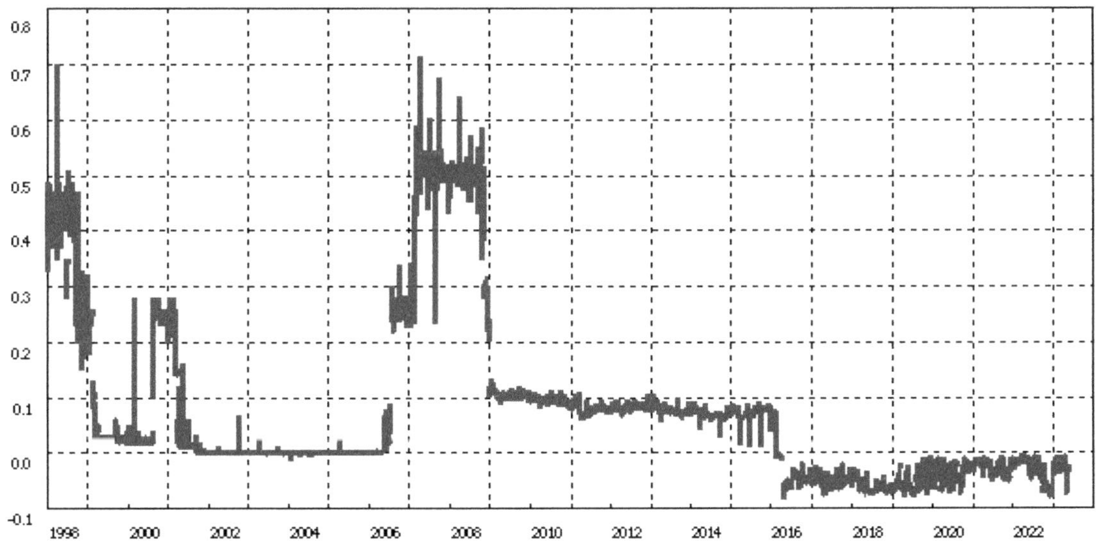

Fig. 6.4 Japan: overnight interbank rate (call rate) (percentage points—daily data 1998/1/5–2023/5/19) (*Data source* Bank of Japan Statistics)

lesser extent, private securities such as Asset-Backed Securities (ABS) and shares. To these were added short-term lending operations to the banking system (against collateral). A limitation of this policy was the fact that purchases were concentrated on *short-term* securities: at that time, the BoJ did not pursue a lowering of the whole yield curve, contrary to what other central banks, and the BoJ itself, would do some years later.

The QE policy was abandoned in 2006, although inflation was close to zero. At that time, GDP was growing at a satisfactory pace: 2% per year between 2004 and 2007. The turnaround was abrupt: by the end of 2007 the size of bank reserves had become less than a quarter of the level reached at the beginning of 2006.

Even with respect to the financial crisis of 2007/2008, which led Japan (like other countries) into recession, the BoJ reacted with some delay. It was not until October 2010 (two years after the Lehman Brothers crash) that *Comprehensive Monetary Easing* was introduced, which led the BoJ to buy several categories of financial assets in addition to government bonds: commercial paper, corporate bonds, exchange-traded funds (ETFs), and Japan real estate investment trusts (J-REITs). However, the amounts of securities purchased were rather small and did not lead to a significant increase in the size of the BoJ's balance sheet.

Kuroda's governorship marked a turning point in BoJ policy. Since 2013, Japanese monetary policy has had an inflation target of 2% (previously it was 1%). In the same year, *Quantitative and Qualitative Monetary Easing* (QQE) began, with the objective of lowering long-term interest rates by purchasing securities on longer maturities. While the term "quantitative" refers to the size of the program, the term "qualitative" refers to the type of securities being purchased: among others, long-term government bonds. The plan gave an immediate acceleration to the pace of purchases (see Fig. 6.5) with a significant impact on the size of the BoJ's balance sheet: in the first year of implementation (from February 2013 to early 2014), the central bank's total assets increased by 38%. In the same period, the average maturity of government bonds held by the BoJ rose from less than three years to over seven. The plan was enhanced in October 2014, further increasing the pace of financial asset purchases.

Since January 2016, the negative interest rate policy (NIRP) has been added to quantitative easing. By adopting *QQE with a negative interest rate*, the BoJ introduced an interest rate of −0.1% on the reserves deposited by banks in their current accounts with the central bank. To limit the burden of this policy for banks, the BoJ introduced a division

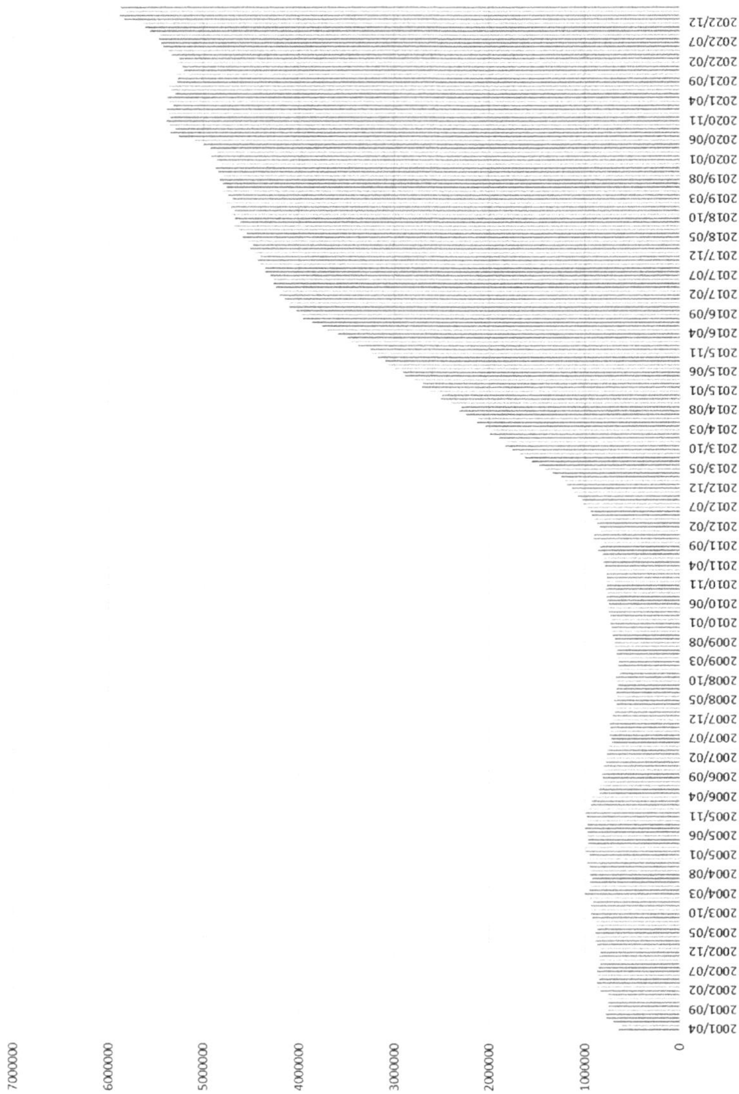

Fig. 6.5 Bank of Japan: holdings of Japanese government securities (stocks—100 million Yen—monthly data, April 2001–April 2023) (*Data source* Bank of Japan Statistics)

of bank reserves into three brackets (*three-tier system*) to which differentiated rates would be applied: +0.1%, 0, −0.1% respectively.[12] This measure, together with the abundant liquidity injected into the money market through financial asset purchases, allowed the BoJ to drive the interbank rate into negative territory: see Fig. 6.4.

In an effort to keep the whole yield curve under tight control and anchor inflation expectations to the 2% target, the BoJ introduced two important innovations in September 2016: *yield curve control* and *inflation-overshooting commitment*. By adopting *QQE with yield curve control*, the BoJ has made a commitment to keeping 10-year JGB yields around zero through its purchases of government bonds. In addition to steering short-term rates by setting the policy rate applied to bank reserves, the BoJ intervenes in the government bond market with fixed-rate purchase operations to steer the level of long-term rates, thus countering any swing in the yield curve.[13] The expansive orientation of this policy was reiterated in the forward guidance of July 2018, when the BoJ announced its willingness to maintain its policy of extremely low interest rates for an extended period of time: both short-term rates (-0.1% on bank reserves) and long-term rates (10-year JGB yields around zero).[14] A specific target range for 10-year JGB yield fluctuations has been introduced by the BoJ in March 2021: +/− 0.25% around zero.[15] To this aim, the BoJ commits to make potentially unlimited purchases ("without setting an upper limit") of government bonds.[16] In addition, the BoJ continues to implement the pre-existing programs with periodic purchases of ETFs, J-REITs, commercial paper, and corporate bonds.

The *QQE with yield curve control* differs from the QE programs adopted by other central banks, and previously by the BoJ itself, in one crucial aspect: instead of specifying the amount of securities it intends to purchase periodically, the central bank announces an interest rate target and adjusts the pace of purchases according to this target. The size of the program thus becomes endogenous. Although effective in controlling the yield curve, this policy implies some risk: namely that the central

[12] For further details, see Bank of Japan (2016a).

[13] See BoJ (2016b).

[14] See BoJ (2018).

[15] This range has been expanded to ±0.5% in December 2022. See BoJ (2022).

[16] See BoJ (2021).

bank might lose control over the size of its own balance sheet.[17] Actually, the pace of JGB purchases has dropped after the yield curve control was announced. The reason is presumably that financial market participants found the BoJ's announcement credible, given the central bank's ability to make potentially unlimited asset purchases to achieve its long-term interest rate target: this was thus largely achieved by acting on expectations.[18]

The objective of anchoring expectations is behind the redefinition of the inflation target. The *inflation-overshooting commitment* envisages that the 2% inflation target should be reached on average over the business cycle. A period of inflation below 2% must be followed by a period of inflation above 2%, in order to strengthen the credibility of the inflation target. In making this commitment, the BoJ starts from an analysis in which it emphasizes the role of adaptive expectations in lowering the expected inflation rate in the presence of an observed rate below 2%. The announcement of the inflation-overshooting commitment is intended to establish a forward-looking mechanism in the formation of expectations.[19] In fact, the BoJ has introduced in 2016 the *average inflation targeting*, anticipating the strategy that would be adopted in 2020 by the Fed (see Sect. 5.3).

References

Bank of England. (2023a). *Bank of England market operations guide: Our objectives*. London.

Bank of England. (2023b). *Bank of England market operations guide: Our tools*. London.

Bank of England. (2022). *Explanatory note: Managing the operational implications of APF unwind for asset sales, control of short-term market interest rates and the Bank of England's balance sheet*. London.

Bank of Japan. (2016a, January 29). *Introduction of "Quantitative and qualitative monetary easing with a negative interest rate"*.

Bank of Japan. (2016b, September 21). *New framework for strengthening monetary easing: "Quantitative and qualitative monetary easing with yield curve control"*.

17 See FRBNY (2018).

18 See Higgins and Klitgaard (2020).

19 See BoJ (2016b).

Bank of Japan. (2018, July 31). *Strengthening the framework for continuous powerful monetary easing*.

Bank of Japan. (2021, March 19). *Further effective and sustainable monetary easing*.

Bank of Japan. (2022, December 20). *Statement on monetary policy*.

BIS. (2019). *Unconventional monetary policy tools: A cross-country analysis* (Paper no. 63 of the Committee on the Global Financial System). Bank for International Settlements, Basel.

FRBNY. (2018). *The Bank of Japan's yield curve control policy*. Federal Reserve Bank of New York and Columbia University.

Hammond, G. (2012). *State of the art of inflation targeting*. Bank of England.

Higgins, M., & Klitgaard, T. (2020, June 22). Japan's experience with yield curve control, *Liberty Street Economics*. Federal Reserve Bank of New York.

Kuttner, K. (2014). *Monetary policy during Japan's great recession: From self-induced paralysis to Roosveltian Resolve* (PIIE Briefing). Peterson Institute for International Economics, Washington, DC.

CHAPTER 7

Future Challenges: CBDC and Greening Monetary Policy

Abstract The Central Bank Digital Currency will open up the possibility for anyone to hold central bank money in digital format. The introduction of a CBDC is motivated by the need to preserve the public nature of money, offsetting the decline in the use of cash and the proliferation of private digital payment tools. The version of CBDC generally preferred by central banks is the digital banknote: unremunerated and available in small amounts for retail payments. Albeit issued by the central bank, the CBDC will be distributed through the banking system in most countries. In this chapter, the issues related to the CBDC will be discussed in general, then some national initiatives will be reported: namely those currently taking place in China, the euro area, the UK, and the US. Central banks pay increasing attention to sustainability issues. The asset purchase programs implemented in recent years have increased the need to control their exposure to climate-related risks and to assess the impact of their investment policy on the environment. In this chapter, we will overview the initiatives taken by the Network for Greening the Financial System and discuss the sustainability policy of the ECB.

Keywords Digital payments · Digital assets · Central bank money · Digital euro · Sustainable finance · Climate-related risks · Market neutrality · ECB's action plan

A. Baglioni, *Monetary Policy Implementation*,
https://doi.org/10.1007/978-3-031-53885-8_7

7.1 Introduction

In the near future, the biggest challenge for monetary authorities will come from technology: they will have to decide whether and how to introduce a *Central Bank Digital Currency (*CBDC). Almost all central banks in the world are seriously thinking about it, but they have not gone so far as introducing it into their economies (with a few exceptions, including some pilot experiments). The introduction of a CBDC would open up the possibility for anyone to hold money issued by the central bank in digital format. So far, this possibility has been reserved for banks, which are entitled to keep their reserves on current accounts at the central bank. Individuals, to the contrary, can hold central bank money only in physical form, namely as banknotes and coins.

The impetus for central banks to consider this innovation comes from the steady decline in the use of cash, which goes in parallel with the proliferation of digital payment services, e-currencies (including stable-coins) and crypto-assets, implying relevant risks to end-users. Central banks fear the threat that private currencies pose to monetary sovereignty and control: ultimately, to the public nature of money. The implications of a CBDC for monetary policy and the economy crucially depend on its design features. If the CBDC will not be remunerated, as it is the case for most projects on the table, the implications for monetary policy will be rather negligible. If, to the contrary, a remuneration rate on the CBDC were to be implemented, that would provide an additional tool to central banks and would enhance the transmission of monetary policy, particularly in a *floor system*. Against these opportunities, the CBDC presents some risks, first of all the possibility that the banking system would be disintermediated, with negative repercussions on financial stability and the supply of credit to the economy. This risk can be controlled by imposing holding limits or disincentives to holding large sums in CBDC, like a two-tier remuneration scheme or no remuneration at all. However, there is a *trade-off*: the stronger these are, the less potential CBDC has as a means of payment/investment and as an additional monetary policy instrument. The version of CBDC prevailing in most national initiatives lies at one extreme of this trade-off: it is intended to be a pure digital banknote, unremunerated and available in small amounts for retail payments, not be seen as an investment opportunity. Finally, in most countries the CBDC will be distributed through the banking system. The central bank, which is the issuer of the digital currency, will retain control of the ledger on which CBDC transfers are recorded, while end-users will access the digital currency and use it to make payments through the services provided by banks and other authorized payment service providers (PSPs). This two-tiered model will avoid the multiplication of access points to the central bank and, at the same time, preserve the central role of banking institutions in the payment system. All these issues will be discussed in the next section, which will also provide an assessment of the national initiatives underway, focusing on China, the euro area, the UK, and the US.

The second topic addressed in this chapter goes under the name of "greening monetary policy". Central banks are increasingly involved in the issue of environmental sustainability, which has become of paramount importance for policymakers in general. Actually, sustainable finance became an issue for private investors even before central banks have begun to pay attention to it, with a huge development of ESG (Environmental, Social, and Governance) investment products. Monetary authorities are involved in this issue both in their capacity as prudential supervisors, ensuring that financial intermediaries identify and manage the climate-related risks to which they are exposed, and in their responsibility to conduct monetary policy and manage their own funds. Under this regard, they are engaged in measuring and controlling their own exposure to climate-related risks and in assessing the impact of their investment policy on the environment. Unconventional policies, with their legacy of large portfolios of financial assets (including private corporate bonds) in the balance sheet of central banks, have made this issue even more urgent than it would otherwise be.

As we shall see, central banks are taking both coordinated and individual actions to address the sustainability implications of their policies. We will briefly overview the initiatives taken by the *Network for Greening the Financial System* (NGFS), a forum involving more than one hundred central banks and supervisory authorities worldwide. Within this network, monetary authorities try to agree on best practices and guidelines in relation to the management and supervision of climate-related risks as well as to the environmental impact of their policies. As far as monetary policy implementation is concerned, there is a broad consensus among members of the NGFS that central banks should adopt adequate risk management measures to protect their balance sheets against the financial risks brought about by climate change, but there is so far no consensus about the specific measures to be taken.

We will then move to the sustainability policy of the European Central Bank. The Ecb, like other central banks, has traditionally followed the "market neutrality" criterion in the selection of securities to include in its monetary policy portfolio and in investing its own funds. The problem with this approach is that, for the reasons that we are going to see, it is not actually neutral: it is biased in favor of some companies and sectors most responsible for greenhouse gas emissions and global warming, such as heavy industry, traditional energy companies (exploiting fossil sources), and transportation. The adoption of the Ecb's Action Plan has opened the way to a departure from the market neutrality approach and it has introduced a roadmap including several initiatives, among which the inclusion of climate-related factors within the criteria used to select the securities purchased in monetary policy operations and accepted as collateral.

7.2 Central Bank Digital Currency

Almost all central banks are considering what could be the biggest challenge for them in the coming years: the introduction of a *central bank digital currency* (CBDC). This is a controversial issue: the CBDC represents a potential progress but also entails some risks. In general, central banks have not yet taken a final decision on this: here we are really at the frontier of possible developments in central banking.[1]

7.2.1 *What CBDC is? (and What Is Not?)*

We can define the CBDC as a sight liability of the central bank, available in electronic form to anyone, in particular to individuals and non-financial firms. To understand the scope of this innovation, we have to go back to the definition of base money, which we introduced in Chapter 3 and which we report here for convenience:

$$BM = R + C \tag{7.1}$$

where R stands for bank reserves and C (cash) is the stock of notes and coins in circulation. Since they are sight liabilities of the central

[1] The book edited by Niepelt (2021) collects a number of contributions discussing the economic, legal, and political implications of CBDC implementation, as well as assessing existing initiatives in several countries.

bank, those holding them can immediately convert them into other assets (financial and real) and into goods and services. In other words, both R and C can be used to make payments with immediate effect. The recipient of the payment gets "central bank money": this gives security and irrevocability to the payment itself. The fundamental difference between R and C is the following. Bank reserves are available in digital format, but only to banks: they can only be used in interbank payments. Cash can be held by anyone and used for retail payments, but it is only available in physical, not digital, format. The CBDC offers the possibility of combining the features of R and C in a single instrument: it is a central bank digital currency available to everyone and usable for retail payments.

According to the approach taken in preliminary studies made by several central banks, the CBDC should not replace bank reserves and cash, but be to some extent complementary to them. Banks will presumably continue to use the reserves deposited with the central bank to settle their payments. The role of cash is declining, but it is difficult to imagine that it will disappear altogether, at least not in all countries and in a few years' horizon. Consequently, CBDC should appear alongside R and C among the items included in the base money:

$$BM = R + C + CBDC \tag{7.2}$$

Moreover, CBDC is expected to be one of the constituent elements of money, defined as the set of short-term liabilities issued by monetary and financial institutions (including the central bank) and held by the public (households and non-financial firms). In this respect, a potential substitution effect from bank deposits to CBDC can be expected, which poses a serious problem of disintermediation of the banking system (I will expand on this below). Money should therefore be redefined as:

$$M = C + CBDC + D \tag{7.3}$$

where D stands for bank deposits. The very fact that the introduction of the CBDC would necessitate a redefinition of (base) money tells us that it represents a quite relevant conceptual innovation. Early reflections on the subject indicate that it might have significant implications for monetary policy, the banking sector and the entire economic system. The actual implications will crucially depend on the design of the CBDC, with regard both to economic and technical features. As we shall see, designing a

CBDC project poses a number of economic, technical, and organizational problems that are not easy to solve.

Before going any further, let me point out what CBDC is *not*: a crypto-currency or crypto-asset, the best-known example of which is *Bitcoin*. It is not for both economic and technical reasons. Economically, the fundamental difference is that CBDC is a currency, whereas crypto-assets are not. As is well-known, a currency is characterized by performing three functions: means of payment, store of value, and unit of account (*numeraire*). The CBDC stems precisely from the idea of making a digital currency issued by the central bank available to everyone. As such, it should be accepted in payments, not only because it is a legal tender, but also because it should enjoy the trust that everyone has in the issuer, as is the case with banknotes. It will have a fixed nominal value, being convertible at par into cash and bank deposits: as such, it can be a risk-free and perfectly liquid form of investment.[2] Of course, the unit of account should be the currency of denomination: euro in the case of the Eurosystem, dollar for the Fed, etc. In contrast, crypto-assets are a highly speculative form of investment: their market value fluctuates widely. The price formation process is opaque, as are the liquidation procedures: this makes the investment not quite liquid. In many cases, there is no clearly identifiable issuer. All this means that crypto-currencies are not generally accepted as a means of payment, with a few rare exceptions. They are therefore quite different from money: both central bank money (currency) and bank money (deposits). Finally, crypto-currencies—like Bitcoin—have a strong negative impact on the environment, due to the high amount of energy consumed by their production technology. This does not apply to the platforms currently used by some central banks to provide real-time payment services, which can be used to provide the CBDC as well.[3]

On a technical level, crypto-currencies generally rely on the *distributed ledger technology* (DLT). This is based on the decentralization and sharing of information: several parties involved in a transaction are custodians of the ledger on which the transaction is written. For reasons related to counterparty identification and confidentiality at the same time,

[2] CBDC could have a nominal yield other than zero, but we will return to this later.

[3] Tiberi (2021) estimates that the TIPS platform, operated by the Eurosystem, has an environmental impact (in terms of CO_2 emissions) 40,000 times less than the Bitcoin system.

extensive use is made of cryptography. CBDC may use DLT and cryptography for some specific purposes, but it does not generally rely on them. The prevailing model of CBDC envisages centralized management, with a single transaction register located at the central bank (*platform model*). However, banks will generally be involved to act as intermediaries between the central bank itself and the end-users, preventing them from directly accessing accounts at the central bank: direct access would pose—among others—obvious organizational problems, multiplying the number of parties that would come into contact with the central bank.

7.2.2 Why Introduce a CBDC?

What motivates central banks to introduce a CBDC? The impetus stems from the transformations that the payment system, and more generally the financial system and society as a whole, are experiencing as a result of technological innovations. Digital payment instruments are gradually marginalizing cash, which traditionally represents public money, issued by the central bank, available to all citizens and considered fully reliable. Faced with this development, it seems necessary to adapt public money to the new technologies by offering a CBDC. The alternative is to allow private digital currencies to take over in everyday use: a scenario that would imply financial risks for users, as well as problems related to competition protection and information management; it would also pose a threat to monetary sovereignty and central bank's control of money.

To analyze this issue, we must start by recalling that central banks are responsible for the proper functioning of the payment system. This means overseeing the safety and efficiency of the means by which payments flow through the economic system. Any gridlock of a payment circuit could cause major damages to the economy, hampering trade and financial transactions. For those who receive a payment, the reliability of the means by which they receive it is of paramount importance: ultimately, the collective trust in the value of money also rests on the reliance we place on the available means of payment. In this respect, maximum reliability is achieved when the beneficiary of a payment receives "central bank money", i.e. a liability issued by the central bank rather than by a private entity: a bank or another (financial and commercial) intermediary. Public money is free from credit, counterparty, and liquidity risks: it is always and immediately convertible into other assets, goods, and services.

Payment systems fall into two broad categories: wholesale and retail. Wholesale systems manage money flows circulating within the financial sector, mainly among banks. They are sophisticated systems that handle large volumes of payments, often of high unit value, particularly when the underlying transaction is financial in nature, such as securities trades. Retail systems, instead, handle payments from end-users, generally of small value and of a commercial nature. These, too, have reached a considerable degree of sophistication and can achieve a large overall size. In many countries, central banks ensure the smooth functioning of wholesale payment systems by directly operating them: this is the case, for instance, with the TARGET2 system operated by the Eurosystem (discussed in Chapter 4). On retail systems, central banks have traditionally limited themselves to a supervisory function, leaving their direct management to private entities: banks, credit card companies, and other payment service providers (PSPs). Consequently, the possibility of making a payment in central bank money has so far been reserved for wholesale payment systems: essentially for interbank transactions. The only exception is cash: this represents so far the only possibility to make a retail payment in central bank money. The introduction of a CBDC is going to be an important innovation in this respect: it will make it possible to extend the use of digital central bank money to retail payments. The security of commercial payments should increase accordingly.

The world of retail payment services is rapidly changing, driven by technological innovation and the initiative of large players in the fields of IT, communication, social networks, and logistics: the *high techs* (or *big techs*). These large companies have, in addition to huge financial resources and high technology, a valuable asset: an enormous network of contacts and information on consumers. Thanks to these resources, they can offer innovative, efficient, and low-cost payment services: in some case integrating them with the services provided by banks, in other cases as an alternative to traditional banking circuits. Some of these companies have introduced electronic currencies: the so-called *stablecoins*, which seek to combine some technical features of crypto-assets with a guarantee of convertibility and/or with an anchor to a portfolio of financial assets, in order to give stability and reliability to their value.

These developments create new opportunities but also some risks. Consumers can take advantage of innovative payment services and benefit from the competition that new entrants bring to traditional banks. Cash is being used less and less, although in some countries it still plays a relevant role. Migration to electronic forms of payment reduces anonymity and facilitates payment tracking: this is good because it hinders illegal activities and tax evasion.

However, new payment services and the issuance of digital currencies by private entities, could disintermediate the traditional monetary circuit: this relies at its core on the issuance of base money by the central bank and downstream on the issuance of bank money (deposits) by banking institutions. Bank deposits are covered by a *safety net* consisting of: (i) the loans provided by the central bank as a lender of last resort, (ii) the insurance that intervenes to reimburse depositors (up to a threshold) in the event of a bank failure, (iii) the prudential regulation and supervision exercised by the authorities. Any private currencies and payment services outside the banking circuit do not enjoy this safety net: this implies greater risk for end-users. Market value volatility is a feature of crypto-assets. But stablecoins also pose the risk, albeit smaller, of changes in (nominal) value: they are issued in a unit of account that may differ from the reference currency and the promise of conversion at par can be broken, particularly in case of a run (when many users at the same time demand the conversion). The proliferation of private entities issuing currencies and providing payment services may increase counterparty risk, especially when the nature of these entities is far from transparent. The possible insolvency of one of these entities, implying losses for end-users, could undermine the public confidence in the payment system as a whole.[4]

Monetary authorities are concerned not only about the above-mentioned risks for the end-users of payment services, but also about the threat that private currencies pose to monetary sovereignty and control. Private currencies compete with the public money issued by the central bank, making the control of the money supply problematic. Actually, this threat comes not only from (domestic and foreign) private issuers, but also from other central banks: an individual central bank may be concerned that another central bank can issue a CBDC and make it available to the citizens of its own country, limiting its monetary sovereignty and exposing its citizens to exchange rate risk, should they decide to use it to any significant extent.

[4] The risks coming from the diffusion of stablecoins are analyzed in the report released by the G7 Working Group on stablecoins (2019).

In the end, the decision to introduce a CBDC responds to a basic need: that of keeping public money available to the economy, offsetting the progressive marginalization of cash. The public nature of money derives not only from the safety features already mentioned, but also from the network effect that characterizes the payment service sector. In a network industry, the utility of each consumer depends on the number of agents using the same service provider. This is as true for payments as it is for telephone services and social networks. The network effect naturally leads to a highly concentrated market structure, where one (or very few) player gets a very large market share: we call it a "natural monopoly". Another possible outcome is the market fragmentation between several incompatible systems: this happens when one service provider prefers to differentiate itself from the others and deny their customers access to its own network. In the presence of the externalities created by the network effect, public intervention can have two purposes: (i) to prevent a single service provider from building a monopoly position and exploiting it to the detriment of consumers; (ii) to favor, or even impose, compatibility between different systems. The CBDC responds to the need of preventing the creation of private monopolies in the retail payment sector, and of providing a means of payment that, thanks to its compatibility with private payment services, guarantees the possibility of transferring (without cost) funds between one system and another.

7.2.3 *The Implications of a CBDC for Monetary Policy*

The introduction of a CBDC might have repercussions on the management and transmission of monetary policy, as well as on the banking sector. The nature and extent of these repercussions depend on some economic features of the CBDC, such as the possible application of a remuneration and holding limits. These properties of CBDC are in principle independent of its technical and organizational characteristics, such as the information technology used and the degree of centralization in the management and distribution of CBDC to end-users (which will be discussed in Sect. 7.2.5).[5]

[5] There is a growing theoretical literature on the likely implications of introducing a CBDC for the management and transmission of monetary policy. The conclusions of this literature are crucially dependent on the assumptions made about the design features of the CBDC: in particular, the remuneration and the payment services linked to a digital

Let us start with the implications for monetary policy. In this respect, it is crucial to distinguish between two different possibilities: CBDC without or with remuneration. The first case is where CBDC does not provide for any form of remuneration. In such a case, the CBDC would be a true *digital banknote* replicating, albeit on an electronic device, the fundamental feature of physical banknotes and coins: that of having a fixed nominal value. Its purpose would essentially be to serve as a means of payment, partially replacing cash, while it would have a much more limited role as an asset for investment. If this is the option chosen by central banks (and most of them actually plan to do so, as we shall see below), the introduction of a CBDC will bear no relevant implications for monetary policy. The only effect will be to tighten the zero lower bound (ZLB) for interest rates, for the following reason.

At present, the lower limit for nominal interest rates may be considered not to be exactly zero, but somewhere in negative territory. Cash can be seen as the closest alternative to bank deposits, so the yield on cash is the reservation rate for holding liquid financial assets. The return on cash is actually negative, albeit for a small amount, because of the risks and costs related to transport, safekeeping, and insurance. Therefore, the *effective* lower bound (ELB) on interest rates is lower than the ZLB.[6] In contrast, the digital banknote has no transport/storage costs and even large holdings should present no risk. Its yield will then be exactly zero, providing a hard lower bound to the yield of other assets, primarily bank deposits.

Quite different would be the implications if the second option were chosen: a CBDC remunerated at an interest rate set by the central bank. In this case, monetary policy would have a new instrument at its disposal, with potentially important implications. Households and non-financial firms would be able to invest in a perfectly liquid and safe asset, capable of providing a return: this would become the benchmark risk-free interest rate for the entire financial system. In a floor system in particular, the rate applied to the CBDC could become the new *floor* for market rates. It would be the reservation rate for the whole economy, not only for banks:

currency account. This literature is reviewed in Infante et al. (2022) and Garratt et al. (2022), who also provide a model of monetary policy pass-through with a CBDC.

[6] See Rogoff (2017).

nobody would lend money at an interest rate lower than this. The possibilities of monetary policy transmission, by applying changes to the *floor rate*, would presumably be expanded.

The implications of the CBDC for the implementation of monetary policy differ depending on the operational framework. In the case of a traditional *corridor system*, in which the operational target of monetary policy is the overnight interest rate in the interbank market, the active management of the supply of bank reserves should be re-calibrated to account for an additional way of holding base money: see Eq. (7.2) above. The supply of reserves would still be described by Eq. (3.19), but the autonomous factors should be redefined as follows:

$$AU = FC - PS - C - CBDC \tag{7.4}$$

If the demand for CBDC were characterized by high volatility, this would pose an additional problem in estimating the liquidity needs of the banking system to be met by open market operations.

To the contrary, such volatility would not be a problem in a *floor system*, particularly so in a *supply-driven floor system*, like the *ample reserves regime* introduced in the US. As we know, in this monetary control framework, it is the large supply of reserves, exceeding the needs of the banking system, that allows the absorption of liquidity shocks avoiding any impact on the equilibrium market rate. In a *demand-driven floor system*, like the one announced by the Bank of England, the liquidity buffer available to offset fluctuations of the autonomous factors is presumably lower. In any case, if the CBDC will be introduced as a pure means of payment (this is the intention announced by several central banks), the demand for the digital currency will be more stable than in the case where it was an asset designed for investment purposes: therefore, the volatility of demand for CBDC could be a minor problem, at least after the introduction phase.

7.2.4 The Impact of a CBDC on the Banking Sector

Let us come to the consequences for the banking system: here lie the main critical issues related to the introduction of a CBDC. This will essentially offer anyone, including individuals and non-financial companies, the possibility of holding an electronic claim on the central bank that can be used in real time to make payments. It is clear that this opportunity would pose a competitive threat to the traditional banking business: deposit-taking and lending. A saver might decide to convert at least part of the sums held in his/her bank account into CBDC, if only because this gives total security. A company could do the same by diversifying the management of its liquid assets. It is also true that this competitive threat is limited by the fact that bank deposits are generally bundled with a number of services, which will not be offered by the central bank, such as: financial advice, savings management, insurance, etc. These create switching costs and make the demand for deposits rather rigid, partially sheltering a bank from potential competitors.

If the conversion of money holdings from bank deposits into CBDC were to take place on a large scale, we would witness a structural disintermediation of the banking sector: a fundamental source of funding would shrink and banks would likely be forced to downsize their assets. In addition to affecting banks, this prospect would be negative for the whole economic system, since the supply of loans to businesses and households would contract, thus interfering with the transmission of monetary policy. It is true that banks could, as an alternative to shrinking assets, expand their recourse to other sources of funding, like bonds sold to retail customers or in wholesale markets; however, these sources are generally more costly than deposits. Banks could also increase their recourse to refinancing with the central bank, but this would have side effects as well: the banking sector would become increasingly dependent on the central bank for funding, and the latter would be forced to expand its exposure to the banking system; not to mention the potential shortage of collateral assets to access refinancing from the central bank.

The substitution effect could become disruptive if some banks suffered a confidence crisis. Financial intermediation theory has shown that the interaction between banks and depositors is characterized by multiple equilibria, which in turn depend on depositors' expectations on banks' solvency. A change in expectations, generated by negative news, can trigger a jump from a normal situation to one in which there is a massive withdrawal of money deposited with a banking institution (*bank run*), making such intermediary incur a liquidity crisis.[7] Actually, retail deposits are more stable than one might think, not least because of the safety net mentioned above. Instability mostly occurs in the wholesale money

[7] There is a large literature on *bank runs*, originating from the seminal contribution of Diamond and Dybvig (1983). See Freixas and Rochet (2008) for a review.

market, but it is also true that most intermediaries operating in this market already have access to digital central bank money in the form of bank reserves. In any case, the possibility of a rapid conversion of bank deposits into CBDC might facilitate the emergence of bank runs, raising some concerns in terms of financial stability.

The risks of disintermediation of the banking sector crucially depend on the choice between the two alternatives introduced above: either an unremunerated digital banknote or a remunerated CBDC. In the first case, the crowding-out effect of bank deposits is expected to be limited, considering that bank deposits, at least time deposits, can provide a positive return: this limits the risk of structural disintermediation. This is the reason why many central banks plan to introduce an unremunerated CBDC, which should play the role of a means of payment, not that of an investment instrument. The risk of bank runs may still be an issue, since depositors might be willing to convert remunerated bank deposits into an unremunerated CBDC in case of panic. However, this kind of risk can be managed by applying holding limits and also by limiting the sums that can be converted from a bank deposit into CBDC in a short time, say in a day. Holding limits might be a feasible solution to limit bank disintermediation also in the case of a remunerated CBDC, which would then become a liquid asset available for investment purposes. There is a technical problem with this solution: once the holding limit has been reached, how would an incoming payment in central bank money (CBDC) be handled? This issue could be addressed by providing that in such a case the payment would be automatically converted into bank money and credited to the beneficiary's bank deposit.[8]

A more flexible solution would be to introduce a disincentive to hold large amounts of CBDC, by applying a *two-tier remuneration scheme*: CBDC holdings would be remunerated at some positive rate up to a certain threshold (*tier 1*); any sums exceeding such threshold (*tier 2*) would be applied a lower rate, possibly zero or even negative. To provide a further limitation to CBDC holdings, access to *tier 1* could be restricted to domestic retail savers.[9]

[8] Meller—Soons (2023) test the efficacy of holding limits, by simulating the introduction of the digital euro with balance-sheet data from over 2,000 banks located in the euro area. They find that a €3,000 holding limit per person would be successful in containing the impact of the CBDC on bank liquidity risk and funding structures.

[9] See Bindseil (2020).

A conclusion, emerging from the above discussion, is that there is a basic *trade-off*. The greater the limitations and/or disincentives to the use of the CBDC, the lower are the implied risks of financial instability and the stronger is the protection offered to the banking system against the threat of disintermediation, but the lower is the potential of the CBDC: both as a payment/investment instrument for its end-users and as an additional monetary policy instrument for the central bank. Under this regard, a pure digital banknote, available in small amounts and to be used for retail payments only, lies at one extreme of the trade-off.

7.2.5 Technical and Organizational Issues

In principle, the introduction of a CBDC might allow all citizens to hold an account at the central bank and be able to make transactions (sending and receiving payments) by directly accessing that account, as we currently do with our bank account. In practice, most central banks have indicated their preference for a (partially) decentralized design of the CBDC, which relies on the intermediation of banks and other authorized payment service providers (PSPs) for the distribution of the digital currency. Under this approach, the central bank is the custodian of the central transaction ledger, and the access to the CBDC by end-users is indirect, namely via the banking system and other PSPs. This solution has the advantage of avoiding a multiplication of access points to the central bank, which at the same time retains control of the ledger on which CBDC transfers are recorded and remains the guarantor of successful payments.

Transfers of CBDC can be of two kinds: either *on-line* or *off-line*. The first ones are channeled through the banking system and finally recorded on the central ledger, while the second ones are not. Off-line transfers of CBDC between two counterparties do not involve any other entity (financial intermediary or central bank): this way of using the digital currency mimics the transfer of physical banknotes between people, thus guaranteeing the anonymity of transactions. However, there is an obvious trade-off between the protection of confidentiality and the need to hinder illegal activities and money laundering: the latter requires the traceability of transactions, which is the reason why authorities in many countries restrict and discourage the use of cash. Therefore, confidentiality should be selectively protected: off-line payments in CBDC should only be allowed for small amounts. All the other CBDC transfers should be recorded on the ledger held by the central bank, ensuring data protection at the same time: access to personal and transaction data should be strictly restricted to the authorized parties, e.g. the financial intermediaries involved in a transaction and the legal authorities.

As far as technology is concerned, off-line transfers of CBDC could take place either by using the *distributed ledger technology* (DLT) or without, relying instead on electronic devices such as prepaid cards and smartphones. The technology, to be used in the management of the centralized ledger, could be provided by the platforms through which central banks currently channel interbank payments: for example, the TARGET2 system in the euro area. The Eurosystem already uses this platform to enable banks to provide retail customers with the service of real-time money transfers: these are the *instant payments* made possible by the TARGET *Instant Payment Settlement* (TIPS) system.

Regardless of the specific technology used, CBDC should be compatible with digital payment services offered by private operators, ensuring interoperability between different retail payment systems. In other words, the transfer of funds from one system to another should not be hindered by technical (incompatibility) or economic (fees) barriers. This is required to maximize the utility of end-users, which increases as the size of the network of compatible payment services grows large, and to support the presence of several providers in the market, thus fostering competition and innovation.

Some of the issues discussed here also emerged in the public consultation carried out by the Ecb between October 2020 and January 2021, with 8,200 participants, mostly private citizens and to a small extent professional operators such as financial intermediaries and tech companies.[10] Privacy seems to be the main concern of citizens: the protection of payment data is the most important requirement for the CBDC. However, they are also concerned that the digital euro might facilitate illegal activities: anonymity is required by a few responders only, while many participants agree that off-line transfers of digital currency should be limited to small payments. Another common need is the compatibility of the CBDC with existing banking and payment services. Diverging

[10] See ECB (2021).

interests emerge among professionals: credit institutions, fearing disintermediation, are in favor of imposing holding limits, while merchants are generally against. Regarding possible remuneration, the *two-tier* solution meets some favor, particularly in the research community.

7.2.6 National Initiatives

More than one hundred central banks in the world are doing research on CBDC and some of them have carried pilot experiments; a few have already introduced their retail CBDC.[11] Of course, these national projects differ among each other for several details, but some common features emerge, namely:

- *No remuneration*: virtually all countries plan to introduce an unremunerated CBDC.
- *Two-tier model*: the largely prevailing organizational model[12] is one where the central bank issues the CBDC and keeps the central ledger, and all the distribution and customer-facing activities are delegated to financial intermediaries.
- *Holding limits*: many central banks have announced their intention to put limitations to the amounts of CBDC that each individual will be allowed to hold in their "digital wallets".
- *On-line and off-line transactions*: in general, citizens will be able to make both kind of transactions, on-line and off-line, where the latter should be limited to small-value retail payments.

The reasons behind these choices have already been discussed above. Let me expand here on the experiences of a few countries: China, the euro area, the UK, and the US.

China. Among these countries, China is the one where the introduction of a CBDC is at the most advanced stage. The first prototype of digital Yuan goes back to 2016, and starting in 2020 the citizens of 23

[11] For details, see the data reported by Lukonga (2023). See also the BIS (2022) survey of 81 central banks: the share of them actively engaged in CBDC work has been steadily increasing over the last few years and it reached 90% in 2021.

[12] Among the central banks surveyed in BIS (2022), 70% are considering a two-tier model.

pilot areas in 15 different Chinese provinces have been able to download some amounts of money in digital Yuan on their smartphones and hold them in *e-wallets*. End-users make this kind of operations through their banks or through the two largest payment service providers in the country: Alipay and WeChatPay. As of end-2021, more than 250 million Chinese people have opened an e-wallet in digital Yuan.[13] The Chinese authorities tried to exploit the 2022 Olympic games to expand the distribution of the digital Yuan to foreign people: in the end, this project has been only partially successful, also because of the Covid-19 pandemic.

The diffusion of the digital Yuan has been further supported by the prohibition, introduced by the People Bank of China in 2021, of making transactions in private crypto-currencies and stablecoins: since then, the only digital currency available to Chinese people to make payments is the public digital Yuan. This move by the Chinese authorities can be seen as a way to gain access to a huge amount of information coming from the mass of retail transactions made by Chinese people. So far, the ability to accumulate this kind of information has been retained by the two large private players: Alipay and WeChatPay. It is also true that the diffusion of the digital Yuan has been presumably favored by the fact that Chinese people are already used to make their payments in electronic money: in Chinese towns, more than 90% of retail payments are made with smartphones and they are handled by Alipay and WeChatPay.[14] Under this regard, the introduction of the digital Yuan responds to the need of providing an alternative to these two private monopolistic platforms.

The digital Yuan shares the above listed features with the planned CBDCs of many other countries. It differs from other projects (like the ones reported below) as it includes the possibility of making the digital currency ***programmable***: in some pilot experiments, the amounts of digital Yuan made available could be used for some specific transactions only and not for general purposes. Finally, the introduction of the digital Yuan can respond to the intention of fostering the international role of the Chinese currency, trying to threaten the dominant position so far enjoyed by the US dollar.

Euro area. In the euro area, the project relative to the introduction of a digital euro has been launched by the Ecb in October 2020, with a report

[13] See Duffie and Economy (2022).

[14] Again, see Duffie and Economy (2022).

outlining the available design options.[15] In the Ecb's view, the reasons for introducing a digital euro, to complement the physical euro banknotes and coins, are essentially the need to preserve the role of public money in the economy, in presence of a constant decline in the use of cash, and to protect the currency's function as a single unit of account in the payment system. The currency issued by the central bank provides an anchor to the monetary system, which is designed following a hybrid model: the central bank provides the base money, while the private sector provides end-users with payment solutions relying on commercial bank money. Other related objectives pursued by the Ecb are: (i) to preserve the European monetary sovereignty, considering that most e-payment services in the euro area are currently provided by companies located outside the EU, and (ii) to support the international role of the euro, offsetting the emergence of other CBDCs which could be used across the borders.[16]

The design of the digital euro exhibits all the above listed features. In particular, the distribution will be delegated to banks and other private PSPs; in addition, some public entities—such as local authorities and post offices—may be designated by the Member States as points of access to the digital euro[17]. End-users will be free to choose between an app provided by such financial intermediaries and an app directly provided by the Eurosystem. Authorized intermediaries will be required to provide (for free) some basic core services, e.g. opening and closing a digital euro account, making transfers and payments (including recurring payments), funding and defunding functionalities, transaction initiation and confirmation. On top of these, banks and PSPs will be free to provide other optional and value-added services, like: pay-per-use enabled via pre-authorization, delivery-versus-payment, splitting payments between multiple payers, and conditional payments. The latter refer to payments that are automatically executed when predefined conditions are met. They should not be mistaken for programmable money, which would entail some units of digital euro being used only to buy specific types of goods/ services. The Ecb has made clear that the digital euro will not be a programmable money, as this would contradict the principle, endorsed

[15] See ECB (2020a).

[16] See ECB (2022a).

[17] In particular, post offices can be a useful point of access for those who do not hold a bank account, thereby contributing to financial inclusion.

by the Governing Council, of guaranteeing the convertibility at par of the digital euro with other forms of the currency (like cash and bank money).[18]

The intermediated distribution model will ensure the protection of personal data. The Ecb will be the issuer of digital euros, but it will not have access to any personal information. More specifically, it will not be able to identify individual end-users and to know what they do with their digital money (this holds for both on-line and off-line payments); it will have access to encrypted data to the extent needed to settle online transactions and support banks and PSPs in performing their tasks.

For financial stability reasons and to avoid a disintermediation of the banking sector, holding limits will be applied, so as to limit the store of value function of the digital euro, which is intended to be a means of payment and should not be seen as an investment option. For the same reasons, no remuneration will be applied to digital euro accounts: the Eurosystem does not intend to develop any functionality to remunerate digital euro holdings. Any individual will be allowed to open several digital euro accounts; in such a case, the holding limit will apply *per person*, i.e. across his/her different accounts. The exact individual limit will be established by the Ecb at some future date closer to the actual implementation of the digital euro. For businesses, merchants, government, and other public authorities the Ecb has already announced that the holding limit will be set to zero[19].

Payments exceeding the holding limit will be handled by an automatic transfer of funds from the digital euro account to the commercial bank account of the payee: this is called the "waterfall" functionality. Symmetrically, the "reverse waterfall" functionality will automatically transfer funds from the commercial bank account to the digital euro account when the digital euro holdings of the payer are not sufficient to complete a payment. This funding process will result in a digital euro issuance, whereby some PSP's central bank money holdings will be converted into digital euros: the commercial bank's account at the central bank will be debited and the digital euro holdings of the end-user will be credited (of course, his/her commercial bank account will be debited accordingly). In the end, some base money will change hands, being transferred from the

[18] See ECB (2023a).

[19] See ECB (2023d).

bank to its client, similarly to what happens when a bank provides physical cash to its depositors. To meet the zero holding limit, business users and public authorities will have any payment received transferred immediately to their commercial bank account, and any payment they make will be instantly funded from their commercial bank account.

On top of holding limits set by the Ecb, transfers of funds from commercial bank accounts into digital euro holdings will also be subject to the conditions each PSP may establish for its own clients concerning the level of funds that can be withdrawn on a periodic (say daily) basis, as is the case for other payments and cash withdrawals today. While these transaction limits are motivated by fraud management considerations, they may also enhance financial stability.

Both on-line and off-line transactions in digital euros will be available. The latter, in particular, can be made without an internet connection, as long as there is physical proximity between the devices of the payer and the payee: as we said already, this way of using the digital money mimics the use of physical cash, including privacy and no intervention by third parties. Specific limits will be set to the size of off-line payments, in order to avoid the use of the digital currency for money laundering or other illegal activities.

Although the final decision to issue the digital euro falls within the sole competence of the Ecb, the above design features are the outcome of the coordination between the Ecb itself and the EU Commission. The latter has issued a formal Proposal for a Regulation on the establishment of the digital euro in June 2023.[20] Among other things, the Regulation includes the rules granting the digital euro the status of "legal tender", which means that merchants located in the euro area need to accept payments in digital euro from consumers, as it happens for cash. To safeguard the function of cash as a means of payment, in the face of the progressive digitalization of payments and of "no-cash policies", the Commission has issued another Regulation Proposal on the legal tender status of euro banknotes and coins,[21] regulating the exact meaning of legal tender for the existing physical currency and ensuring consistency between the two forms of public money: physical and digital euro.

[20] COM (2023) 369 final.

[21] COM (2023) 364 final.

In October 2023, the Ecb has completed the two-year investigation phase, the findings of which (reported in Ecb 2023d) have provided the basis for the decision taken by the Governing Council to launch the next phase of the project: the preparation phase, started on 1 November 2023 and planned to last two years.[22] In this phase, the Eurosystem will finalize the digital euro rulebook and select providers to develop the platform and infrastructure. This phase, which also includes testing and experimentation of technical solutions and functionalities, will pave the way to the final decision to issue the digital euro. While this decision is expected to be taken in a few years, it will be officially considered by the Governing Council only after the legislation on this matter (namely the two above-mentioned Commission's proposals) is adopted.

United Kingdom. The Bank of England's approach[23] to the introduction of the CBDC is very similar to that of the Ecb. The basic reasons behind the introduction of a digital pound are the decline of cash as a means of payment and the proliferation of cards and other private digital payment services: hence the need to provide a public digital money, free from credit, market, and liquidity risks. The organizational model is the above-mentioned two-tier model ("platform model" in BoE's terminology). The BoE issues the digital pound and provides the central infrastructure, while banks and other private (approved) financial firms provide the interface between the BoE and consumers: they will offer "digital wallets" to end-users, where to store their digital pounds and make transactions. Such wallets may be integrated into other payment services provided by financial intermediaries. In order to protect privacy, the holdings of digital pounds will be recorded anonymously on the BoE's core ledger; end-users will directly interact with their wallets only and not with the central bank. The BoE has explicitly excluded monetary policy as a motivation for introducing the digital pound: this is not intended to be an additional tool to implement monetary policy. For this reason, no interest (either positive or negative) will be paid on digital pound holdings. The digital pound is intended to be a means of payment (digital banknote), not a savings product. To limit its potential impact on the banking sector, the BoE plans to put holding limits: an individual limit

[22] See the press release "Eurosystem proceeds to the next phase of digital euro project", 18 October 2023.

[23] See BoE (2023).

between £10.000 and £20.000 has been proposed. Based on the roadmap outlined by the UK authorities (BoE and Treasury), the process that may lead to the introduction of a digital pound is currently in the "design" phase, including the technical development and the design of the platform. At the end of this phase, around the middle of the decade, a decision will be made on whether or not to proceed to the "build" phase, including the development of prototypes and the execution of pilot tests. The final "launch decision" will presumably be taken in the second half of the decade.

USA. Contrary to the central banks examined so far (PBOC, Ecb and BoE) the Federal Reserve Bank is still at an early stage in considering the introduction of a CBDC. The Fed is currently in the research and consultation phase, comparing the different options on the table and seeking for comments from the public. It is active in doing experiments related to a hypothetical CBDC.[24] No schedule has been released as to the steps to be taken in the coming years and when a final decision will be made. Before proceeding with the issuance of a CDBC, the Fed will need the approval of the US Congress.

The motivations for introducing a CBDC in the US are the ones already discussed in general. The decline in the use of cash (the share of cash payments over total has declined from 31 to 20% in the five years up to 2022) and the emergence of private digital currencies (stablecoins and crypto-currencies) make it necessary to preserve the role of public money in the economy. In the case of US, a specific motivation is the need to preserve the international role of the dollar, which is currently the most widely used currency in cross-border payments and investments: this reduces the transaction and borrowing costs for US households, businesses, and Government. The emergence of other CBDCs in the world might threaten the dominant position enjoyed by the US dollar in the global financial system.[25]

[24] Examples include: (i) a multiyear exploratory research project (*Project Hamilton*), conducted by the Boston Fed in collaboration with MIT's Digital Currency Initiative, to investigate the technical feasibility of a CBDC that could be used by an economy the size of the United States, (ii) an Innovation Center at the New York Fed to facilitate collaboration with the BIS on a number of financial innovations, (iii) a Technology Lab at the Board of Governors that has several CBDC experiments under way.

[25] See Brainard (2022).

The discussion paper released by the Fed in January 2022, which has provided the basis for a public consultation, leaves several issues open.[26] One thing that has been already defined is the organizational model: the introduction of a digital US dollar, if any, will rely on the intermediated (two-tier) model. The Federal Reserve Act does not authorize direct Fed accounts for individuals. The management of CBDC holdings and payments will be done via commercial banks and other regulated financial service providers, which will provide end-users with digital dollar accounts and digital wallets. The intermediated model will rely on private sector's existing privacy and identity-verification tools. The adoption of an unremunerated CBDC together with the application of holding limits are considered by the Fed good options to preserve financial stability and to limit the disintermediation of bank deposits; however, no decision on these matters has been taken so far.

As far as monetary policy is concerned, the Fed's discussion paper argues that under that current "ample reserves regime", where the daily fluctuations in the quantity of bank reserves generally have little effect on the level of the federal fund rate and other short-term interest rates, the volatility of the demand for a non-interest-bearing CBDC would not be a problem for the implementation of monetary policy, provided the supply of bank reserves remains large enough to provide an adequate buffer to offset such fluctuations: the ability of the central bank to keep the FF rate in line with its target would not be affected. If, to the contrary, the CBDC were remunerated at levels comparable to other safe assets, the interaction between CBDC and monetary policy would be more pronounced and complex: on the one hand, the level and volatility of the public's demand for CBDC could be quite substantial; on the other hand, the rate applied to the CBDC could be a new policy tool in the hands of the central bank. These conclusions are in line with the arguments made in the above discussion (subsection 7.2.3).

[26] See Fed (2022) and Fed (2023).

7.3 Greening Monetary Policy

7.3.1 *Sustainable Finance and the Role of Public Policy*

The topic of environmental sustainability has entered the agenda of central banks in the wake of the enormous development that ESG (*Environmental, Social, and Governance*) issues have had in recent years, gaining centrality in the public policy debate. The financial sector has quickly adapted to this trend: the market for sustainable investments, from ESG-funds to green bonds, is expanding worldwide. Among sustainable investment strategies, the most common is *negative screening*, which excludes certain sectors or companies, such as those that are particularly polluting (linked to fossil fuels) or active in the production of weapons or tobacco, from the investment targets. Alongside this, other strategies are increasingly adopted: (i) the inclusion of ESG factors in the financial analysis guiding the asset allocation of investment funds, (ii) the selection of the best companies, on the basis of ESG-scores, in their sector of activity (*positive screening/best-in-class*), (iii) active participation in the life of the target company, at least at the shareholders' meeting, to guide its choices according to sustainability criteria (*corporate engagement* and *shareholder action*). A remarkable trend is the growing interest of retail investors in sustainable investments, which often leads them to give up part of their return in order to invest in "green" securities: several studies have documented the existence of a negative yield premium (*negative greenium*) that allows issuers to pay (on average) lower yields on green bonds than on conventional bonds.[27]

Policymakers act in the area of sustainability along several dimensions. One is *fiscal policy*, through the investment of public funds to foster the conversion to a "carbon-free" economy. Think for example of the huge public spending programs introduced in Europe in the last few years: Green Deal, Next generation EU (which includes a large share devoted to green policies), and Repower EU. Another line of action is *regulation*. After many years in which the classification of sustainable economic activities and investments remained in the hands of private entities and associations of financial intermediaries, the need has emerged

[27] See, for example, Ehlers and Packer (2017). An EU study (Fatica et al., 2019) documents how the *greenium* is significantly higher for corporate and supra-national issuers than for financial issuers, such as banks: for the latter, it seems to be more difficult to signal their commitment to green project financing.

for a regulation introducing commonly accepted classification criteria and transparency requirements. The European strategy in this area was outlined in the EU Commission's *Action Plan on financing sustainable growth* (March 2018), which takes as a starting point the 2015 Paris Agreement and the fundamental goal of limiting global warming to below 2 °C (increase over pre-industrial level). The Action Plan includes several initiatives aimed at channeling private funds towards sustainable investments, including climate-related risks into risk management practices, and fostering transparency. Downstream of the Action Plan, several steps have been taken: from the *Taxonomy of Sustainable Activities* to non-financial reporting requirements for corporations (*Corporate Sustainability Reporting Directive*) and disclosure requirements for investment products (*Sustainable Finance Disclosure Regulation*), to the definition of European standards (EU *green bond standard* and *Ecolabel*).

Two policy tools that can be used, in addition to their traditional tasks, to pursue sustainability goals are in the hands of central banks: *banking supervision* and *monetary policy*. In the first area, central banks are engaged (together with other authorities) in supervising that financial intermediaries (banks, investment funds, and insurance companies) put in place adequate policies to control the risks related to climate change: physical risks (related to extreme events such as hurricanes and floods) and transition risks. The latter are due to the conversion process towards a sustainable economy, which may make some economic activities obsolete (think of coal and oil extraction) and impose high adaptation/conversion costs on some productive sectors (think of the energy sector). Climate-related risks can have a relevant impact on the level of financial risk to which banks and other financial intermediaries are exposed to. Through multiple transmission channels, both physical and transition risks can turn into some of the typical banking risks: credit, market, liquidity, and operational risks.[28]

In the EU, the *European Banking Authority* (EBA) has issued guidelines[29] that require credit institutions to include ESG factors in their risk management policies, in particular for credit risk: risk assessment procedures must consider the possible impact of climate risks on borrowers' financial condition. The EBA guidelines are not binding, but competent

[28] See BIS (2021) and Bolton et al. (2020).

[29] See EBA (2020).

supervisory authorities (including the ECB) are expected to comply with them, unless a motivation to the contrary is given. In December 2022, the EBA has released a roadmap on sustainable finance covering several areas, such as: transparency and market discipline, risk management and stress testing, and prudential treatment of exposures.[30]

In November 2020, the ECB issued a *Guide on climate-related and environmental risks*,[31] in which it outlines its supervisory expectations regarding the management and reporting of risks related to climate change. The Guide, albeit not formally binding, provides the standards to which banks should align. It covers several areas, such as: strategy, governance, organization, risk measurement and management, and non-financial reporting. The ECB's expectations require banks to adapt their organization and decision-making processes to take account of climate and environmental factors. As part of its supervisory activity, the ECB conducted in 2022 its first climate stress test on 104 significant banks in the euro area.[32] The main purpose of the exercise is to assess the banks' ability to conduct internal stress analyses in relation to climate risks: in particular, the banks' ability to develop a framework for analyzing climate risk, to estimate different climate risk factors, and to make projections in this area.

With regard to monetary policy, the large asset purchase programs, carried out under the QE policies, raise an issue: which is the environmental impact of central banks' investment decisions, in particular of corporate bond purchases? The question applies even after a central bank has eventually abandoned the QE policies, since the securities portfolio accumulated has to be managed for several years ahead: the central bank has to decide whether and how to re-invest the proceeds from maturing securities. A similar problem arises in relation to the range of assets accepted as collateral in central bank's lending operations to the banking sector. In addition, central banks have to manage their own reserves, held for purposes other than monetary policy: these can also play an important role in channeling financial resources towards the most environmentally virtuous activities. Given the public nature of their mandate, it seems natural for central banks to take account of the externalities arising from

[30] See EBA (2022).

[31] See ECB (2020b).

[32] See ECB (2022b).

the impact of their investment decisions on the environment. Some initiatives have already been taken on this front, others are under discussion. In the following, we will focus on the activities of the *Network for Greening the Financial System* (NGFS), involving many central banks, and on the policies introduced by the ECB in this area.

7.3.2 The Network for Greening the Financial System

The NGFS, established in December 2017, is a forum among 127 central banks and supervisory authorities worldwide, which aims to define best practices in relation to the management and supervision of climate-related risks in the financial sector and the mobilization of resources in favor of the environment. The documents produced by the NGFS are not binding, but work as a coordination device among the several institutions belonging to the network. In its first report, *A Call for Action*,[33] the NGFS formulated six recommendations, addressed primarily to central banks and supervisors, but also to financial intermediaries. They range from the need to incorporate environmental risks into the risk management policy of financial institutions, and the related prudential supervision, to the transparency criteria to be adopted in relation to these issues. For our purposes, the most relevant recommendation is to incorporate sustainability factors into the management of central banks' financial resources: primarily their own funds, but potentially also the financial assets purchased under monetary policy operations.

The latter recommendation has been expanded in a second document: a sort of "sustainable investment guide" addressed to central banks[34]. It starts by distinguishing between the different types of portfolios held by central banks:

1. *Policy portfolio*: assets accumulated under asset purchase programs and other monetary policy operations; foreign exchange reserves.
2. *Own portfolio*: assets held as investments of the own funds (paid-up capital, general reserves and provisions for financial risks) and not for monetary policy purposes.
3. *Pension portfolio*: assets allocated to retirement funds.

[33] See NGFS (2019a).

[34] See NGFS (2019b).

4. *Third-party portfolio*: assets held on behalf of third parties, e.g. local governments. For the Eurosystem, this category includes foreign exchange reserves held by national central banks.

Flexibility in the management of financial resources, including the possibility of applying sustainability criteria, varies according to the type of reserves. It is higher for the *own portfolio*. For the *policy portfolio*, it is limited by the institutional purposes related to monetary policy and by the principle of *market neutrality* (see below). For the *pension portfolio*, a constraint comes from the need to ensure a return to stakeholders, while for the *third-party portfolio* it comes from the fact that the financial resources are not fully available.

Environmental factors, for central banks as well as other financial institutions, can be considered in both directions: from the environment to investments and vice-versa. On the one hand, we should consider the risks, both physical and transitional, that may affect the value of financial assets. On the other, we should consider the environmental impact of investments, measured by the intensity of the greenhouse gas emissions made by the financed entities. For a company, the volume of emissions can be measured as a ratio to the company's size; for public debt securities, the volume can be measured as a ratio to GDP or *per capita*.

Among possible investment strategies, the most frequently used is the *negative screening* approach, namely the exclusion of issuers operating in controversial sectors (e.g. armaments or highly polluting productions): their exclusion from the range of possible investment targets contributes to the reputation of central banks. Reputational issues may play a role in the sustainable investment strategy of central banks, especially for those that require supervised financial intermediaries to control climate-related risks and to include ESG factors into their business strategies. The *best-in-class* approach, namely the selection of the most virtuous companies in a sector as a target for investment, is less frequently followed, since it implies a strong dependence on indices and ESG-scores provided by private rating agencies. Finally, a tool commonly used by central banks to implement their sustainable investment strategy is the purchase of green bonds.

Environmental issues have implications not only for the allocation of central banks' investments, but also for the conduct of monetary policy through their impact on macroeconomic variables.Consider, for example, the effects of transition policies towards a carbon-free economy on the prices of different energy sources and thus on inflation; more generally, the effects of such policies on the allocation of investment, production, and consumption. The NGFS recommends that central banks take environmental factors into account in their macroeconomic and forecasting models, in assessing the transmission channels of monetary policy, in designing their strategy, and in their communication policy.[35]

The NGFS has paid specific attention to the operational framework of monetary policy. In a report devoted to this topic, it recommends that central banks "consider the effect of climate-related risks on their operations as well as the effects of their actions on exposures of other entities, including the financial sector, to climate-related risks"[36]. However, while there is a broad consensus among members of the NGFS that central banks should adopt additional risk management measures to protect their balance sheets against the financial risks brought about by climate change, there is so far no consensus about the specific measures to be taken. Table 7.1 provides a summary of the wide range of different options on the table.

Finally, the NGFS has provided a guide for central banks on producing their own climate-related disclosures.[37] Under this regard, monetary authorities are expected to lead by example and to demonstrate accountability. The guide covers three areas: governance, strategy, and risk management. (i) Central banks should report how their governance structures for monetary policy, asset management, financial stability, and internal operations encompass climate-related risks. Disclosures should reflect the different portfolios of assets held for various goals as part of their institutional functions. (ii) Central banks should disclose their strategies for identifying and assessing inward and outward impacts of climate factors on their activities. Disclosures should report any adaptation of areas and functions, as well as changes to the operational framework. (iii) Central banks are recommended to describe how climate-related risks are integrated into their existing risk-management frameworks. Disclosures should include the methodologies to identify and assess climate-related exposures associated with credit facilities and investment portfolios, as well as data sources and limitations.

[35] See NGFS (2020).

[36] See NGFS (2021a).

[37] See NGFS (2021b).

Table 7.1 Options for adjusting the operational framework to climate-related risks

	Asset purchases
Tilting approach	Skew asset purchases according to climate-related risks of issuers
Negative screening	Exclude some issuers from purchases if they fail to meet climate-related criteria
	Credit operations
Pricing	Make the interest rate for lending facilities conditional on the extent to which a counterparty's lending is contributing to climate change mitigation
Eligibility	Make access to some lending facilities conditional on a counterparty's disclosure of climate-related information or on its low-carbon/green investments
	Collateral
Haircuts	Adjust haircuts to account for climate-related risks of pledged assets
Negative screening	Exclude otherwise eligible collateral assets, based on their issuers' climate-related risk profile
Positive screening	Accept sustainable collateral so as to incentivize banks to fund projects/ assets that support environmentally-friendly activities (e.g. green bonds/ loans)
Collateral pools	Require counterparties to pledge collateral such that it complies with a climate-related metric at an aggregate pool level

Source Adapted from NGFS (2021a)

7.3.3 The Ecb from Market Neutrality to Green Monetary Policy

The environmental sustainability objective is within the scope of the Ecb's mandate: not only because climate change affects price stability and the transmission of monetary policy, but also because the Ecb has a statutory duty to provide support for EU policies aimed at ensuring sustainable growth for EU Member States, although this second objective is conditional on not conflicting with price stability (as we have seen in Chapter 4).[38] The measures recently taken (reported below) contribute to align the Ecb's policy with the general orientation of the EU, which

[38] Arguments supporting this view have been provided by two members of the Executive Board: Schnabel (2021) and Elderson (2021).

aims to channel financial flows, both private and public, towards sustainable investments. Sustainability is among the issues addressed in the Ecb's 2020/21 strategy review.

It is also true that the Ecb must contribute to realizing the principles of free market and efficient allocation of resources, affirmed by the EU Treaty (Art. 127). For this reason, asset purchase programs, especially corporate bond purchases, should follow the principle of *market neutrality*, according to which purchase operations should not distort the market (relative) pricing mechanism, even though they are obviously intended to have an impact on the general level of yields. At the operational level, this translates into a composition of the policy portfolio that replicates the basket of securities available for purchase and able to meet the criteria to be included in a specific program: the so-called "*eligible universe*".

The problem with market neutrality is that, from an environmental perspective, such principle is not actually neutral and it conflicts with sustainability. The reason is that, in the corporate bond market, some large companies, operating in the most polluting sectors, are over-represented: the value of their bond issues is generally higher than their relative size. As a consequence, the eligible universe is skewed towards sectors characterized by higher levels of polluting emissions: heavy industry, fossil energy, and transportation. In contrast, the service sector, which is generally less polluting, is under-represented. One factor behind this distortion of the market portfolio is that the most polluting companies are often those with more physical capital, which can be pledged as collateral for issuing debt securities. Another factor may be that innovative companies, such as those active in the renewable energy sector, generally raise more funds through equity (like venture capital) rather than debt securities. Whatever the origin, the distortion of the eligible universe is mirrored in the distortion of the purchases made by the Eurosystem under the *Corporate Sector Purchase Programme* (CSPP), the composition of which has been guided until recently by the market neutrality principle: this has led the Eurosystem to hold a portfolio of corporate bonds unbalanced in favor of the more polluting companies.[39]

[39] See the evidence provided by Papoutsi, Piazzesi, and Schneider (2021). The relationship between market neutrality and environmental sustainability is discussed in Bernardini et al. (2021).

For the above reasons, the principle of market neutrality has been questioned in the policy debate. Indeed, it should be amended to take account of environmental sustainability factors. One direct approach in this direction is to exclude certain sectors, which are particularly polluting, from the (corporate) asset purchase programs. Another, more indirect, way of addressing this issue is the so-called "tilting approach", which consists in changing the composition of the basket of corporate bonds under purchase: under-weighting those issued by companies operating in carbon-intensive sectors (e.g. oil, gas, and raw materials) and over-weighting other bonds that are characterized by lower carbon-intensity (CO_2 emissions per unit of production/sales).[40] In this way, the central bank could help reduce the cost of debt for the less carbon-intensive companies. As for companies operating in "brown sectors", the higher cost of funding should provide an incentive to make investments aimed at reducing their negative impact on the environment. Note that these adjustments could be applied not only to net asset purchases, but also in the reinvestment of the proceeds from maturing securities. The tilting approach could also be applied to haircuts applied to assets accepted as collateral in monetary policy operations, penalizing more carbon-intensive securities with higher haircuts.

The adoption of the Ecb's Action Plan[41] to include climate change considerations in its monetary policy strategy and implementation framework opened the way to a revision of the market neutrality approach, starting from an analysis of the potential biases in the market allocation and leading to the proposal of alternative benchmarks for the purchase of financial assets, in particular within the CSPP. The Action Plan has introduced a roadmap including several initiatives, such as: the inclusion of climate-related factors within the criteria used to select the securities purchased in monetary policy operations and accepted as collateral; the introduction of sustainability disclosure requirements for private sector assets as a new eligibility criterion or as a basis for a differentiated treatment for collateral and asset purchases; an assessment of the Eurosystem's exposure to environmental risks, including climate stress tests of the Eurosystem's balance sheet; and deepening the understanding of the

[40] See Schoenmaker (2019).

[41] The Action Plan was announced together with the outcomes of the 2020–21 strategy review: see the press release of 8 July 2021.

implications of climate change, and of related policies, on the macroeconomic framework, the transmission of monetary policy, and financial stability.

Some steps of the roadmap have been implemented. The Governing Council has taken decisions addressing several issues, such as: (i) the composition of corporate bond purchases made in monetary policy operations; (ii) the criteria for selecting the range of assets that can be pledged as collateral when borrowing from the Eurosystem.[42]

As for the first issue, the Ecb has adopted the above-mentioned *tilting approach*. Accordingly, the composition of the corporate bond holdings should deviate from that of the "market portfolio", defined as a portfolio that merely replicates the universe of eligible securities, each weighted according to its market capitalization. The issuers with a high climate score, based on greenhouse gas (GHG) emissions, should be overweighted, while those with a low score should be under-weighted. More specifically, the *overall climate score*, used to tilt bond holdings, combines the following three sub-scores:

1. *Backward-looking emissions sub-score*. It is based on issuers' past emissions and it looks at how companies perform compared with their peers in a specific sector as well as compared with all eligible bond issuers.
2. *Forward-looking target sub-score*. It is based on the objectives set by issuers to reduce their GHG emissions in the future. Companies with more ambitious decarbonization targets receive a better score. This should provide an incentive to reduce their emissions.
3. *Climate disclosure sub-score*. It is based on the assessment of issuers' reporting of GHG emissions. Those issuers with high-quality disclosures receive a better score.

This tilting policy has become operational in October 2022. Issuers' climate scores affect their relative weighting in the benchmark guiding the Eurosystem's reinvestment purchases of corporate bonds: both those bonds purchased under the CSPP and those purchased under the

[42] See the press releases of July 4 and September 19, 2022.

pandemic program (PEPP).[43] Such policy has a twofold purpose: on the one hand to reduce the Eurosystem's exposure to financial risks arising from climate change, and on the other hand to support the transition to a carbon–neutral economy, consistent with the environmental targets set by the EU. The tilting approach should not interfere with the monetary policy stance set by the Governing Council, as the overall volume of securities to be purchased continues to be determined solely by monetary policy considerations, consistent with the target of price stability.

It should be noted that, even before the adoption of the Action Plan, the Eurosystem had deviated from the market neutrality principle by purchasing green bonds for amounts larger than their share in the basket of eligible securities. Interestingly, green bond issuances are mainly concentrated in the most polluting sectors: companies operating in these sectors issue green bonds to finance conversion activities towards lower GHG emission technologies and the use of renewable energy sources. According to the Ecb's estimates, the CSPP helped to reduce green bond yields by 25 basis points.[44] The announcement of the program seems to have stimulated an increase in green bond issuance, thus contributing to the development of the European market for these bonds. As part of the PSPP, the Eurosystem has also purchased sovereign green bonds, issued by national governments and supranational institutions.

As for the Eurosystem's collateral framework, two new criteria have been introduced. The first one aims to limit the carbon footprint of financial assets pledged by banks to obtain central bank funding, by imposing a cap on the securities, issued by companies with a high carbon footprint, as a share to the total securities portfolio deposited by a bank with the Eurosystem. The second criterion (to be implemented by 2026) concerns the transparency in non-financial reporting: only securities issued by companies that comply with the climate-related disclosure requirements of the Corporate Sustainability Reporting Directive (CSRD) will be accepted. These criteria add to a measure previously taken, aimed to support innovation in sustainable financial products: the inclusion

[43] The reinvestment of the proceeds from maturing securities purchased under PEPP should continue until the end of 2024, while the reinvestment of CSPP securities has been discontinued in July 2023.

[44] See ECB (2018).

of *sustainability-linked bonds* (SLBs) in the range of eligible securities.[45] SLBs are fixed-income securities whose coupons are linked to the achievement of predefined sustainability performance targets, such as the reduction of GHG emissions: the issuer commits to pay higher interests if those targets are not met; alternatively, there is a coupon reduction if those targets are met. An SLB differs from a green bond in that the financial resources raised are not tied to investment in specific projects.

Finally, the Eurosystem has taken an important step towards greater transparency on climate-related risks and environmental impact of its securities holdings, by publishing two reports: one covering the monetary policy portfolio and another covering the non-monetary policy portfolio.[46] The first one shows the decarbonization path followed by the corporate bonds held under the CSPP and PEPP. The carbon footprint of these portfolios (measured by several metrics) has been steadily declining between 2018 and 2022, as a result of two factors: the reduction of GHG emissions by companies and the above-mentioned tilting approach in selecting the securities under purchase. The second report shows that the Ecb staff pension fund's corporate investments (equity and bonds) have decarbonized since 2019, with a reduction of GHG emissions by more than 50%, thanks to a reallocation of investments following a best-in-class methodology. As for the own funds portfolio (mainly consisting of sovereign bonds), the share of it invested in green bonds shows a remarkable increase (from 1 to 13%) between 2019 and 2022.

References

Bernardini, E., et al. (2021). *Central banks, climate risks and sustainable finance*, Bank of Italy, Questioni di Economia e Finanza, (608).

Bindseil, U. (2020). *Tiered CBDC and the financial system* (Working Paper No. 235). European Central Bank.

BIS. (2021). *Climate-related risk drivers and their transmission channels,* Bank for International Settlements.

BIS. (2022). *Gaining momentum—results of the 2021 BIS survey on central bank digital currencies*. BIS Paper No. 125, Bank for International Settlements.

[45] See the ECB press release of 22 September 2020.

[46] See ECB (2023b; 2023c). These reports, released in March 2023, will be followed by annual disclosures of climate-related information on both portfolios.

BoE. (2023). *The digital pound: A new form of money for households and businesses?* Consultation Paper, Bank of England and HM Treasury.
Bolton, P., et al. (2020). *The green swan. Central banking and financial stability in the age of climate change*, Bank for International Settlements.
Brainard, L. (2022 May 26). *Digital assets and the future of finance: Examining the benefits and risks of a U.S. Central bank digital currency*. Testimony before the Committee on financial services, U.S. House of representatives.
Diamond, D., & Dybvig, P. (1983). Bank runs, deposit insurance, and liquidity. *Journal of Political Economy*, 91(3).
Duffie D., & Economy, E. (2022). (Eds). *Digital currencies: the US, China and the world at a crossroads*. Hoover Institution Press.
EBA. (2020). *Guidelines on loan origination and monitoring*. European Banking Authority.
EBA. (2022). *EBA roadmap on sustainable finance*. European Banking Authority.
ECB. (2018). *Purchases of green bonds under the Eurosystem's asset purchase programme*. ECB Economic Bulletin No.7/2018.
ECB. (2020a). *Report on a digital euro*. European Central Bank.
ECB. (2020b). *Guide on climate-related and environmental risks. Supervisory expectations relating to risk management and disclosure*. European Central Bank.
ECB. (2021). *Eurosystem report on the public consultation on a digital euro*. European Central Bank.
ECB. (2022a). *The case for a digital euro: key objectives and design considerations*. European Central Bank.
ECB. (2022b). *2022 Climate risk stress test*. European Central Bank.
ECB. (2023a). *Progress on the investigation phase of a digital euro—third report*. European Central Bank.
ECB. (2023b). *Climate-related financial disclosures of the Eurosystem's corporate sector holdings for monetary policy purposes*. European Central Bank.
ECB. (2023c). *Climate-related financial disclosures of the ECB's non-monetary policy portfolios*. European Central Bank.
ECB. (2023d). *A stocktake on the digital euro. Summary report on the investigation phase and outlook on the next phase*. European Central Bank.
Ehlers & Packer. (2017, September). *Green bond finance and certification*, BIS Quarterly Review.
Elderson F. (2021). *Greening monetary policy*. ECB Blog, 13 February.
Fatica *et al.* (2019). *The pricing of green bonds: are financial institutions special?* JRC (Working Paper No. 2019/7).
Fed. (2022). *Money and Payments: the US Dollar in the age of digital transformation*. Board of Governors of the Federal Reserve System.
Fed. (2023). *Money and Payments: the US Dollar in the age of digital transformation*. Summary of public comments.

Freixas, X., & Rochet, J.-C. (2008). *Microeconomics of Banking*. MIT Press.
Garratt, R., Yu, J., & Zhu, H. (2022). *The case for convenience: how CBDC design choices impact monetary policy pass-through*. BIS (Working Papers No. 1046).
G7 Working Group on stablecoins. (2019, October). *Investigating the impact of global stablecoins*.
Infante, S., Kim, K., Orlik, A., Silva, A. F., & Tetlow, R. J. (2022). *The Macroeconomic Implications of CBDC: A Review of the Literature*, Finance and Economics Discussion Series 2022–076. Board of Governors of the Federal Reserve System.
Lukonga I. (2023). *Monetary policy implications of Central Bank Digital Currencies*, IMF (Working Paper No. 23/60).
Meller B. & O. Soons. (2023). *Know your (holding) limits: CBDC, financial stability and central bank reliance,* ECB (Occasional Paper No. 326).
NGFS. (2019a, April). *A call for action. Climate change as a source of financial risk*. Network for Greening the Financial System.
NGFS. (2019b, October). *A sustainable and responsible investment guide for central banks' portfolio management*, Network for Greening the Financial System.
NGFS. (2020, June). *Climate change and monetary policy. Initial takeaways*. Network for Greening the Financial System.
NGFS. (2021a, March). *Adapting central bank operations to a hotter world. Reviewing some options*, Network for Greening the Financial System.
NGFS. (2021b, December). *Guide on climate-related disclosure for central banks*, Network for Greening the Financial System.
Niepelt, D. (2021). (Ed.). *Central Bank Digital Currency: Considerations, projects, outlook*. CEPR Press.
Papoutsi, M., Piazzesi M., & Schneider, M. (2021). *How unconventional is green monetary policy?* Working paper.
Rogoff, K. (2017). Dealing with monetary paralysis at the zero bound, *Journal of Economic Perspectives*, 31(3).
Schnabel, I. (2021, March 3). *From green neglect to green dominance?* speech at the webinar Greening monetary policy—Central banking and climate change.
Schoenmaker, D. (2019). *Greening monetary policy*, CEPS (Discussion Paper No. 13576).
Tiberi, P. (2021, May.). *The carbon footprint of the TIPS system: A comparative analysis with Bitcoin and other infrastructures*. Bank of Italy.

Index

A. Baglioni, *Monetary Policy Implementation*, https://doi.org/10.1007/978-3-031-53885-8

F

N

O

P

GPSR Compliance
The European Union's (EU) General Product Safety Regulation (GPSR) is a set of rules that requires consumer products to be safe and our obligations to ensure this.

If you have any concerns about our products, you can contact us on

ProductSafety@springernature.com

In case Publisher is established outside the EU, the EU authorized representative is:

Springer Nature Customer Service Center GmbH
Europaplatz 3
69115 Heidelberg, Germany

www.ingramcontent.com/pod-product-compliance
Ingram Content Group UK Ltd.
Pitfield, Milton Keynes, MK11 3LW, UK
UKHW020835290926
15470UKWH00004B/1355
* 9 7 8 3 0 3 1 5 3 8 8 4 1 *